Law and Human Gene

Law and Human Genetics

Regulating a Revolution

Edited by

Roger Brownsword
W.R. Cornish
Margaret Llewelyn

·H A R T·
PUBLISHING

OXFORD – PORTLAND
Hart Publishing

Oxford and Portland, Oregon

Published in North America (US and Canada) by
Hart Publishing
c/o International Specialized Book Services
5804 NE Hassalo Street
Portland, Oregon
97213-3644
USA

Distributed in the Netherlands, Belgium and Luxembourg by
Intersentia, Churchillaan 108
B2900 Schoten
Antwerpen
Belgium

Distributed in Australia and New Zealand by
Federation Press
John St
Leichhardt
NSW 2000

First published 1998
Reprinted 1999

First published as Volume 61, No. 5 of the Modern Law Review by
Blackwell Publishers, 108 Cowley Road, Oxford OX4 1JF

Hart Publishing Ltd is a specialist legal publisher based in Oxford, England.
To order further copies of this book or to request a list of other
publications please write to:

Hart Publishing Ltd, Salter's Boat Yard, Oxford, OX1 4LB
Telephone: +44 (0)1865 245533 or Fax: +44 (0)1865 794882
e-mail: mail@hartpub.co.uk

British Library Cataloguing in Publication Data
Data Available
ISBN 1 84113-006-0

Printed in Great Britain on acid-free paper
by Biddles Ltd, Guildford and King's Lynn

Contents

Human Genetics and the Law:
Regulating a Revolution

Roger Brownsword,[*] *W.R. Cornish,*[**]

and Margaret Llewelyn[***]

Whilst the science of genetics, which dates back to Gregor Mendel's pioneering work in the last century, is hardly new, its public profile has never been higher. At every level, genetic technology and its applications — whether concerning the isolation and location of particular human genes (such as the BRCA-1 and BRCA-2 genes for breast cancer), the cloning of the Edinburgh sheep, or the mixing and marketing of modified soya — is the subject of media attention and public debate. Genetics, without question, is hot news; whether, however, it is also good news is altogether more moot. For this is a science that elicits vastly different reactions: at one pole, we find celebration and boundless optimism; at the other, we have profound suspicion and dire prediction; and, between these extremes, there is a broad spectrum of opinion in which a positive view of genetics is qualified by expressions of caution and concern. Most dramatically, perhaps, it is the Human Genome Project — a prodigiously expensive international voyage of scientific discovery — that prompts our deepest uncertainties and equivocations: do we really want to unravel the mysteries of the biological dimension of human life; do we really want to have the knowledge and power to control and fine-tune that dimension; do we really want such awesome responsibility? Whatever our response, it is no exaggeration surely to say that we stand at the threshold of a revolution — a revolution in biotechnology, but equally a revolution in the terms of human social existence.[1]

On the face of it, the legal community, with its tendency towards gentle incrementalism, is not particularly well-equipped to handle any kind of revolution, let alone a revolution of the proportions indicated by modern genetics. As one writer has recently put it, once we let the genetics genie out of the bottle, we will (among other things) 'tie the lawyers up in ... knots .... '[2] In some areas — patents is perhaps the best example — lawyers have already grappled with some of these knots. Thus, while the politicians in the European Union have spent a decade debating, and finally agreeing, the terms of the Directive on the Legal Protection of

---

[*] Faculty of Law, University of Sheffield
[**] Faculty of Law University of Cambridge
[***] Faculty of Law, University of Sheffield

1   See, eg, Patrick Dixon, *The Genetic Revolution* (Eastbourne: Kingsway Publications, 1993); and Daniel Callahan, 'The Genetic Revolution' in David C. Thomasma and Thomasine Kushner (eds) *Birth to Death: Science and Bioethics* (Cambridge: Cambridge University Press, 1996) 13.
2   Tim Radford, 'Double Jeopardy' *The Guardian Weekend*, May 23 1998, 20, 22.

Biotechnology,[3] the intellectual property lawyers at the European Patent Office have developed a highly controversial jurisprudence addressing *inter alia* the patentability of genetically modified plants and animals, as well as that of products based on human genes.[4] We can be confident, however, that the puzzles presented by modern genetics will not be limited to nice points about patentability, nor for that matter to proprietary points such as those raised by the famous Californian case of John Moore (in which a cell-line was developed from Moore's tissue).[5] Consider, for instance, just one of the more obvious questions arising from the rapid developments in human genetics: will it be possible (or, indeed, desirable) to confine the results of viable genetic testing to those who are directly parties to a particular test? Or will genetic testing be seen as a basis for new classifications, giving rise to new possibilities for discrimination by third parties? If so, will certain genetic profiles then be read as 'good/bad risks', 'socially desirable/ undesirable', and so on? How are these possibilities to be handled by medical lawyers, insurance and employment lawyers — and, no less by family lawyers, as embryos, fetuses and mates are found to be more or less genetically eligible? How is such sensitive information to be viewed by public lawyers, civil liberties lawyers and criminal lawyers?[6] Inevitably, it seems, the lawyers of the next century will feel the impact of genetics across a broad sweep of their practice.

Against this background, this collection of essays seeks to inaugurate amongst British lawyers an informed debate about the implications of the genetic revolution. The principal focus for the collection is *human* genetics (although other forms of genetics are touched on in some of the papers). This, it should be emphasised, is not to discount the importance of debating the regulation of plant and animal genetics.[7] However, the closer that genetics gets to fully mapping the human genome, and to routinely screening, testing, and intervening in it, the more urgent it becomes that lawyers should debate their regulatory options and objectives. It is imperative, too, that lawyers should open the channels of debate with non-lawyers as well as understanding that this is a debate that knows no local boundaries. Thus, whilst the majority of contributors to this collection are lawyers, and British lawyers at that, the project is informed both by a spirit of inter-disciplinarity and by an awareness that the genetic revolution is a phenomenon that has global significance.

In the United Kingdom, the seeds of a general debate about human genetics were sown by two reports from the Nuffield Council on Bioethics, one on screening and testing,[8] the other on the use of human tissue,[9] and by the BMA's publication *Our*

---

3 Directive 98/44/EC (OJ L 213, 30.7.1998, p. 13) — the approval of the European Parliament finally having been secured in May 1998. However, behind the facade of formal agreement, there remain deep divisions of opinion, the weakening of earlier opposition to the Directive reflecting not so much a rivision of principle but a practical accommodation withthe commercial importance of patentable biotechnology.

4 The three leading cases at the European Patent Office are: *Harvard Onco-mouse* [1989] OJ 451, [1990] OJ 476, [1992] OJ 590; *Plant Genetic Systems* [1995] EPOR 357; and *Relaxin* [1995] EPOR 541.

5 *Moore v Regents of the University of California* (1990) 793 P2d 479.

6 What, too, will lawyers make of diagnostic genetic test kits (which might be more or less reliable) becoming available 'over the counter' to mass consumer purchasers?

7 For a range of issues arising from the latter, see, eg, Peter Wheale and Ruth McNally (eds), *Animal Genetic Engineering: Of Pigs, Oncomice and Men* (London: Pluto Press, 1995). Of course, in the context of patents, much of the groundwork in determining appropriate regulatory parameters for *human* genetics, was undertaken in relation to plant and animal genetics.

8 Nuffield Council on Bioethics, *Genetic Screening: Ethical Issues* (London, December 1993).

9 Nuffield Council on Bioethics, *Human Tissue: Ethical and Legal Issues* (London, April 1995).

Genetic Future: The Science and Ethics of Genetic Technology.[10] However, the issue was formally brought into the public domain by the House of Commons Science and Technology Committee when it identified the field of human genetics as one that was ripe for review and regulation.[11] According to the Committee:

> The fast moving pace of the science of human genetics, its actual and potential importance in clinical medicine and its bearing upon deep concerns of humanity, mean that it is necessary to keep matters under public review, and to provide for appropriate legislative and regulatory response when this is called for ... .
>
> At the same time the rate of development means that situations and problems will change not only within a human generation, but may over-take primary legislation and the development of case law. It is therefore necessary to be flexible and to keep the development of the scientific possibilities under review, not only in the genetics peer groups, but also in public understanding, so that as far as possible issues are anticipated, and research and development and legislation and regulation are conducted with as full as possible an appreciation of the consequences.[12]

To meet this challenge, the Committee recommended 'the establishment of a Human Genetics Commission which would be able to monitor developments in genetics and give advice to the government on the implications of such developments across a wide field.'[13] Acting on this recommendation, in 1996, the Government set up the Human Genetics Advisory Commission (HGAC) as a non-statutory advisory body. One of the key tasks for the HGAC — whose terms of reference include advising on how public understanding of, and confidence in, human genetics might be improved[14] — is to cultivate a rational and reflective public discourse about a range of emotive and controversial issues. This important aspect of the HGAC's remit is discussed in the opening paper of the collection by Sir Colin Campbell, the first chair of the Commission.

If the Commission is to orchestrate an informed debate about the practice and applications of human genetics, the non-scientist public, including the lawyers, must understand what, technically speaking, genetics can and cannot do (which is *not* to say, of course, that the discourse of science and technology should be privileged in any such debate). In their paper, Julian Kinderlerer and Diane Longley outline the present state of the art, identifying both the promise and the present limitations of human genetics. Their conclusion, that a strong regulatory framework is essential if decision-making is to be responsive, accountable and legitimate, ties in closely with Julia Black's critique of regulatory processes — particularly her analysis of the problem of the 'gap' that exists between the views of regulatory insiders and regulatory outsiders, and her concern that regulation should aspire to be strong, in the sense not merely that outsiders are integrated into regulatory discourses, but that genuine communication between the many different perspectives should be facilitated. Kinderlerer and Longley's conclusion also ties in with Deryck Beyleveld and Roger Brownsword's analysis of the principle of

---

10 British Medical Association, *Our Genetic Future: The Science and Ethics of Genetic Technology* (Oxford: Oxford University Press, 1992). See ch 9 for a sketch of the regulatory position as it stood in the early 1990s.

11 Select Committee on Science and Technology, Third Report, *Human Genetics: The Science and its Consequences* HC 1994–95, HC Paper 41.

12 *ibid* paras 2 and 3.

13 *ibid* para 285.

14 See Human Genetics Advisory Commission, *First Annual Report* (London: DTI, 1998) Annex A. The HGAC operates alongside the Advisory Committee on Genetic Testing (ACGT) and the Gene Therapy Advisory Committee (GTAC), the latter two specialist committees having a narrower remit than the HGAC. See *ibid* para 4.6.

respect for human dignity, a principle which, together with respect for human rights, is widely seen as setting the bounds within which human genetics is legitimately practised.[15] Without doubt, human genetics gives rise to a host of ethical concerns,[16] but whether human dignity justifiably grounds those concerns, or merely functions as an expressive signal of certain negative reactions to genetics, is more open to question.

Because much of human genetics will have its applications in medical contexts, regulation of this field is essential. However, as both Sheila McLean and Ruth Deech highlight in their papers, more genetic information, coupled with an expansion of (or, at any rate, the apparent expansion of) reproductive choice, is not an unqualified good. Regulators need to be sensitive to the subtlety of the cultural consequences liable to be wrought by the genetic revolution in reproductive contexts, particularly the pressures and expectations that might insinuate themselves in medical and familial settings, the possible assumption of new responsibilities (for example, parental responsibility for the production of 'perfect' children, or at least the avoidance of 'imperfect' children), and the emergence of old risks in new forms (especially the tendency to disvalue others or to treat them as less than equal). The complex interplay of risk and responsibility is a central theme, too, in Onora O'Neill's account of the current debate about the use of genetic information in insurance, as it is in Celia Wells' reflections on the way in which the criminal justice system is likely to react by selectively incorporating such genetic information as it finds functional. In the final paper in the collection, Alain Pottage's wide-ranging discussion takes us back to questions of patentability and exploitation. As the angry exchanges, in Europe and elsewhere, about the patentability of the processes and products of modern biotechnology clearly testify, genetics invites a radical revision of traditional (and confident) assumptions concerning not only what is patentable, but also what (and who) is available for commercial exploitation. Moreover, Pottage (like Wells) finds in genetics a force that threatens, on an altogether broader front, to destabilise and blur the distinctions and dualisms on which our conceptual frameworks are founded. Such subversion of the conventional wisdom can be anticipated not merely at the level of local legal doctrine (for example, with regard to the distinction between invention and mere discovery, or that between person and property) but, more generally, at the level of the relationship between science, law, and society. Human genetics, in other words, challenges us to re-think in the most fundamental sense what we are and how we interact with the environment in which we find ourselves.

In many ways, this collection underlines the shifting and paradoxical nature of risk and responsibility in technologically sophisticated post-industrial societies. For, as quickly as human genetics eliminates one kind of risk, it replaces it with another; and, as quickly as the narrative of genetics (biographical and biological) portrays us as less responsible, we find ourselves being offered more choice and, concomitantly, more responsibility. This, however, is not all. Writing in the mid-

---

15 In particular, see the Council of Europe, *Convention for the Protection of Human Rights and Dignity of the Human Being with regard to the Application of Biology and Medicine: Convention on Human Rights and Biomedicine* (DIR/JUR (96) 14) (Strasbourg: Directorate of Legal Affairs, November 1996); and the UNESCO *Universal Declaration on the Human Genome and Human Rights* (adopted by the General Conference in November 1997).

16 For general discussion of the ethical questions posed by human genetics, see, eg, Hille Haker, Richard Hearn, and Klaus Steigleder (eds) *Ethics of Human Genome Analysis* (Tübingen: Attempto Verlag Tübingen, 1993); Michael J. Reiss and Roger Straughan, *Improving Nature?* (Cambridge: Cambridge University Press, 1996); and Robert Schwartz, 'Genetic Knowledge: Some Legal and Ethical Questions' in David C. Thomasma and Thomasine Kushner (eds), n 1 above, 21.

1980s, Ulrich Beck,[17] one of the leading commentators on the post-industrial condition, warned of the inexorable march of 'progress'. In a striking passage dealing with genetics, he said:

> The fear of the 'advances' in genetic technology is widespread today. Hearings are held. Churches protest. Even scientists faithful to progress cannot shake off their uneasiness. All of this takes place, however, like an *obituary* for decisions taken long ago. Or rather, no decision ever occurred. The question of 'whether' was never waiting at the door. No committee ever let it in. It has always been on the way. The age of human genetics, the reality of which people are debating today, actually started long ago. One can say 'no' to progress, *but that does not change its course at all.* Progress is a blank check to be honored *beyond* consent and legitimation.[18]

And, in this, Beck surely is right. Genetics already has more than a head start; debates tend to be opened only after 'progress' is reported. The science underpinning the genetic revolution is already well developed; and the social implications of that science become more visible, more debatable, by the day. If lawyers, in Britain and elsewhere, are to shape the regulation of those implications in a way that meets the requirements of democratic consent and legitimacy, the sooner they join the debate about the genetic revolution the better.

---

17 Ulrich Beck, *Risk Society* (trans Mark Ritter) (London: Sage Publications, 1992) (first published in German, 1986).
18 *ibid* 203.

A Commission for the 21st Century

*Colin Campbell**

New insights into the structure, function and control of genes and how they influence our health, have produced a dramatic expansion in our understanding of what causes disease. The application of genetic technologies can be used to advance medical research and clinical care, including, for example, the discovery and development of new pharmaceuticals, vaccines and diagnostic tests. Although this technology offers much promise, some developments have also raised wider concerns. Given the huge potential of genetic advances, it is important to consider the ethical and social consequences now, and not be taken unaware. The Government has recognised the significance of these issues and the Human Genetics Advisory Commission (HGAC) has been given the task of advising Ministers.

The Human Genetics Advisory Commission

The Human Genetics Advisory Commission was established, in December 1996, as a non-statutory advisory body. It provides independent advice to UK Health and Industry Ministers on issues arising from developments in human genetics that have social, ethical and/or economic consequences. The Commission was also asked to advise on ways to build public understanding of the new genetics. Its full terms of reference are to:

(i)   keep under review scientific progress at the frontiers of human genetics and related fields;
(ii) report on issues arising from new developments in human genetics that can be expected to have wider social, ethical and/or economic consequences, for example, in relation to public health, insurance, patents and employment;
(iii) advise on ways to build public confidence in, and understanding of, the new genetics.

The Commission has a facilitative and advisory role. It aims to improve the level of informed debate about the issues which arise from advances in human genetics. To this end, it endeavours to make the issues accessible to as wide an audience as possible. We are committed to open and public debate and will try to ensure that the debate is well informed. This should help to enable the Government and Parliament to address difficult and complex issues with the right information, understanding and analysis.

Challenges faced by the HGAC

The HGAC faces a number of key challenges:

(i)   how to make complex issues accessible to a wider audience;

* Chairman, Human Genetics Advisory Commission, London.

(ii) how to ensure that its advice reflects the broad range of opinion, with the correct analysis; and

(iii) how to ensure that the systems that emerge to address issues in human genetics are worthy of public confidence.

Making complex issues accessible to a wider audience

The HGAC believes that greater public discourse about human genetics will improve the policy making process. However, many groups within our society are effectively excluded — or feel excluded — from public debate about the implications of complex developments in human genetics. The Commission wishes to take steps to improve this situation.

It has been impressed upon the Commission that the language used can have an impact on the public's perception. This is especially true of emotive issues such as cloning. In the course of our work on the implications of the birth of 'Dolly' the sheep for human cloning, we have highlighted the importance of making a distinction between on the one hand, *human reproductive cloning*, where the intention is to produce identical fetuses or babies (this, it has to be stressed, is banned in the UK) and, on the other hand, what may be called, *therapeutic cloning*. This includes other scientific and medical applications of the nuclear replacement technology such as the production of replacement skin for victims of serious accidents. If we are to encourage wider discussion of the issues, and involve lay people, we must establish a common lexicon for the purposes of this public discourse and debate.

The Commission is also committed to listening and making itself accessible to wider public views. We recognise the need to use a variety of methods to achieve this. The HGAC considers, on an on-going basis, how best to involve the public in consultation with other bodies that have experience in this area. A key element is to ensure that those involved in discussions are appraised of the facts; this is not always easy when dealing with scientifically complex problems and fast moving technologies. To achieve this end, we give presentations about developments in genetics and the work of the HGAC to a range of audiences and, as Chairman of the Commission, I have participated in many public discussions. Examples include the Ashmolean Club, a conference on 'Advances in Health Care and Ethical Constraints' at the University of Hertfordshire and a conference on 'The Implications of Genetic Testing for Insurance'. Other audiences have included industrialists, academics, civic forums and school children.

Openness is vital in encouraging wider public debate. The Commission publishes its reports, which are also available on its World Wide Web Site (www.dti.gov.uk/hgac), along with the press notices that are issued after every main HGAC meeting. The publication of the HGAC's advice to Ministers on insurance, *The Implications of Genetic Testing for Insurance*, and the consultation document on cloning, *Cloning Issues in Reproduction, Science and Medicine* (a joint exercise with the Human Fertilisation and Embryology Authority), were both accompanied by press briefings. Human genetics attracts media interest and, in response, the Chairman and other members of the Commission give radio and television interviews, as well as providing articles for journals and other publications.

If we are to make these issues more accessible to the wider public, we need to convey effectively the concept of risk. More thought needs to be applied to how this can be achieved. In the course of our work it has also become apparent that we in the UK need to improve our information about the ethical, legal and social implications of advances in genetics. In 1997, the Wellcome Trust announced plans to fund research into the ethical, legal and social implications (ELSI) of developments in biomedicine, and sought advice from the HGAC and others on the content of this research programme. The HGAC recognises this work as important, as results of the programme are likely to provide useful information for the Commission and others. New conceptual frameworks and evaluation criteria will have to be articulated as genetic understanding — and new uses of this knowledge — increases.

Ensuring HGAC advice reflects the broad range of opinion on a subject

The Commission recognises that there is much existing expertise in the field of genetics. A great deal of work has already been done and a number of specialised bodies are considering specific issues. Proceeding by way of consultation is therefore a key element of the HGAC's work. The Commission believes that only by consulting widely can it ensure that its advice to Ministers reflects the range of opinion on the issues under consideration and takes account of the latest developments, both in scientific and other areas, in the UK and abroad.

In 1997, the Commission held a series of consultative meetings with the aim of developing its thinking on the issues. The objectives were to initiate an exchange of information with interested parties, to discuss current and emerging developments and also to discuss public knowledge of human genetics, along with ways of building public understanding of the subject. Given the HGAC's remit of keeping under review scientific progress, the first consultative meeting with scientists discussed current and expected developments in the field of genetics. Other meetings were held with journalists and industrialists, as well as those involved with consumer groups and people concerned with the social policy implications of genetic advances. A number of common themes emerged from these meetings — concern was expressed about the possible misuse and misinterpretation of genetic tests, and the potential for new forms of discrimination; the need to consider genetics in the wider context (for instance, looking at privacy and ethical issues) was seen as important, as was informing the public and those who advise them (eg health care professionals and others).

Building on the knowledge imparted at consultative and other meetings, the Commission has to date issued two consultation papers to seek a wider range of views. The insurance consultation paper was based around specific questions and was aimed primarily at those involved with the insurance industry. The consultation exercise on cloning was targeted at a much wider audience. The HGAC will continue to collaborate with the Human Fertilisation and Embryology Authority on cloning. The HGAC's consultative documents have set out background information, to render complex and opaque issues in clear terms so that lay people are enfranchised in following and contributing to the debates. The Commission membership have endeavoured to keep abreast of scientific developments by means of expert presentations and briefings prior to main meetings.

The HGAC is fortunate in that Revd Dr John Polkinghorne of the Advisory Committee on Genetic Testing (ACGT) and Professor Norman Nevin of the Gene Therapy Advisory Committee (GTAC) are members of the Commission. The

HGAC has a broader remit than these two specialist committees and complements their work. The dual membership of the GTAC and ACGT chairmen ensures that there should be no duplication of effort.

The Nuffield Council on Bioethics is also a key UK organisation in considering the ethical issues arising from developments in genetics. Members of the HGAC and the Nuffield Council met in February 1998 to discuss their workplans and ensure that they are complementary. Dr Onora O'Neill, immediate past chairman of the Nuffield Council on Bioethics is also a member of the HGAC.

Genetics knows no boundaries. Although cultural and social contexts differ and one nation has little influence over the culture and politics of another, there are areas of common agreement and concern, and much can be learnt from the experiences in other countries. Thus, the HGAC has been developing international contacts.

I have held discussions with representatives of bodies examining the issues in other countries. In addition to meeting Dr Harold Shapiro, the Chairman of the US National Bioethics Advisory Commission, I attended the Third Standing Conference of National Ethics Committees in January 1998 and a meeting organised by the British Council and *Nature* about the approaches adopted in Britain and France to deal with bioethics. We recently met with members of the European Group on Ethics in Science and New Technologies.

The HGAC will continue to keep a watching brief on international developments in genetics and biomedicine, such as the UNESCO 'Universal Declaration on the Human Genome and Human Rights' and the Council of Europe 'Convention for the Protection of Human Rights and Dignity of the Human Being with regard to the Application of Biology and Medicine'.

Improving public confidence in, and understanding of, systems that emerge to address human genetics issues

The Commission believes that it needs to be flexible and responsive, given the fast pace of developments in genetics. For example, public concern has been expressed in the UK about the implications of genetic testing for insurance. The relationship between genetics and insurance is inevitably a complex one. The insurance industry is of long standing and its operations are built on well established principles. Genetics is an emerging discipline, at the cutting edge of science, and even those closest to it cannot yet see its full implications. Our role has been to examine the point of contact between these two areas, with a view to ensuring maximum public understanding of any new systems which emerge.

We have published advice to UK Ministers which recommends that insurers respect a voluntary moratorium on the requirement to disclose genetic test results. This would allow time to establish independently verified evidence on the extent to which genetic test results can be used reliably to predict life expectancy or the onset of ill health, a robust appeals mechanism and a sound body of research in the UK on the ethical, legal and social implications of advances in human genetics.

There must be a continuing dialogue with the insurance industry about how the situation can be monitored, with active research on how to translate test results. I am confident that this dialogue can be realised. An impressive range and variety of organisations are already actively considering the complex issues in this area. For example, the Association of British Insurers (ABI) published a genetics Code of Practice. The Commission welcomes the considerable progress made by the ABI. A broad range of people and organisations assisted us in developing our report:

these included actuaries, underwriters, the Genetic Interest Group and other patient associations, clinicians, representatives of consumer groups and industry. They met with us, sent in submissions or responded to our consultation document. The debate is becoming better informed.

Conclusion

We are entering a period of unpredictable change in genetics. We are told that advances in genetic science will revolutionise health care provision over the next ten years, yet we are also concerned about the potential for abuse. If we are to realise the promise of this technology it is necessary for it to be controlled sensibly. As a first step, however, there must be wide public debate. We have to embark on open social negotiation to determine what is and what is not acceptable. This process of social negotiation should inform our decisions about the role of the law in regulating the development and application of genetic science. The following articles are a welcome and important contribution to a process which, if undertaken seriously, should stand us in good stead in the 21st Century.

Human Genetics: The New Panacea?

Julian Kinderlerer and Diane Longley*

Considerable advances have been made in human genetics in recent years, often outstripping the knowledge and understanding of the medical professions as well as the general public and taking regulators by surprise. In this paper, we seek to give a realistic indication of the many developments in human genetics and of what might or might not be scientifically possible in time, without the clutter and sensationalism of media hype. This, we feel, is an essential exercise to enable certain key elements and concerns to be taken on board, putting developments in context prior to any fresh consideration of the need for and potential effectiveness of regulation of human genetics.

The elucidation of the structure of DNA during the 1950s[1] provided a model for understanding the process for the transfer of genetic information between generations of the same organism. In bacteria and fungi identification of a variety of enzymes capable of modifying this group of large molecules has made possible the science termed 'modern biotechnology', and opened up our understanding of the mechanisms which lead from information molecule to function. Until the identification of these new enzymes scientists had used a variety of mutagenic devices (including, for example, ultra-violet light) to modify the genetic information in bacteria and fungi and observe the change in characteristics (or phenotype). From the late 1970s it became possible both to insert and remove genes in bacteria and to observe the consequences. An understanding of the control mechanisms followed rapidly. It became possible to sequence and extract genes from higher organisms and insert them into bacteria. Numerous quantities of the bacteria could then be grown, which meant that the amount of both the gene and the protein derived from that gene was relatively large, allowing analysis.

In 1990 a fateful decision was made. The entire human genome was to be sequenced. A 'genome' is the complete set of genes and chromosomes of an organism.[2] The intention was to construct a 'high-resolution genetic, physical and transcript map' of the human, with ultimately, a complete sequence. The Human Genome Project is the largest research project ever undertaken with the intention of analysing the structure of human DNA and determining the location of the estimated 100,000 human genes. According to Hieter and Boguski:

> The information generated by the human genome project is expected to be the source book for biomedical science in the 21st century and will be of immense benefit to the field of medicine. It will help us to understand and eventually treat many of the more than 4000 genetic diseases that afflict mankind, as well as the many multi-factorial diseases in which genetic predisposition plays an important role.[3]

About 40,000–50,000 genes have been identified, although for a majority the

* Sheffield Institute of Biotechnological Law and Ethics.

1 J.D.Watson and F.H.C. Crick, 'A Structure for Deoxy-ribose Nucleic Acid' (1953) 171 *Nature* 737.
2 P. Hieter and M Boguski, 'Functional Genomics: It's All How You Read It' (1997) 278 *Science* 601.
3 *Human Genome News* (1998)9,1–2. http://www.ornl.gov/TechResources/HumanGenome/project/project.html.

function is still unknown.[4] Whilst more than 95 per cent of the human genome
remains to be sequenced, the acceleration in the process as new techniques are
introduced means that the 15 year timescale originally envisaged for the completed
project is likely to be met.[5]

It should be pointed out that a complete sequence does not provide information
that allows an understanding of the mass of data. It can (to some extent) be
compared to the possession of a very large encyclopaedia written in an unknown
language. The complete sequence will not be 'sufficient to understand its
functional organisation, neither for individual units nor at a more integrated level'.[6]
The emphasis will quickly shift from the huge databases that store the recorded
information to a functional analysis. It is assumed that there are about 100,000
genes with specific functions in the genome. The function of most of these is
unknown. 'In the past we have had functions in search of sequence. In the future,
pathology and physiology will become "functionators" for the sequences'.[7]

DNA profiling and similar techniques show very clearly that (virtually) no two
individuals share the same genome. There will be differences in many of the genes on
their chromosomes. Whose genome is, therefore, being sequenced? Sequences are not
being determined for an individual, but rather for the genetic information of a large
range of persons. This has resulted in an appreciation of the 'polymorphism' in our
genetic make-up. Many of the amino-acids found in the linear sequence of a protein
cannot be changed, for the change is likely to have a deleterious impact on the
function. As proteins are directly coded in the DNA, there must be a similar constraint
on the DNA. Many of the proteins found in humans are also found in other organisms.
Even though the function is the same or similar, their sequence differs significantly.
Hence exact replication is unnecessary. The DNA sequence that makes up many genes
will differ from organism to organism, and even from person to person.[8]

Duboule[9] raises the question that lies at the heart of this article. How will it be
possible to assimilate the mass of newly available information and translate it into
clinical practice 'in a way that fulfils scientific criteria and respects ethical as well
as social concerns'?

Genetic and biological advances

For obvious reasons, development of modern biotechnology proceeded apace in
bacteria, viruses and fungi much earlier than in higher organisms. Within bacteria,
fungi and plants it is now possible to move almost *any* 'gene'[10], from *any* one

---

4   L. Rowen, G. Mahairas and L. Hood, 'Sequencing the Human Genome' (1997) 278 *Science* 605 and
    Schuler *et al* 'A Gene Map of the Human Genome' (1996) 274 *Science* 540–546.
5   S.E. Koonin, 'An Independent Perspective on the Human Genome Project' (1998) 279 *Science* 36.
6   D. Duboule, 'The Evolution of Genomics.' (1998) 278 *Science* 555.
7   D. Tosteson, Symposium on 'Genomics and Gene Therapy: Meaning for the Future of Science and
    Medicine' (1997) Harvard Institute of Human Genetics, Cambridge MA 26 March 1997: cited in P.
    Hieter and M. Boguski, n 2 above.
8   D. Wang *et al* 'Large Scale Identification, Mapping and Genotyping of Single-Nucleotide
    Polymorphisms in the Human Genome' (1998) 280 *Science* 1077.
9   See n 6 above.
10 Gene is defined as 'The fundamental physical and functional unit of heredity. A gene is an ordered
    sequence of nucleotides located in a particular position on a particular chromosome that encodes a
    specific functional product (i.e., a protein or RNA molecule).' Gene expression is defined as 'The process
    by which a gene's coded information is converted into the structures present and operating in the cell.
    Expressed genes include those that are transcribed into mRNA and then translated into protein and those
    that are transcribed into RNA but not translated into protein (e.g., transfer and ribosomal RNAs).' The
    definitions are taken from *A Primer on Molecular Genetics* (1992) US Department of Energy, Office of
    Energy Research, Office of Health and Environmental Research, Washington, 36.

organism to *any* other. The use of 'gene' here includes the coding sequence that provides the information necessary to produce the gene product (protein)[11] and any sequences that identify when, where (in which tissue, within the cell or in interstitial fluids) and how much of the product will be produced. Scientists are now able to choose a known gene product from virtually any source, identify its DNA sequence, manufacture it in the laboratory modifying the sequence so that it will be better expressed in the organism into which it is to be placed — attach to it the various signal sequences needed to identify:

- **when** in the life cycle of the cell or organism that product will be expressed;
- **where** in the cell or organism expression will occur; and
- **how much** will be produced; and

insert this new construct into an organism of choice. Clearly non-human biotechnology genetic modification knows few bounds. As a consequence, efforts have been made to establish international regulatory measures, it being considered inappropriate to leave regulation to the market and industrial initiatives in most countries. There are negotiations currently in progress to produce a protocol to the Convention on Biological Diversity[12] to ensure the safe transport of genetically modified organisms between countries, and the United Nations Environmental Programme (UNEP) has produced a set of guidelines which define minimum standards for the safe manufacture and use of modified organisms.[13]

The transformation of bacteria and viruses is now routine. Viruses carry a small number of genes, and for many viruses the function of most of these is known. Insertion of a gene into a specific position is easily accomplished, and in general, the effect is predictable. Live viruses are often used as vaccines — the pathogenic impact for human and animal viruses having been attenuated by a variety of techniques. However, in many cases, the mechanism of attenuation is still poorly understood, and the impact on the virulence of the organism due to an inserted gene has to be investigated before the modified virus may be used on human or animal tissue.

There remain many limitations to the use of genetic modification in higher organisms. The transformation of some plants remains difficult, and insertion of genes into large animals is problematic as the normally long generation time means that a very high yield of transformed animals is needed if the technique is to be used effectively. In general we cannot choose where the construct is inserted into the genome of the host plant or animal, even if the complete sequence of that genome is known. In many instances the insert may go into the middle of a vital gene, rendering the cell incapable of growing. Techniques presently available for insertion of genes into plant cells make it likely that a number of copies of the gene

---

11   'A gene product is the biochemical material, either RNA or protein, resulting from expression of a gene. The amount of gene product is used to measure how active a gene is; abnormal amounts can be correlated with disease': *ibid* 36.

12   Article 19 para 2 of the Convention on Biological Diversity (CBD) requires the Parties to the Convention to 'consider the need for and modalities of a protocol setting out appropriate procedures, including in particular, advance informed agreement, in the field of the safe transfer, handling and use of any living modified organism resulting from biotechnology that may have adverse effect on the conservation and sustainable use of biological diversity'. The CBD is a legally binding agreement (Rio de Janeiro, 1992) which has been signed by over 150 countries. It came into force on 29 December 1993.

13   *UNEP International Technical Guidelines for Safety in Biotechnology* (1996). These Guidelines arose from the requirement in Chapter 16 of Agenda 21 (adopted at the United Nations Conference on Environment and Development in Rio de Janeiro in 1992) for the 'Environmentally Sound Management of Biotechnology'.

will be inserted randomly into the genome. For plants, traditional breeding practices (over a period of time) allow choice of a plant carrying both a small number of insertions and with as little loss of other characteristics as possible. As these separate 'constructs' are inserted into different places within the plant genome, selection over time means that they segregate, and it is possible to choose plants that demonstrate a particular, desirable characteristic.

The efficiency of transformation of plant cells is extremely low. Only a small proportion of the targeted cells is usually modified successfully depending on the technique.[14] There are, however, a very large number of cells in the tissue targeted for transformation and in most plants it is possible to regenerate a complete plant from a single cell. By using markers such as antibiotic resistance, or herbicide resistance, it is possible to select those cells which have survived and are not susceptible to (say) the antibiotic — implying the resistance marker is present and is being expressed. Even where the conversion is only one in a million, selection systems are able to find the successfully transformed single cell and grow it into the entire organism, or grow numerous copies.

The insert used is usually a small piece of DNA. Even for a large protein, the number of bases[15] in the 'gene' is likely to be less than 5000. In addition most of the DNA in a chromosome has no known function and is thought of as 'junk'. Insertion of a gene into these regions is unlikely to have a significant impact on the characteristics of the organism.

Table 1 shows the size (in base pairs) of the genome or chromosome for a number of different organisms. A gene may require a few hundred to a few thousand base pairs, and, as we have said, even in humans, there are thought to be less than a hundred thousand genes. If a new gene is inserted into the genome amongst the 'junk' it ought to have no impact on other than the desired characteristics for the modification. Bacteria and viruses have almost no junk DNA, but the modification of their genetic information can be achieved precisely.

Table 1[16]

Comparative Sequence Sizes	Base pairs
Largest known continuous DNA sequence (yeast chromosome 3)	350×10^3
Escherichia coli (bacterium) genome	4.6×10^6
Largest yeast chromosome now mapped	5.8×10^6
Entire yeast genome	15×10^6
Smallest human chromosome (Y)	50×10^6
Largest human chromosome (1)	250×10^6
Entire human genome	3×10^9

---

14   Between 1 in 1,000 and 1 in 10,000,000 cells are successfully transformed.
15   DNA is made up of a set of 4 monomeric units called bases that are linked together in a linear chain to form a very long molecule. Each of the bases is able to associate in a specific manner with one of the others, providing 2 pairs of 'base-pairs'. The DNA molecule is in general actually two, complementary strands wound around one another in a double helix. The four bases are usually named A, C, G and T. A and T pair, as do C and G. If a strand of DNA has the sequence AACGTAAGCTGGG, its complementary strand will have the sequence TTGCATTCGACCC. The two strands will be aligned as

AACGTAAGCTGGG
|||||||||||||
TTGCATTCGACCC.

16   n 10 above, 7.

Plant cells are routinely modified using a variant of *Agrobacterium tumifaciens*. This bacterium possesses an element (termed a plasmid) capable of entering a plant cell and taking over the function of the cell in order to produce a chemical upon which the bacterium lives. Scientists have subverted this plasmid, removing some of the genes that are deleterious to the plant and inserting the 'construct' of choice. There are many plants, however, that are not susceptible to the bacterium, and a ballistic method is used instead. The technique, termed biolistics, literally involves firing fine particles of a metal, usually gold, that have been soaked in the 'construct' at a leaf or similar plant tissue. The DNA is taken up by a very tiny number of cells in the tissue. The selection procedures allow for the destruction of all cells other than those that contain genes resistant to the antibiotic or herbicide used. The remaining cells are those in which insertion has been successful and the inserted genes are working. These may then be cajoled into reforming an entire plant.

It was realised from the inception of the use of this technology in organisms other than humans that there existed a potential for harm. Consequently regulatory structures were put into place that attempted, primarily, to identify the potential hazards and that endeavoured to reduce risk to within acceptable limits.

The regulatory structures for *non-human use* of biotechnology were designed initially to examine risk only, and were largely confined to the identification of risk to human health and safety resulting from the manufacture of new organisms with new properties. At first the risk was considered only to be to those working in the environment in which the technology was being used. However, it was soon realised that there was a significant risk to the environment in the event of escape of organisms modified to be fitter than their corresponding wild-type in particular conditions. Risk to the environment therefore has to be seriously considered. In many instances, however, scientists working with modified organisms may forget that humans are part of the environment and the risk to humans outside the confines of the laboratory, factory or hospital may be notable.

Today, virtually every country in the world has instituted some form of regulatory regime for the use of modern biotechnology in micro-organisms and plants. These are almost exclusively concerned with the minimisation of risk to human health and safety, or with minimisation of risk to the environment. The UNEP guidelines introduced in 1996 constituted an attempt to ensure a minimum baseline for regulatory structures in all countries.

Conversion of animal cells is much more difficult. Although it is possible to select those where transformation has had some success — for example in animals that have extremely short generation times, as is the case with many insects — in general, generation times are too long. It is not possible to regenerate an entire animal from a single cell in the same way as has been achieved for plants. Insertion of DNA sequences into animal cells usually involves micro-injection, whereby the DNA construct is injected into individual cells. The proportion of successful insertions is relatively high — it must be at least 70 per cent for the process to be considered useful. If the fertilised egg is used as the host cell, *all* the cells of the animal will contain the insertion. If the DNA is inserted into one of a group of cells that will eventually form the embryo, the resulting animal is a chimera. Some of the cells contain the construct, others do not, as only those cells which derive from that transformed will contain the inserted genes. If the construct produces 'gene-products' (proteins) which are only important within the cell in which the gene is found, then the chimaeric nature of the animal will be obvious. If the gene is intended to be manufactured within a cell, but used outside the cell, either in the whole body or in a particular organ, the chimaeric nature becomes less important. This particular factor may be important for gene therapy in humans, where a specific gene cannot be inserted into the correct tissue. As long as the gene is present and expressed somewhere, the therapy may be effective.

For reasons identified above, the techniques are not able to be applied directly to humans or, for the most part, animals. Not only are some procedures ethically questionable, but they may not be possible scientifically. We do not, as yet, have the scientific knowledge that would allow the regeneration of an entire human from a single cell. Nor would it be acceptable to use a selectable marker that would 'kill' off the vast majority of those we chose to modify. The insertion of genes, at will, into the genome of individual humans is therefore not yet a viable proposition. On the other hand, the technology is developing rapidly, and it may become possible to insert a particular sequence near to a sequence known to occur in a genome. Although there are only four bases that provide the alphabet for a DNA molecule, there are 1,024 different random sequences each consisting of five bases and over a million different sequences consisting of 10 bases. Recognition of a sequence of bases is a fundamental element to this technology and it is likely that systems that must be in existence already in some organisms will be found which are capable of directed insertion of a construct into a particular position in a DNA molecule.

It is clear that many aspects of biotechnology already impact directly on humans, or will do so in the near future. Modification of plants and animals (by traditional means) so that they provide more effective foods is a centuries old practice. Modification of viruses, bacteria and fungi so that they act as less effective pathogens, or are usable as vaccines, is also a process that has been available for some generations. It is now possible to introduce 'human' genes into a whole range of organisms so that they can be used as factories to produce proteins that are important in food or in medicine; as models to allow a better understanding of the function of particular genes or gene products; as media for the growth (and study) of human pathogens; or for the preparation of cells or organs which will ultimately be used in human medicine.[17]

'Genetic disease'

Advances in human genetics over the last few years — particularly those resulting from the greater understanding that the human genome project is providing — are staggering. It is this aspect and the inherent possibilities, however remote, that have caught the imagination of so many. Technology now provides an opportunity to link many characteristics and 'pathologies' with the product of a gene, even where we are not sure of the actual function of that product. As the human genome project proceeds, it has become apparent that there are many variations in the standard complement of genes that identify each one of us as a unique individual. There are many natural modifications of individual genes in the population, most of which have no (as yet) discernible impact on the individual. What we observe are characteristics, or 'phenotype', not the presence or absence of a particular form of a gene. These characteristics may be the result of a multitude of causes to which many genes may contribute. The presence of a

---

17   All cells have on their surfaces factors which allow them to be recognised as self, and therefore prevent them being destroyed by the immune system. The humanisation of organs in animals such as the pig requires these factors to be replaced by those found on human cells.

particular 'allele'[18] or gene product may also result in alterations in multiple characteristics.

Significant modification or mutation in a vital part of many genes would result in loss of function of the gene product, and in most cases, a failure to develop into a viable organism. Many mutations, however, result in disease, or increased susceptibility to disease, or simply to 'undesirable' characteristics.

Up to 3,000 diseases so far have been identified as having a genetic element; approximately two per cent of new-born children suffer from a perceptible genetic disorder. All of the characteristics we possess are decided by both the genes we carry (nature) and by the environment in which we live (nurture). Whilst it has been debated over many years as to which is the more important, for the purpose of this paper, it is of no concern — if there is a 'gene' which is implicated in a particular characteristic, then modification of that gene may result in a modification of the characteristic. It is now possible to test for the absence of a normal gene, or the presence of an abnormal one, even where the function of the gene is unknown. If tests are available to detect the gene, or any modification of it that has occurred, in an individual, the results may be used for both the alleviation of a condition, or for discrimination against the carrier. The development of tests thus presents us with a double-edged sword. In addition, for many conditions, we can identify the cause of the 'deviation from the norm' — which we might term 'disease' — but we have no way of mitigating the impact of that deviation or of modifying the person. Intended modification of a gene or its expression by human intervention may modify the expressed characteristic, even though it is not the only gene involved, but other changes may also be observed.

The definition of disease is, of course, problematic: to some, blond hair may be seen as normal, and dark hair would then be seen as pathological. *Perceived disease* (colour of hair, gayness, cystic fibrosis, likelihood of contracting cancer, diabetes, thallasaemias, Lesch Nyhan syndrome, Tay-Sachs disease, Huntington's disease) may be due to: presence or absence of a gene or allele different from that preferred; absence of expression, although the coding sequence would appear to be present; expression of too much or too little of the gene product; or wrong time or timing of the appearance of the gene product.

Many genetic diseases are due to changes in just a single gene (monogenic), such as adenosine deaminase (ADA) and purine nucleoside phosphorylase (PNP) deficiencies. More than two hundred specific enzyme defects cause known human clinical syndromes, and over a hundred other genetic diseases have been biochemically characterised.[19] Cystic fibrosis is the most common genetic disease, affecting some 30,000 individuals in the United States; about 2,000 children suffering from the disease are born each year.[20] Tay-Sachs disease[21] and

---

18 An 'allele' is an alternative form of a genetic locus; for example, at a locus for eye colour there might be alleles resulting in blue or brown eyes; alleles are inherited separately from each parent. The allele is the actual nucleotide sequence of a gene on a chromosome. Changes in sequence from one allele to another arise as a result of mutation in the germ-line and can be transmitted to the next generation.

19 J.B. Stanbury, J.B. Wyngaarden, D.S. Fredrickson, J.L. Goldstein and M.S. Brown, *The Metabolic Basis of Inherited Disease* 5th ed (New York: McGraw Hill, 1983) ch 1.

20 US Congress, Office of Technology Assessment, *Genetic Counseling and Cystic Fibrosis Carrier Screening: Results of a Survey–Background Paper*, OTA-BP-BA-97 (Washington, DC: US Government Printing Office, September 1992).

21 Tay-Sachs disease is a recessive disorder that affects the central nervous system to cause mental retardation and early death. It is a disease which predominantly occurs among Jews of Eastern and Central European descent and populations in the United States and Canada descended from French Canadian ancestors.

Table 2

Disorder	Number of Patients
Adenosine deaminase deficiency	40–50 worldwide
Purine Nucleoside Phosphorylase deficiency	9 patients in 6 families, worldwide
Lesch-Nyhan Syndrome	1:10,000 males
Arginosuccinate synthetase deficiency	53 cases known
Ornithine carbamoyl transferase deficiency	110 cases known

Huntington's disease[22] are both associated with a single gene defect. However, although there are numerous diseases that may be genetically linked, as Table 2 shows, the number of individuals affected by particular monogenic disorders is quite small.[23]

Familial history and epidemiology used in conjunction with modern gene technology make it relatively simple to identify a gene associated with a particular condition. There is very little that can be done, in terms of mainstream clinical procedures, to alleviate the symptoms of most monogenic diseases.[24] *Theoretically,* treatment of many such monogenic diseases by means of gene therapy is fairly straightforward. If it were possible to replace the gene by one that does not cause disease, in the same place in the genome, then the disease would be removed. But, modern gene technology has not, as yet, provided us with the tools that allow the removal of a gene within a chromosome and its replacement by a corrected form. It is not presently possible to replace genes in the 'right' place with absolute precision. However, if the disease is a result of the absence of a gene product, the provision of that product may alleviate all or most of the symptoms of the disease — insulin for diabetes is an obvious example of one such treatment.

Multigenic disorders have always been seen as much more problematic in terms of treatment. In multigenic disease a number of genes, or their products, interact and very little is known about how changes in one gene or product may affect the interaction with others. However, even though other genes are involved, if a single gene modifies the 'defective' characteristic, then in time it may be possible to 'alleviate' the condition using that gene or gene product.

It is the genes that indicate a predisposition to a disease that are most likely to cause ethical and moral dilemmas when their 'treatment' is considered. If an individual has an increased susceptibility to a particular disease, then genetic information may be used to attempt to ensure that the individual is (so far as is possible) isolated from the vectors that carry the disease. If, however, there is an increased likelihood of developing an auto-immune disease, or suffering from breast cancer later in life, due to the presence of an allele different from that found in the normal population, the question arises as to whether that information should be available to the individual concerned. In the first case there is currently no treatment or prophylaxis. In the latter case the impact of any treatment on the development of the disease is not known.

---

22 Huntington's disease is a dominant trait encoded in chromosome 4 that causes a debilitating brain disease that usually becomes evident only in a patient's 40s or 50s (after reproductive decisions have been made). All who carry the gene will develop the disease.

23 *Human Gene Therapy — A Background Paper* (Washington, DC: US Congress, Office of Technology Assessment, OTA-BP-BA-32, December 1984).

24 E. Tracy, C.R. Childs and Scriver (1995) 56 *American Journal of Human Genetics* 359, cited in N.A. Holtzman, P.D. Murphy, M.S. Watson and P.A. Barr, 'Predictive Genetic Testing: from Basic Research to Clinical Practice' (1997) 278 *Science* 602.

Probably more at issue than the treatment of disease which has a genetic base will be the identification of such diseases, and of individuals who are likely to be affected. If tests are developed which identify those likely to suffer, or those with a predisposition to a pathological condition, a variety of choices become available.

Advances in gene technology present a number of possibilities:

- to link a particular gene or gene product to a characteristic or to test for the presence or absence of a particular allele, and use the information to predict disease or predilection to disease. It may or may not be possible to offer treatment;
- to replace the gene and thereby alleviate all or some of the unacceptable characteristics;
- to replace the gene product and alleviate some or all of the unacceptable characteristics. The obvious example is diabetes, where treatment with insulin, originally derived from pigs and now manufactured, alleviates some of the disabilities suffered. Phenylketonuria is another example which is 'treated' by ensuring that the diet is deficient in phenylalanine.

Genetic testing and screening

There is a growing number of tests for diseases that might have a heritable element. In some cases there is a chemical present in abnormal quantities within body fluids and testing for the difference from the norm is an indication of a disease state. This method of disease detection or corroboration has long been used in medicine. Where a mutation has occurred within an allele, the identification of the absence of the 'normal' gene may depend on relatively simple genetic tests. If the exact mutation has to be identified, then sequencing of the gene may be required. Genetic testing is defined in a recent report by the National Institutes of Health (NIH) Task Force on Genetic Testing, as

> [t]he analysis of human DNA, RNA, chromosomes, proteins, and certain metabolites in order to detect heritable disease-related genotypes, mutations, phenotypes, or karyotypes for clinical purposes. Such purposes include predicting risk of disease, identifying carriers, and establishing prenatal and clinical diagnosis or prognosis. Prenatal, newborn and carrier screening, as well as testing in high risk families, are included. Tests for metabolites are covered only when they are undertaken with high probability that an excess or deficiency of the metabolite indicates the presence of heritable mutations in single genes. Tests conducted purely for research are excluded from the definition, as are tests for somatic (as opposed to heritable) mutations, and testing for forensic purposes.[25]

Testing can allow for the identification of 'diseases' in individuals before the appearance of any symptoms. If a gene has been implicated in an increased probability of a pathological condition developing, then the test informs the patient of a possible increase in the likelihood of their becoming 'ill' or affected at some time in the future.

Many questions arise about the use of genetic testing which have ethical and subsequently legal implications. If there is no available therapy to alleviate a disease that might be predicted by a test, questions have to be asked about whether

---

25   Neil A. Holtzman and Michael S. Watson (eds) *Promoting Safe and Effective Genetic Testing in the United States* (1997) — Genetic Testing: Task Force, National Institutes of Health — Department of Energy Working Group on Ethical, Legal, and Social Implications of Human Genome Research (http://nhgri.nik.gov) (NIH Task Force on Genetic Testing); and Holtzman, Murphy, Watson and Barr, n 24 above.

it should be performed. Even for those diseases which have been identified as being essentially monogenic — a single defective gene being responsible for the condition — we have no effective means of preventing the disease, and in most cases have little in the way of treatment to alleviate the worst features. Of course, in some instances we have been able to use therapies which improve the quality of life of those who suffer from a particular disease, and even ensure that the individuals live beyond the age of reproductive competence. Insulin dependent diabetes and cystic fibrosis are both examples. But the prognosis or time of onset of a disease cannot be detected by genetic testing.

The impact of tests is so important that it is crucial that those performing them are competent, and that those tested understand fully the implications of choosing to take them. Cultural attitudes to illness and abnormality 'run deep'.[26] These attitudes may be important in the application and interpretation of genetic testing and genetic screening procedures. Where a test indicates a likelihood of impairment, and is performed before birth or before implantation, should the provision of the test imply abortion? Predictive tests may have severe implications for the applicant or their family to obtain health or life insurance. Positive test results might not mean the disease will inevitably develop, or even anticipate the severity of the disease. For late onset diseases, there can be no reliable prediction of the age at which the disorder will manifest itself, the degree of debilitation, or the response to treatment.

Markel suggests that '[u]nrelenting vigilance is necessary on the validity of tests and the reliability of the laboratories providing them, both as the tests are developed and as they are used on large numbers of people'.[27] This is also highlighted by the NIH Task Force which recommends that 'the genotypes to be detected by a genetic test must be shown by scientifically valid methods to be associated with the occurrence of a disease. The observations must be independently replicated and subject to peer review'.[28]

The symptoms observed in many illnesses might have many causes. Genetic testing may provide an additional diagnostic tool, a method of identifying which of the causes is responsible for the symptoms in an individual, and hence indicate the likely therapy. Can the information derived from genetic tests be limited to determining the therapy (as is done currently with blood tests)? However, in many cases, symptoms of one disease may be linked (genetically or otherwise) with a predisposition to other problems. The question then arises as to whether the results of the test should be used to inform the patient about those other problems.

Tests provide information about a particular individual, but also provide information about their family — not only parents or siblings. This raises issues about individual autonomy, the possibility of making informed choices and the nature of the wider relationship between individuals and society. If a test has been performed on an individual's genetic material, should the information be made available to all those who may also be affected? Should permission for the test be obtained, not only from the person directly affected, but also from those whose lives might be altered following the test? The impact of what are often uncertainties resulting from testing may affect an individual's identity, their privacy and their relationships. These decisions cannot be made by the scientist, but are extremely important in determining what should and should not be done.

Because of the methods by which deleterious mutations are identified, many of the new pathological conditions that have been associated with unusual alleles

---

26 H. Markel (1997) Appendix 6 of the Report of the NIH Task Force on Genetic Testing (*ibid*).
27 *ibid*.
28 n 25 above.

have been attributed to Ashkenazi Jews. The number of diseases now being described might suggest that Jews from Eastern Europe are the carriers of rather a large number of genetic disorders. That this is an artefact of the methodology may often be forgotten. A recent US Government report, for example, quotes the discovery of a genetic alteration that, in early studies, appears to double a person's risk of colon cancer: 'The genetic alteration, which can be identified with a $200 blood test, is most prevalent among Jews of Eastern European descent. Once identified, people who carry this mutation can use regular colon examinations to detect cancer growth early when it is most easily treated'.[29]

The NIH Task Force on Genetic Testing points out that '[it] is unacceptable to coerce or intimidate individuals or families regarding their decision about predictive genetic testing.'[30] Respect for personal autonomy is regarded as paramount, informed consent must be obtained and it must be made clear that testing is voluntary. Prior to any predictive test in clinical practice, health care providers should describe not only the features of the test but its potential consequences. Whatever decision potential test recipients make, their care is not to be jeopardised.

Testing also carries profound implications for those unable to give consent or fully understand the implications. Should tests be undertaken, for example, on children? Tests are already carried out on almost all children born in the United Kingdom or the United States to determine whether they have phenylketonuria, but this is of direct benefit to the child, as avoidance of foods containing phenylalanine serves almost as a complete 'cure' for the disease. If a test is undertaken on children, should this only be where there is an immediate or direct benefit?

The NIH Task Force has also recommended that: 'No individual should be subjected to unfair discrimination by a third party on the basis of having had a genetic test or receiving an abnormal genetic test result. Third parties include insurers, employers, and educational and other institutions that routinely inquire about the health of applicants for services or positions.'[31] For this recommendation to be effective it would require the introduction of innovative legislation in most countries of a proactive rather than reactive nature. For example, in January 1998, the Vice-President of the United States called for federal legislation to bar employers from discriminating against employees on the basis of their genetic make-up. 'Progress in genetics should not become a new excuse for discrimination,' he said. 'Genetic discrimination is wrong — and it's time we ended it'.[32]

Notwithstanding discrimination, genetic testing is likely to be an important tool in identifying individuals susceptible to disease, not only for attempting to protect them (or their offspring) from the consequences of the disease, but for the future consideration of determining priorities and allocation of resources within health services. It is important that the technology is regulated to ensure that: information is accurate; individuals are provided with information about the identified problem in order to make informed choices; the implications for relatives of those tested are clearly understood by the individual undergoing the test; testing does not result in unfair discrimination at work or for life and health insurance; and priorities and resource allocation decisions are based on as sound evidence as possible taking account of 'the state of the art'.

---

29 *Genetic Information and the Workplace*, Department of Labor, Department of Health and Human Services, Equal Employment Opportunity Commission & the Department of Justice — 20 January 1998.
30 n 25 above.
31 *ibid.*
32 (1998) 9 *Human Genome News*, 1–2.

Gene therapy

If a gene product is known to be faulty, or absent, it may be possible to treat the condition simply by providing the missing chemical that would have appeared had the gene-product not been absent. This has proved extremely difficult in many cases because it is not easy to place the required chemicals at the correct site (within a cell) at the time or with the timing needed. Instead of providing the protein, or the chemicals that result from the presence of the protein, it may be possible to provide the gene. Thus:

> Gene delivery can be achieved either by direct administration of gene-containing viruses or DNA to blood or tissues, or indirectly through the introduction of cells manipulated in the laboratory to harbour foreign DNA. As a sophisticated extension of conventional medical therapy, gene therapy attempts to treat disease in an individual patient by the administration of DNA rather than a drug.[33]

A major goal of 'gene therapy' is to provide the patient with healthy copies of missing or flawed genes.

It is theoretically possible to replace a gene that is absent or not being expressed, but we have little in the way of mechanisms for the removal of a gene within human tissue. If an abnormal gene product is being expressed, and this is resulting in a disease condition, the presence of a gene expressing the normal gene product may not alleviate the condition. Identification of the presence of genes that are associated with abnormal conditions does not necessarily provide a solution. In the case of the genes BRCA1 and BRCA2 that have been linked with a significant increase in the likelihood of breast or ovarian cancer, possible therapy includes the complete removal of the 'offending' tissue but there is no evidence as yet that this radical procedure would relieve the problem.

There have been a number of attempts to *mask* the effect of genes, in effect *removing* them by using anti-sense oligo-nucleotides[34] that are believed to bind to the RNA before translation or to the DNA and stop the formation of the protein gene-product.

Therapies that involve 'changing the gene' may include:

- gene insertion, in which a new version of a gene is introduced into a cell;
- gene modification, in which a gene already in place is altered; and
- gene surgery, in which a particular gene is excised and may also be replaced by its normal counterpart.

At present, only the first of these alternatives is available.

It is not only the replacement of defective genes that may be important. If a gene is available which can allow the targeting of particular cells, then its insertion into a patient may allow novel therapeutic action. Anti-tumour cytokines is an example where the aim is to enhance the *in vivo* production of therapeutic chemicals. A further use of the technology involves the insertion of *suicide genes* into unwanted cells (such as cancers) the gene-product of which is capable of converting relatively benign drugs circulating in the bloodstream into cyto-toxins.

It is possible to place a 'new' gene in germ-line cells (sperm or egg cells) which

---

33   Stuart H. Orkin and Arno G. Motulsky, *Report and Recommendations of the Panel to Assess the NIH Investment in Research on Gene Therapy* (1995) National Institutes of Health, Washington DC.

34   An oligo-nucleotide is a short length of DNA or RNA. As DNA is double stranded and consists of two complementary strands, the production of a piece of DNA or RNA which is complementary to that which is translated to form a protein ('anti-sense') may stop translation and little or no gene product is produced.

would result in the inserted information being passed from that generation to all succeeding generations. Germ line gene therapy is not considered acceptable at present because of its permanence, and the lack of precision in the use of the technology. To some, the technique is 'immoral', as exemplified in the Directive on the Legal Protection of Biotechnological Inventions that was agreed earlier this year in the European Parliament. Germ line gene therapy remains unacceptable at the present time, and will remain so until we have much more control and understanding of the processes, both immediate and delayed, that may result from the insertion of a gene into what would be all the cells within that person and their offspring.

The alternative is to place the replacement genes into the genome within 'somatic' cells. Somatic cell gene therapy involves the introduction of a gene into cells with the expectation that the gene will be expressed and that a disease state will be alleviated. The gene is expressed only in those cells and is not passed on to future generations. It is hoped that the gene will remain in the cell and be expressed for a reasonable period of time, but it is not necessarily inserted into the genome within the cell. The technology may be performed *in vitro* on explanted autologous or other cells. The desired gene is inserted into the cell that is then placed within its human host. It is also possible to introduce the gene *in vivo*.

Gene therapy may also be administered simply by using the gene in a way similar to a drug, providing the patient with an encapsulated gene capable of providing, for a short period, the necessary gene products and functions. Such genes would not be incorporated into the genome and would, in general, be lost ultimately from the target cells.

None of these techniques is without problems. Only a small proportion of cells is modified using any of the processes mentioned above. Generally, in humans, modified virus particles would be used to act as vectors for the insertion of genes into the human genome, and the number of cells infected may be small. The amount of gene product expressed may then be significantly less than might have been expected. It is not usually possible to insert the replacement gene into the affected tissue, ie the organ in which the normal gene product would be produced. For example, insulin is produced in the Islets of Langerhans in the pancreas. It may not be necessary to produce the insulin at that same site, as the functional site is different. If it were necessary to introduce the gene into that tissue, the difficulties might well be insurmountable. Many genes appear to function at a particular time or in response to particular environmental stresses or changes. It has not, as yet, proved possible to mimic the time at which a gene is switched on, or the response to stress. In addition, the gene product may not be produced continuously. Until we have a greater understanding of the promoter and signal sequences attached to genes, it will remain difficult to mimic the control.

The insertion of 'foreign' genes into a patient is not new. All transplant patients carry genes which may be different from their own, and which may be expressing a slightly different protein with different properties that impact on the whole patient. Blood transfusion also involves the transfer of genes that may (for a short time) express proteins different from those in the patient. Somatic gene therapy is therefore part of the natural progression in medical science. The technology may enable the alleviation of many disease conditions and even the cure of human disease including cancer, and AIDS.

It was originally envisaged that gene therapy would be used to treat monogenic disorders, but this has not proved to be the case. The number of individuals who are suffering from any single monogenic disease is too small to make the research effort economically viable, and the majority of protocols for gene therapy throughout the world have concentrated on diseases of concern to much larger groups of individuals.[35] For the first 2,300 patients where treatment has been attempted, only 10 per cent have been for a range of monogenic diseases, 60 per cent have been for cancer, and about 18 per cent for infectious diseases (primarily AIDS).[36] At the beginning of 1998, approximately three hundred protocols had been approved, involving 2,293 patients.[37] The vast majority of patients have been in the USA (75 per cent, 1,708 of 2,293); 367 patients have been treated in the European Union and Switzerland, of whom 95 patients have been treated in the UK. The diagram below shows the number of patients treated for identified problems.

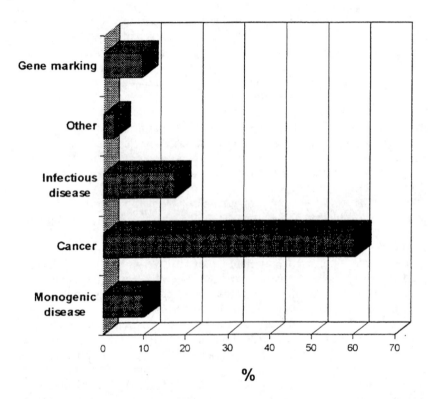

Gene therapy protocols for work with cancer patients have included both gene marking and 'true' gene therapy. Amongst the major areas of work have been: use of suicide genes which provide drug sensitivity to cancer cells; use of cells carrying genes which confer drug resistance into non-malignant blood stem cells to protect them from chemotherapy; insertion of tumour suppression genes into cancers; boosting of the host anti-tumour immune system; transfer of oncogene down-regulating genes to shut off cancer-inducing genes; and use of anti-sense genes to block the expression of cancer-promoting genes.

Getting the gene into the relevant cell in a live human remains problematic. If an attenuated virus is modified so that it is capable of infecting the patient and carrying the required genes into appropriate cells, there is a possibility that the

---

35   http://www.wiley.co.uk/genetherapy/diseases.htm (January 1998).
36   http://www.wiley.co.uk/genetherapy/ (5 March 1998).
37   http://www.wiley.co.uk/genetherapy/genes.htm (January 1998).

virus may regain virulence, or infect persons other than the target. There are a wide variety of vectors used to insert the DNA into the desired cells. Techniques include micro-injection, where naked DNA is inserted into isolated cells, complexed DNA within liposomes, retroviral RNA vectors and DNA viruses (eg adenovirus, herpes and pox viruses). As Table 3 shows, retroviruses are best understood, and have therefore been used in most protocols, although they have the disadvantage of only infecting dividing cells. The virus is incorporated into the host genome in a random position. Adenoviruses have the advantage of being able to infect non-dividing cells, are said not to integrate within the genome, but are highly immunogenic.

Table 3[38]

Vector	Protocols	Patients
Adeno-associated virus	3	21
Adenovirus	34	265
Electroporation	2	8
Gene gun	4	30
Liposome	56	433
Liposome/Adenovirus	1	3
Naked DNA	9	54
Poxvirus	16	121
Retrovirus	139	1100
Retrovirus/gene gun	1	6
Retrovirus vector producing cells	22	155
RNA transfer	1	0
Transfection	5	94
Totals	*301*	*2293*

The tools are available to allow a very considerable expansion in the use of genes in providing new ways of treating disease but the problems highlighted in terms of the application of the technology must first be overcome.

The NIH Panel that reported on the use of gene therapy in 1995 was extremely critical of that which had been done at that stage. They were excited by the promise of gene therapy but were concerned that 'clinical efficacy had not been definitively demonstrated at this time in any gene therapy protocol, despite anecdotal claims of successful therapy and the initiation of more than one hundred Recombinant DNA Advisory Committee (RAC)-approved protocols'.[39] The Panel identified difficulties in almost every aspect of the technology. They were concerned not only about the vectors used but that the scientific basis for comprehending the manner in which some vectors interact with human tissue was not well understood. There was concern that the basic research required to underpin much of the work in human patients had not yet been done adequately, and 'in the enthusiasm to proceed to clinical trials, basic studies of disease pathophysiology, which are likely to be critical to the eventual success of gene therapy, have not been given adequate attention'.[40] The Panel believed that these studies could have been attempted in animal models before their use in humans, and that such studies could well have offered alternative treatment procedures. On the other hand, the report went on to

---

38   http://www.wiley.co.uk/genetherapy/vectors.html (5 March 1998).
39   See n 33 above.
40   *ibid.*

identify the need for further clinical studies to evaluate the gene therapy approach. This makes it clear that animal experiments cannot provide complete information. In particular, it is important to use human clinical studies for cystic fibrosis, cancer and AIDS.

The Panel was unsure about the interpretation of the results of many of the gene therapy protocols that had been attempted at the time of their report. Problems of 'very low frequency of gene transfer, reliance on qualitative rather than quantitative assessments of gene transfer and expression, lack of suitable controls, and lack of rigorously defined biochemical or disease endpoints'[41] were cited. The overall impression of the Panel was that only a minority of clinical studies had been designed to yield useful, basic information. A further problem highlighted was that the 'hype' regarding the results achieved implied a greater degree of success than had actually been observed. The Panel emphasised that this could undermine confidence in the integrity of the field and might ultimately hinder progress in development of the successful application of gene therapy to human disease.

Xenotransplantation

Modern biotechnology may also be used to overcome rejection of transplanted animal tissues. This procedure would reduce the problem of many more organs being required for transplantation than are currently available. The transplantee acutely rejects animal organs unless the immune system has been suppressed (or modified). This happens normally when the donor is human, but careful choice of donor and the use of immuno-suppressive drugs slows or stops rejection. Rejection of animal organs is likely to be much more severe than that of human organs. It will be possible to make the animal tissue 'closer' to that of the human into whom it is to be placed by changing a variety of 'recognition sites' which occur on the surface of all cells. This would decrease the amount of suppression of the immune system required to allow acceptance of the new tissue whilst retaining the capacity to resist disease. There are many scientific issues which might be addressed, including the similarity of physiology between the donor and human tissue, sterility of donated tissue, and the possibility of transfer of dormant viruses to the immuno-suppressed human (or animal). Scientists are working on the 'humanisation' of animals, particularly pigs — seen to be the most likely donors of organs — and many of the problems of rejection have been solved. The UK is likely to allow transplantation from pigs to humans, but has ruled out the use of primate organs both for moral and safety reasons.

The risks of disease transmitted from animal to man through xenotransplantation are significant. Even where organs are humanised, the patient will still require suppression of their immune system, and any infectious agents in the animal tissue may be passed on. In order to maintain 'sterility' the animals will have been kept in isolation, and are likely to have been born using caesarean section. It is possible to screen for known pathogens likely to infect humans, whether immuno-suppressed or immuno-competent, and only use animals that appear not to be infected. There are, however, likely to be dormant viruses incorporated into the genome of the animal which, under the new physiological conditions, could be activated to affect the transplanted tissue within the patient, the patient's own tissue, or even be

---

41 *ibid.*

transferred from the patient to the general public. It is well established that most new emerging human infectious diseases generally have their origins in other species.[42] The risks to the general public are extremely small, are impossible to estimate, and may be too small to justify monitoring patients over an extended period of time. Such risks may well be considered worth taking, but the hazard may be substantial.

An editorial in *Nature* in January 1998 strongly advises a worldwide moratorium on the use of xenotransplantations, arguing that the rejection problem requires much more work, and that the potential risks of disease transfer are currently too great to accept.[43] Given the potential risk to the public, the issue is first and foremost an ethical one. Before introducing a regulatory framework driven by technical considerations, an informed public debate is needed so that the public can decide whether it wishes to consent to clinical xenotransplantation at all and, if so, under what conditions.[44] The United Kingdom currently takes one of the most stringent positions, having introduced a moratorium on clinical trials until further research shows that transplants are safe and that the science is sufficiently developed to offer transplant recipients real benefits.[45] The government has set up a Xenotransplantation Interim Regulatory Authority, and is expected to produce legislation later this year.

Artificial organs and human cells and tissues provide alternatives to xenotransplantation, and would avoid the risk of xenozoonoses. One company is to market an artificial skin, based on cultured human cells, for example, while stem cells extracted from umbilical cord blood offer a promising alternative to bone marrow transplants.[46]

Cloning

The debate about cloning has concentrated on the possibility of individuals attempting to make identical copies of themselves, and the repugnance felt by many that this might be possible. It is likely that the scientific lessons derived from the cloning of animals will lead primarily to the cloning of tissue rather than of whole organisms. The brunt of the discussion on cloning has concentrated on the development of techniques to produce exact genetic copies of an individual (with respect to nuclear DNA). The main advantages of experiments on cloning would appear to be the identification of the biochemical and physiological controls which might allow the reconstitution of an organ from a small number of cells. Thus: 'Nuclear replacement research can improve our knowledge about physiological processes and the genotype. For example, it is hoped that this work will offer a greater insight into the origins of cancer and other cellular development processes such as ageing and cell commitment.'[47]

---

42 See eg, B. Hjelle *et al* 'A Novel Hantavirus Associated with an Outbreak of Fatal Respiratory Disease in the Southwestern United States: Evolutionary Relationships to Known Hantaviruses' (1994) 68 J Virol 592; S.S. Morse and A. Schluederberg, 'Emerging Viruses: The Evolution of Viruses and Viral Diseases' (1990) 162 J Infect Dis 1; F.A. Murphy, New, emerging, and reemerging infectious diseases' (1994) 4 Adv Virus Res 1.

43 'Halt the Xeno-bandwagon: Xenotransplantation's Risks Make a Moratorium Essential' (1998) 319 *Nature* 309.

44 F. H. Bach and H.V. Fineberg 'Call for Moratorium on Xenotransplants' (1998) 391 *Nature* 326; and R. A. Weiss 'Transgenic Pigs and Virus Adaptation' (1998) 391 *Nature* 327.

45 (1997) 385 *Nature* 285.

46 (1996) 382 *Nature* 99.

47 *Cloning Issues in Reproduction, Science and Medicine. A Consultation Document* Human Genetics Advisory Commission (HGAC) and Human Fertilisation & Embryology Authority (HFEA), (1998) Department of Health.

Development of therapeutic agents

The development of gene products which will be significant as therapeutic agents in other organisms (clotting factors in sheep's milk, or vaccines in plant products) is already important in the pharmaceutical industry. The use of products derived from human tissue is problematic because these may contain factors capable of infecting humans. It has long been held that recombinant blood products (produced in yeasts or bacteria), such as blood clotting factors used for haemophiliacs, are much safer than those derived from human blood as contaminating agents are absent. This is theoretically true, but currently both serum-derived Factor VIII and recombinant factor VIII are stabilised by the addition of serum albumin. In the United Kingdom, the cost of the recombinant factor VIII is more than double that of factors derived from pooled human serum. Because of concerns about the infectivity of new-variant CJD, the Government has recently decided that it will not use pooled serum from within the UK. The production of human gene-products in plants in particular is likely to provide a source of relatively safe products, indistinguishable from those derived from human tissue in large quantities and at reasonable prices.

Conclusion

Clearly there are many avenues open to the scientist to use biotechnology in humans or in other organisms for the benefit of humans. All of these are being explored. Many of these approaches may carry considerable risks, or may prove unacceptable. Human genetics may or may not succeed in becoming the new panacea. In the meantime we may have been presented with a veritable Pandora's Box. Whilst scientists and physicians are capable of identifying the possibilities which may advance therapeutic procedures, they are no better equipped than anyone else to identify the social and moral issues that might result from their use. Only society can ultimately decide the degree of importance to be attached to the benefits, hazards and impact of these. Such fundamental decisions within an area of inherent uncertainty can only be made within a properly constituted regulatory framework. Only law can provide the mechanisms that can facilitate effectively the negotiation between fact and value and the taking of necessary decisions about the nature and direction of scarce resources for both research and policy. Regulation also carries with it a number of other advantages. By ensuring that controversial developments and the practices of scientists and clinicians are properly authorised and monitored a potent regulatory framework can assist public acceptance of 'cutting edge' techniques such as those discussed above. Besides being instrumental in the policy process law thus promotes legitimacy and accountability.

The issue of which regulatory devices are to be given preference is of course a matter of conjecture and debate,[48] but lessons can surely be drawn from the growing provisions and literature on their use in the field of non human biotechnology, in addition to those in the ever widening field of innovative medical technologies.

---

48   cf the discussion in Julia Black's paper in this volume.

Regulation as Facilitation: Negotiating the Genetic Revolution

*Julia Black**

Regulation of genetic technology, some would claim, is an oxymoron. Genetic technology is simply out of control.[1] If you turn to ask what structures exist to regulate genetic technology, however, then you find a mass of legal regulations, non-legal rules, codes, circulars, practice notes, international conventions, and ethical codes. There exists an enormously complex set of advisory bodies, regulatory bodies, committees, professional bodies, and industry associations, operating at an international, national and sub-national level. In the UK, at the national level alone, there are over eleven different bodies involved in the regulation of some aspect of genetic technology. Surely in this morass of regulation someone, somewhere, must be exerting some form of control?

But the charge is more complex: it is essentially that control is not being exercised over what it should be. That regulation is not finding the right answers, or indeed asking the right questions. Moreover, that science is defining the agenda: in Beck's phrase, the debate about its course occurs as an obituary for activities begun long ago.[2]

Indeed, one of the striking aspects both of the debate about genetic technology and of its regulation is the number of different conceptualisations of the 'problem' which genetic technology poses and thus of the solutions that should be found. It is seen variously to be an issue of risk (to health, the environment), a question of choice (of patients, consumers), a matter of property rights (to patents, an individual's DNA), of confidentiality (against employers, insurance companies, other family members), or a question of ethics. Moreover, the definition of the problem which is adopted by regulation and the solutions proposed are not always those that others would share.

Given these fundamental divergences of views, it is suggested that regulation has a role to play which is not, or not simply, about control, but rather about facilitation. Regulation has an important role to play in connecting the arguments of participants, in facilitating the integration of the wide range of views as to the appropriate course that the technology and its regulation should take. The first task of this article is to explore the extent to which this occurs at present: to examine just what questions the current regulation of genetic technology asks, and what questions others consider it should be asking. What do the regulatory systems and

* Law Department, London School of Economics and Political Science.
My thanks go to Rob Baldwin, Anne Barron, Damian Chalmers, Tim Cross and Gunther Teubner for reading and commenting on an earlier draft, and to the participants of the Modern Law Review conference on Law and Genetics for their responses to the paper given at the conference. Responsibility for views, errors and omissions remains my own.

1 A view most forcefully put by Beck: U. Beck, *Risk Society: Towards a New Modernity* (London: Sage, 1992, trans M. Ritter); further U. Beck, *Ecological Politics in an Age of Risk* (London: Polity Press, 1992, trans A. Weisz); id, *Ecological Enlightenment: Essays on the Politics of the Risk Society* (New Jersey, Humanities Press, 1995).

2 Beck, *Ecological Politics in an Age of Risk,* ibid 203.

their participants consider their purpose and rationale to be, and what gaps exist between that internal perspective and that of those outside the regulatory system as to the central issues which should be addressed.

The main purpose of the article is then to consider how regulation may facilitate the integration of those different perspectives. Integration does not mean the replacement of a multitude of perspectives with the regulatory imposition of just one. Rather integration is the full recognition of different perspectives in the regulatory process. The call for integration in this form is one which is often made. The ways to achieving that integration, it is frequently advocated, are the development of forms and forums of consensus-building and co-operation, and the adoption of communicative, procedural models of regulation. The labels vary across writers and disciplines: 'proceduralisation',[3] 'civic science',[4] 'scientific proceduralism',[5] or simply 'democratisation',[6] but they share a common desire. That is to open up the decision process, to deny any one voice authority in that process, and through the integration of views and perspectives to arrive at accepted solutions to intractable problems. The negotiation of regulation.

To the extent that the facilitation of such negotiative, or integrationist, models requires simply institutional re-design, then finding ways to achieve this is complicated although solutions can probably be found, at least at the level of policy formation. However it is suggested that facilitating integration also requires that attention be paid to other dimensions of regulation which are sometimes overlooked, notably those of cognition and communication. In particular, attention has to be paid to the standing of different parties in that negotiation, to the weight or authority which will be ascribed by participants to each voice, and to the barriers to communication which it is suggested that different cognitive systems give rise.

With respect to the issues of standing and of cognitive authority, then, at present, the scientific voice is that which is granted the status of objectivity, and thus, in the current rules of debate, authority and legitimacy. Lay views are often seen as irrational, based in ignorance, as mere emotions or prejudices. As such they have only such weight as is necessary to afford them in a democratic society. They are either an irritation or something which should be indulged, depending on your view of popular politics. But the scientific language is that which is accepted; it is the official language of debate. For 'lay' views to be accepted, then (to an extent) they have to re-translate themselves into the language of science, and in so doing accept the scientific definition of the problem. For a negotiation to occur which fully recognises and gives standing to other voices, there is a need for a reorientation of the cognitive aspect of regulation. This requires in part a re-conceptualisation of the view that 'expert = objective, lay = irrational'. It is on such an exercise that a number of writers have embarked, and the nature of that exercise will be explored in part here.

---

3 R. Mayntz, 'The Conditions of Effective Public Policy: A New Challenge for Policy Analysis' (1983) 11 *Policy and Politics* 123; G. Teubner, 'Substantive and Reflexive Elements in Modern Law' (1983) 17 *Law & Soc Rev* 239; G. Teubner, 'After Legal Instrumentalism? Strategic Models of Post-Regulatory Law' in G. Teubner (ed), *Dilemmas of Law in the Welfare State* (Berlin: de Gruyter, 1985); H. Willke, 'Societal Regulation through Law?' in G. Teubner and G. Febbrajo (eds), *State, Law, Economy as Autopoietic Systems* (Milan: Guiffre, 1992).

4 T. O'Riordan, 'Exploring the Role of Civic Science in Risk Management' in C. Hood and D. Jones (eds), *Accident and Design: Contemporary Debates in Risk Management* (London: UCL Press, 1996).

5 K.S. Shrader-Frechette, *Risk and Rationality: Philosophical Foundations for Populist Reforms* (Berkeley: University of California Press, 1991).

6 Beck, *Ecological Politics in an Age of Risk*, n 1 above.

There is a more fundamental problem, however, which it is suggested here faces an approach to regulation which seeks to facilitate integration. It is one which occurs on the communicative dimension, and is one which the idea of 're-translation' emphasises. It is that the languages of science, commerce, ethics, ecology, law are foreign to each other; neither can hardly understand what the other is saying, let alone why they are saying it. Until this problem is addressed, simply focusing on the structural dimension, providing the structures in which different actors can participate, will not lead to a negotiated agreement. This is because the different participants speak different languages. The conditions for real communication do not exist. This 'dialogue of the deaf' is particularly striking in the context of genetics. What is needed, it is suggested, is the means by which this language barrier can be overcome. This cannot be provided by the development of a common language, however, for the cognitive differences are too fundamental. Nor should it be provided by an 'official' language, for that would represent the dominance of one cognitive perspective over all others. Rather, it is suggested, regulation needs to facilitate communication by taking on the role of interpreter or translator: putting the views of each set of participants into a language that the others can understand. It can thereby enable the integration, the negotiation of regulation, which is required.

Regulation: structural, cognitive and communicative dimensions

In analysing the regulation of genetic technology it is proposed to focus on three dimensions of regulation: the structural, the cognitive and the communicative. There are thus other dimensions which are here excluded, notably that of preferences: the article will not explore the different interests which participants have nor how they are pursued.[7]

The structural dimension is essentially the institutional context in which regulation occurs. The ability of actors to enter a particular regulatory or decision making forum is structured by institutional rules and norms, both legal and non-legal.[8] Some may be able to access that forum relatively easily, others may find that they are excluded from it, or can only enter in a limited way. So there may be insiders and outsiders with respect to a particular forum: those who have access to a particular forum and those who do not.

The cognitive dimension refers to the perceptions of participants, their 'world views', their rationalities, their operating logics.[9] The communicative dimension refers to the communicative interaction between participants.[10] The dimensions may interact. Thus the non-legal norms which may define entry to a particular forum or the standing of a participant in that forum may themselves be defined by

---

7   There are a number of analyses of the relationship between preferences and perceptions: for a discussion of the relationship between the cognitive aspect and that of preferences in the context of institutional analysis see J. Black, 'New Institutionalism and Naturalism in Socio-Legal Analysis: Institutionalist Approaches to Regulatory Decision Making' (1997) 19 *Law and Policy* 51.

8   I am here drawing on sociological institutionalist analyses of decision making: see in particular R. Scott, *Institutions and Organizations* (California: Sage, 1995); W. Powell and P. DiMaggio (eds), *The New Institutionalism in Organisational Analysis* (Chicago: Univ Chicago Press, 1992).

9   For a discussion see for example the references cited in n 8 above, and R. Friedland and R. Alford, 'Bringing Society Back In: Symbols, Practices and Institutional Contradictions' in Powell and DiMaggio, n 8 above.

10 It thus clearly has resonance with the communicative models of Habermas; most recently J. Habermas, *Between Facts and Norms: Contributions to a Discourse Theory of Law and Democracy* (Cambridge: Polity Press, 1996).

the cognitive dimension: the institutional actors' own sense of who should have access and who should not. Institutional structures may facilitate communication. Indeed it is the adjusting of such structures to this end which is advocated by many as the solution to the problem of cognitive fragmentation (fundamental divergences of perspective or world views).

Focusing on these three dimensions of regulation illustrates very clearly the task facing regulators in facilitating negotiation and integration. It is that cognitive fragmentation itself places a considerable barrier to communication. Different cognitive structures simply have different languages. This barrier thus exists even if the appropriate institutional structures are in place. Participants in the debates on the course and regulation of genetic technology simply speak different languages; simply providing the structures in which they can all participate in a decision will not serve to overcome this communication barrier. Focusing on the structural, communicative and cognitive dimensions of regulation indicates the differences in perspective which different actors have as to the definition of and solution to the 'problem' of genetic technology and the implications which this has for the languages in which issues relating to genetic technology are debated, and the role for regulation which this entails.

The next three sections of the article explore three different aspects of genetic technology: genetically modified organisms (GMOs) and genetically engineered products (GEPs), genetic technology in the human and medical context, and that of the rights to the exploitation of genetic technology. With respect to each, the analysis will focus on the structural dimension of the regulation, and ask who has access to the regulatory or decision making fora and who does not ('insiders' and 'outsiders'), on the cognitive dimension, asking what the different conceptualisations are of the problems posed or issues to be addressed, and on the communicative dimension, the languages which are used. Whose definition of the problem is the definitive one? What language dominates? Which discourse do others have to adopt in order to be heard? Is the language of science, or medicine, for example the only one which is seen as valid; do all other arguments have to re-translate themselves into this language in order to be recognised as ones that have to be addressed? To what extent, finally, is there an attempt to negotiate a regulatory decision between different participants and what form does that negotiation take?

Regulating GMOs and GEPs

Techniques of genetically modifying organisms are well advanced, and an increasing number of genetically engineered products are being developed and marketed.[11] Regulation of this aspect of genetic technology is fragmented and there are a number of different regulatory fora in which issues concerning research into genetic engineering and the development and marketing of genetically engineered products are raised. The principal actors are scientists, both in universities and in

---

11 Genetically engineered maize, soya, cotton, tomatoes and potatoes are being grown in the US and Canada, and a tomato puree made from genetically modified tomatoes was first sold in the UK in 1996. In total 124 consents for the release of GMOs had been granted between 1993 and June 1997; in December 1996 the European Commission decided to give its approval to authorise the marketing of GM maize for unrestricted use; approval has been given for a GM oilseed rape, and several other applications are pending. Details are given in ACRE's newsletters (available at http://www.shef.ac.uk/doe).

industry, industry itself, and a plethora of regulatory bodies whose membership reflects the traditional corporatist relationship of government, business and unions. There are few opportunities for the wider public to enter the regulatory fora, and they are recognised principally in their capacity as consumers. The issues or problems raised by genetic engineering are seen solely in terms of risk. The organising principle of the regulation is thus risk, and moreover, whilst there is some recognition in principle that different perceptions of risk may exist it is not clear to what extent a technical, scientific measurement is discounted in favour of public perceptions of risk.[12]

There are tensions which arise between those who are inside the regulatory fora, the regulators and regulated, but these are as to whether or not the regulation is accurately targeted towards the right risks, not as to whether risk is the most appropriate organising principle. The concerns of those who are outside are often much broader and more fundamental, often going not to issues of risk, although those are raised, but to the activity of genetic engineering itself, and to the wider implications it can have with respect to related issues of for example, intensive farming, the growth and dominance of agri-business, or the disadvantaged position of smaller farmers particularly in developing countries. Such 'ethical' objections are however effectively excluded from the regulatory fora.

Regulatory fora and principal actors

The conduct of genetic research and the development and marketing of GEPs is regulated by laboratories themselves and by governmental bodies who bear a wealth of acronyms. The key regulatory instruments are the Code on Good Laboratory Practice, and the regulations on contained use[13] and deliberate release,[14] both of which implement EU directives.[15] The contained use regulations are issued under the Health and Safety at Work Act 1974 (HSWA) and their operation is principally the responsibility of the Health and Safety Executive (HSE), acting in consultation with the Department of the Environment (DoE). In practice this is undertaken by the Advisory Committee on Genetic Modification (ACGM), a non-statutory body. The ACGM advises on the granting of consents, on policy development and EU negotiations, and produces guidance.[16] Enforcement is the function of the HSE, which has specialist inspectors for the purpose. The deliberate release regulations are issued under the Environmental Protection Act 1990 (EPA), and their administration is principally the responsibility of the DoE, acting in consultation with the HSE. Again, in practice this task is undertaken by

---

12 On the distinctions between them, see further below.
13 GMO (Contained Use) Regulations 1992, SI 1992/3217; amended by the GMO (Contained Use) (Amendment) Regulations 1996, SI 1996/967 and the GMO (Risk Assessment) (Records and Exemptions) Regulations 1996, SI 1996/1106 (exemption from risk assessment with respect to human health for imported or acquired GMOs).
14 Genetically Modified Organisms (Deliberate Release) Regulations 1992, SI 1992/3280 (as amended), made under Part IV of the EPA 1990.
15 Council Directive on the contained use of genetically modified micro-organisms 90/219/EEC OJ No L 117/1 and Council Directive on the deliberate release into the environment of genetically modified organisms 90/220/EEC OJ No L 117/15. These Directives were based on the OECD's report, *Recombinant DNA Safety Considerations*, OECD, 1986. In addition, the Advisory Committee on Dangerous Pathogens publishes advice on work with dangerous pathogens, and GMOs may also be biological agents under the Control of Substances Hazardous to Health Regulations 1994.
16 The latter task has now been given to a permanent Technical Sub-Committee, established in 1996. See further ACGM Newsletter No 21, February 1997.

an advisory body, the Advisory Committee on Releases to the Environment (ACRE), which is established under the EPA.[17]

The regulation of products which are to be placed on the market is also governed by regulations rooted in EU directives. The regulation of genetically engineered products, or products containing GMOs, initially occurred under the deliberate release regulations but gradually several discrete systems of regulation are being developed for different types of products, or where appropriate the regulation is being assimilated into existing regulation of similar products. So whereas the initial 1992 regulations covered the marketing of all GMOs,[18] subsequent changes have created separate regimes for medicines and veterinary products,[19] animal feed additives[20] and foods and food products which are produced from GMOs or contain GMO products.[21] The change is often described as a move from 'process' to 'product-based' regulation: from scrutinising any act of genetic modification to scrutiny of the product itself.[22] In fact process regulation continues, and moreover GM products are still subject to a risk assessment which is over and above that which is applied to products of the same type.

The principal actors in this regulatory environment are thus scientific researchers in universities and industry, industry itself, and those who sit on the different regulatory quangos. Regulation occurs within laboratories and industry, and those working with GMOs or producing GEPs are required to have local safety committees to advise on risk assessments. The membership of ACGM and ACRE follow a corporatist model, combining government, industry and union representatives. All have a scientific background and the latter are meant to have some kind of broad remit to represent the public, and they include a number of ecologists.[23]

Access

The operation of the regulation is structured essentially as a series of discrete and individualised negotiations between applicant and regulator. Those working with

---

17 ACRE used to be the sub-committee of the ACGM on releases to the environment.

18 But not non-living GMOs or products derived from GMO products which were not themselves GMOs (bread containing modified wheat, for example).

19 Under the Genetically Modified Organisms (Deliberate Release) Regulations 1995, SI 1995/304, implementing EC Directive 94/15/EC OJ No L 103, the authorisation and supervision of medicinal products for human and veterinary use is to occur on a European basis: Council Regulation EEC No 2309/93 (OJ No L214) lays down an EC procedure for their authorisation and supervision and establishes a European Agency for the Evaluation of Medicinal Products. The Regulation provides for the specific risk assessment of medicinal products containing or consisting of GMOs.

20 The change was again introduced by the 1995 Deliberate Release Regulations, which provide that with respect to the marketing of additives which fall under the Feeding Stuffs Regulations 1991 (SI 1991/2840, as amended by SI 1993/1442, 1994/499 and 1994/2510) incorporated or to be incorporated in any feeding stuff, a specific risk assessment of additives containing GMOs has to be undertaken. The 1995 regulations implement Directives 70/524 OJ No L270, and 93/114/EC OJ No L334.

21 The Genetically Modified Organisms (Deliberate Release and Risk Assessment Amendment) Regulations 1997, SI 1997/1900 add to the exemptions from the requirement for consent novel foods or ingredients containing GMOs which fall under Regulation EC No 258/97 OJ No L 43 concerning novel foods and food ingredients. The regulation provides for specific environmental risk assessment of novel foods or novel food ingredients which contain or consist of GMOs and introduces a labelling regime. It is administered in the UK by the Advisory Committee on Novel Foods and Processes and MAFF.

22 For a discussion of the distinction see J. Tait and L. Levidow, 'Proactive and Reactive Approaches to Risk Regulation: The Case of Biotechnology' (1992) 24(3) *Futures* 219.

23 For an early assessment of the composition of ACRE see L. Levidow and J. Tait, 'Advice on Biotechnology Regulation: the Remit and Composition of Britain's ACRE' (1993) 20 *Science and Public Policy* 193.

GMOs are required to notify HSE of the intention to use premises for genetic modification work for the first time and for certain subsequent individual activities, and in some cases await specific consent from HSE before starting the work. Those intending to release or market GMOs must apply for consent to the appropriate body, usually ACRE. The controls to be adopted are negotiated between the applicant and the regulator.

There is some attempt to broaden the conversation which currently occurs between regulator and applicant to include third parties. This is made through the publication of a register of notifications and approvals for both contained use of GMOs and their release. The HSE maintains a register of notifications of contained use which is open to public inspection.[24] It is required to publish a specified minimum amount of information concerning the identity of the notifier, the type of activity being undertaken, plans for monitoring the GMO and for emergency response, and the valuation of any foreseeable effects of the GMO.[25] The applications for deliberate release are also placed on a public register,[26] and the ACRE Guidance requires applicants to provide a summary conclusion of the risk assessment which would be comprehensible to a layman.[27] Applications to release for non-market purposes must in addition be publicised in one or more newspapers which circulate in the locality of the release, and must contain a statement of the purpose and nature of release to be made and which other specified bodies have been notified.[28] ACRE's advice as to consent will also be entered on the register. Although there is no formal mechanism for public objections to be made or taken into account, the ACRE guidance indicates that ACRE will consider public comments prior to the final decision; to this end its advice is entered at least two weeks before the final decision.[29]

There is a tension, however, between providing transparency of the regulatory system and protecting the confidentiality of the regulated. To this end, beyond this minimum amount the notifiers under the contained use regulations can claim that the information should not be disclosed as it would adversely affect their competitive position or ability to obtain a patent (on the basis that the information has to have been previously unpublished).[30] The onus is however on the notifier to give full justification of this claim.[31] Under the deliberate release regulations information may be witheld from publication (but not from ACRE) if it is commercially confidential.[32] Applicants have tried to make extensive use of these exclusions, marking all information as commercially confidential and on occasion witholding information from the regulators themselves on that basis, practices which the regulators have criticised.[33] Further, following pressure from applicants

---

24   Reg 16. The register is not complete in that it only contains those notifications for which express consent has to be given by the HSE, that is first uses of Group II organisms, and Type B operations with Group II organisms.
25   Reg 15.
26   Reg 17.
27   Guidance, paras 3.32, 3.44 and 3.90(g).
28   Reg 8.
29   ACRE guidance, para 3.91.
30   See further below.
31   Reg 15(2).
32   EPA s 123(3)(a). The criterion used for deliberate release is thus slightly different than that which applies under the Contained Use Regulations, which applies to information which would adversely affect the applicant's competitive position. Note in any event that the Environmental Information Regulations 1992, SI 1992/3240, apply, governing freedom of information with respect to the environment.
33   ACRE Newsletter, Issue No 7, June 1997.

that the information put on the register was allowing protesters to vandalise the release sites, the regulations were amended in 1995. Information to be included in advertisements for crop plants now does not have to include details either of the dates of release or their location.[34]

The principal way in which the public enters the area of decisions as to the research and development of genetically engineered products is as a consumer. Participation takes the form of either buying or refusing to buy genetically modified products. In order that consumers can participate even in this way, they need information as to whether the product has been genetically engineered or contains engineered ingredients. Parts of the industry have resisted labelling on the basis that consumers will not understand the information which is being given and will be scared off buying the food, or have said that it is not feasible because of the practices adopted by suppliers: in the US, companies have refused to separate out genetically modified soya from normal soya. Nevertheless, in November 1997 an EU regulation came into force requiring the labelling of genetically engineered foods.[35]

Conceptualisation/definition of the problem

The issue at which the regulation is addressed is that of risk. Risk has been the defining conceptualisation of the problems posed by GMOs throughout the development of the regulation. Initially focused on the risk to human health, the regulation subsequently broadened to include risks to the environment.[36] In its Thirteenth Report, which was to a considerable extent the precursor to the regulation, the Royal Commission on Environmental Pollution considered the range of impacts, particularly undesirable impacts, which the release of GMOs could have on the environment.[37] The manipulation of a virus, for example, could unintentionally alter its virulence or widen the range of susceptible organisms; indirectly, it could change the range of insects who carry the virus, so bringing it into contact with previously unaffected plant species. Projects that engineered plants to produce toxins may have the danger that the toxin will appear in a part of the plant that might be eaten by non-target animals or humans; the cultivation of the crop on a wide scale may encourage the development and spread of insects resistant to it. Herbicide resistant genes could spread to weeds, which could lead to greater use of herbicides overall. The release of antibiotic resistant genes could accelerate the dissemination of antibiotic resistant genes in pathogens. Genes inserted into new host organisms may transfer after release to other organisms with undesirable consequences. Non-pathogens could be converted to pathogens. Finally, consideration has to be given to the extent to which the effects of the release of GMOs could be reversed: whether the GMOs could be recovered or eradicated, and how their disposal would be managed, particularly if they had the capacity to become converted into novel pathogenic agents.

The solution proposed and adopted was to adopt a precautionary approach to risk

---

34   1995 Deliberate Release Regulations, taking into account Commission Decision 94/730/EC OJ No L 292.

35   Regulation (EC) No 258/97; as yet no guidance has been issued by MAFF, or indeed any other member state, as to the implementation of the regulation.

36   However an amendment which would have introduced an ethics commission was rejected during the passage of the EPA: see L. Levidow and J. Tait, 'The Greening of Biotechnology: GMOs as Environment Friendly Products' in V. Shiva and I. Moses (eds), *Biopolitics* (London: Atlantic Highlands, 1995) 134.

37   Royal Commission on Environmental Pollution, Thirteenth Report, *The Release of Genetically Engineered Organisms to the Environment*, Cmnd 720 (London: HMSO, 1989) chapters 4 and 5.

management. A precautionary approach to risk is one in which the risks which are potentially posed are assessed in advance and attempts made to reduce or eliminate them.[38] In Wildavsky's phrase, it attempts to ensure 'trial without error'.[39] Controls are put in place even in the absence of information on the extent of the risks posed. It contrasts with a reactive approach, in which a product is assumed to be safe until a particular hazard is identified and proven. The rationale underlying the regulation was that the act of genetic modification itself posed risks above and beyond those posed by traditional breeding techniques. It is this idea that genetic engineering is inherently risky, coupled with a precautionary approach and a case by case assessment of risks, which was thus adopted by the 1990 EU directives on contained use and deliberate release which form the basis of the current system of regulation.[40]

The regulation implements this precautionary approach by adopting a strategy of individualised assessment and approval, rather than the formulation of rules which attempt to prescribe in advance what is or is not permitted, or to set out particular safety requirements that have to be met. Release of GMOs is permitted only after an assessment has been made of their capacity to cause harm to the environment or to the health of humans or other living organisms, or to human senses or property.[41] For both non-marketing and marketing releases the regulations require a detailed assessment of the risks to the environment including potential impacts on the ecosystem (eg genetic stability and mobility, pathogenicity, ecological and physical traits, antibiotic resistance, ecological aggressiveness) and the risks to human and animal health. The applicant must also give details of measures to monitor and control the spread of GMOs, means of cleaning up waste and emergency plans to abort the release.[42] The precautionary approach to risk regulation is maintained with respect to GEPs by the deliberate release regulations. Moreover, as noted, even though the regulation is moving to the development of separate product regimes, the risk assessments which are required parallel those required by the deliberate release regulations.

Internal debates

Although those within the regulatory fora agree that the issue to be addressed is that of risk, they disagree on whether or not the regulation is appropriately targeted and as to what degrees of risk are posed. The contained use regulations

---

38 The precautionary principle was originally enunciated by the West German government in 1976 in the field of pollution control, and has become highly influential in debates both on environmental regulation and on approaches to risk regulation more generally. See further T. O'Riordan and J. Cameron, *Interpreting the Precautionary Principle* (London: Earthscan, 1994).

39 A. Wildavsky, *Trial Without Error: Anticipation vs Resilience as Strategies for Risk Reduction* (London: CIS, 1985).

40 The precautionary principle underlies the Government's sustainable development strategy in environmental regulation: *Sustainable Development. The UK Strategy*, Cm 2426 (London: HMSO, 1994).

41 There are exceptions which recognise that the purpose of releasing some genetically modified organisms may be to further pest control or to break down toxic wastes; in these cases the provisions on prohibition notices and the powers of inspectors where they fear imminent harm are disapplied: 1992 Deliberate Release Regulations, reg 4.

42 Regs 6 and 11; Schedules 1 and 2. The GMO (Deliberate Release) Regulations 1995, SI 1995/304 introduced a simplified system of notification for higher plants. The GMO (Deliberate Release and Risk Assessment) Regulations 1997, SI 1997/1900 added a requirement with respect to applications for marketing that they contain information which could be relevant to the establishment of a possible register of modifications introduced into a species; and information about proposed labelling to indicate that the product contains or consists of GMOs.

have been strongly criticised by scientists, industry, and by the regulators themselves on the ground of lack of 'fit' with scientific understandings and laboratory practice.[43] In its report on the competitiveness of the biotechnology industry, the Select Committee on Science and Technology found that the original categorisation of organisms adopted in the regulation, which was meant to be based on the degree of risk which they pose, was 'risible' in the eyes of scientists, with the consequence that the whole risk assessment system was being brought into disrepute.[44] The need for any system of regulation over and above that required by existing standards of good laboratory practice is itself questioned. Many scientists engaged in genetic engineering take the view that the hazards presented are low or even minimal, and that a precautionary regulation focused specifically on genetic products is unnecessary: genetic engineering poses no more hazards than the introduction of non-indigenous species and is in fact more precise than traditional cross breeding techniques.[45] Indeed even the chairman of the ACGM which administers the regulations stated that there was no evidence that the technique of modification was itself hazardous.[46] Industry argues strongly that the regulations place it at a considerable competitive disadvantage vis à vis the US and Japan, and that it should be relaxed and refocused.[47] In the words of the BioIndustry Association, 'much of the regulation put in place by the European Commission is based on old science and reflects concerns that have not proved justified.'[48]

Outsider perspectives

The regulation thus sees the problem posed by genetic engineering as one of risk, and within those fora the debate is as to the appropriate fit of the regulation to the degree of risk which is in fact posed. The debate about genetic engineering which occurs outside the regulatory fora shares the risk-based conceptualisation of the issue, but adopts a very different perception of the risks which are posed. But in contrast to the regulatory focus, those who at present are outside the regulatory fora do not see the issues to be confined to risk. So not only do the conclusions which are reached differ given the common definition of the problem, but that definition is itself challenged. The conceptualisations of the issues and the language in which they are expressed are thus fundamentally different.

Attitudes to genetic engineering, in particular to its acceptability, tend to be rooted in a wide range of factors. Evidence from a number of public attitude surveys conducted indicates that acceptability is linked, *inter alia*, to the perceived need of the technology or its products, to the interaction of genetic technology with

---

43   See for example comments in ACGM Newsletter No 19, April 1996.
44   Select Committee on Science and Technology, *Regulation of the UK Biotechnology Industry and Global Competitiveness*, 199–203, HL Paper 80, paras 5.25–5.26. The basis of distinguishing between Group I and II organisms was altered in 1995, and the classification is now based not on the detailed characteristics of the organism, but on a qualitative assessment in each individual case of whether it is likely to cause adverse effects to humans, animals, plants or the environment: EC Directive 94/51/EC; The GMO (Contained Use) (Amendment) Regulations 1996, SI 1996/967. Guidance on the application of the criteria is contained in EC Decision No. 95/1579/EC, and further in ACGM, *A Guide to the GMO (Contained Use) Regulations 1992, as amended in 1996*. Both this distinction and that between Type A and B operations is to be abolished under proposals for a fundamental revision of the Contained Use Directive.
45   Evidence to the SCST, Report on Biotechnology, *ibid* paras 5.8–5.12.
46   *ibid* para 5.11.
47   See further *ibid*.
48   BioIndustry Association, *A Charter for Biotechnology*, 1997, 9.

other practices of which the person may not approve, and to the attitude taken to the wider social impacts it is perceived that the use of genetic technology will have.[49] Thus it is resisted on the basis that it may lead to more intensive farming, the use of pesticides, or exploitation of farmers in developing countries ('genetic imperialism'). The use of the growth hormone rBST, for example, is opposed on the basis that it will simply be to the benefit of large agri-businesses at the expense of smaller farmers; genetically modified seed because of its impact on the issue of farmers' rights[50] or on developing countries' farming practices.

Opposition is manifested in a number of ways. There has been strong resistance to genetic engineering from environmental groups and consumers in both the US and Europe. In Austria, for example, a referendum last year on the continuation of the ban of genetically altered corn received 1.2 million supporting signatures. A referendum in June 1998 in Switzerland on the 'gene protection initiative' proposed a ban on, *inter alia*, the breeding and purchase of transgenic animals and the release of GMOs into the environment (the proposal was actually defeated). In November 1997 Greenpeace filed petition with the US Environmental Protection Agency demanding that it revoke permits for certain GE crops, and English Nature is pressing for a three year moratorium on such crops.[51] Others have taken more direct action, for example digging up crops.[52] In April 1997 a week long 'Global Days of Action Against Biotechnology' was organised, with over 200 groups in 24 countries participating.[53]

Attempts at negotiation

An attempt at negotiating or mediating between the different perspectives is perhaps made in the definition of risk which appears to be adopted by the regulatory bodies. It has been suggested that in its membership ACRE embodies a tension between technical risk assessment and policy issues irreducible to scientific evidence,[54] a tension which is explored further below. In the absence of empirical evidence it is not clear exactly how that tension in practice is resolved. The guidance issued by ACRE does however recognise the essentially qualitative nature of much risk assessment. It states that whilst risk is to be assessed as far as possible on the basis of technical and scientific measurements, given the uncertainties which pervade consideration of the possible impacts of GMOs on human health or the environment much of that assessment is necessarily qualitative rather than quantitative in nature.[55] The requirement is thus that the risk assessment statement should comprise a reasoned appraisal based on the best available quantitative or qualitative measure of risk to the environment and human health.

---

49   See generally, D.P. Ives, *Public Perceptions of Biotechnology and Novel Foods: A Review of the Evidence and Implications for Risk Communication* (Norwich: Centre for Environmental and Risk Management, UEA, 1995); J. Durant (ed), *Biotechnology in Public: A Review of Recent Research* (London: Science Museum, 1992).

50   The ability to retain a certain proportion of seeds from that year's crop to sow for the following year (which obviously reduces the amount of seed which the farmer will buy from the seed seller/manufacturer).

51   *The Guardian*, 12 April 1998.

52   For example, in Ireland the Gaelic Earth Liberation Front dug up the first field of a genetically engineered crop (sugar beet) to be planted in there: *Nature Biotechnology* vol 15, November 1997, 1229, and crops have been dug up in Scotland: *The Guardian* 12 April 1998.

53   The week was organised by Jeremy Rifkin's Foundation on Economic Trends and the Pure Food Campaign (both in the US). For details see B. Nasto and J. Lehrer, 'Antibiotech week raises tension over transgenic food', *Nature Biotechnology*, vol 15, June 1997, 499.

54   Levidow and Tait, n 23 above.

55   ACRE Guidance, para 4.5.

This view is shared by the HSE and by a recent interdepartmental committee on risk assessment.[56]

There are necessarily limits, however, to the extent that the risk assessment process can be used as a means of mediating the different perceptions which surround this aspect of genetic technology. For whilst the regulation is firmly risk-based, risk is not seen by those outside the regulatory fora to be the only problem which is posed by GMOs and GEPs. There is an opposition to the very activity of genetic engineering, issues of risk aside. There is no formal venue in the regulatory or approval process for these concerns to be expressed, and industry is very opposed to there being one. The BIA's *Charter for BioIndustry* urges the government to 'stand firm against attempts from whatever direction, to attach ethical considerations to safety or indeed, other technical legislation.'[57] However, the result is a closure, structural and cognitive, of the regulatory system to the concerns voiced by those who do not have access, formally or informally, to the regulatory fora in which decisions are taken. The legal remits of the regulatory bodies define the issue in terms of risk, and risk is the only acceptable regulatory criterion for many of those who seek regulatory approval. The result is that those who argue against the release of genetically engineered crops or the sale of genetically engineered seeds or foods on the grounds that they will, for example, contaminate organic crops, or lead to undesirable farming and commercial practices, are simply met with the answer that release is safe, or that the risk can be controlled. That safety is not, or not the only, point, is not a debate in which the regulatory system will currently engage.

Human and medical genetics

Issues of human and medical genetics are also addressed in a number of different regulatory fora, and the main actors are scientific researchers, the medical profession, and a number of regulatory or advisory bodies which are staffed principally by scientific and medical professionals. The principal contrast between the regulation of human and medical genetics and that of GMOs and GEPs is the broader definition of the problems which are raised. The issues which are raised by genetic technology in the human and medical context are seen not solely in terms of the risks posed but of the appropriate adaptation of medical ethics to accommodate that technology. Ethical issues appear in turn to be defined and driven in large part by the medical profession. Non-medical or scientific professionals enter principally in their capacity as patients, although the Advisory Committee on Genetic Testing and the Human Genetics Advisory Commission have a remit to consider the wider social implications of genetic engineering. Again, however, there are differences in cognition, in the conceptualisations of the problem and the perceptions of the issues to be addressed between those who are within the decision making and regulatory fora and those who are outside it. Attempts to negotiate or mediate between these different perspectives have been patchy; an exception is with respect to cloning, where there is currently a concerted effort to address the matters which non-scientists and medical practitioners consider to be important.

---

56 *Use of Risk Assessment within Government Departments: Report prepared by the Interdepartmental Liaison Group on Risk Assessment*, HSE 1996; and see further, The Deregulation Initiative, *Regulation in the Balance: A Guide to Risk Assessment*, DTI 1993; DTI, *The Use of Scientific Advice in Policy Making*, DTI 1997.

57 n 48 above, 9.

Regulation of genetic technology in the human and medical context is fragmented, and not nearly so structured as that which relates to GMOs and GEPs. For that reason, we will look first at the different regulatory fora,[58] their principal participants and the main access points, but then explore the dimensions of cognition and communication in more depth with respect to three different contexts in which genetic technology is deployed. These are testing (which is increasingly routine), gene therapy (which in scientific and clinical terms is a nascent technology, but in which research trials is occurring) and cloning (which is nascent).

Regulatory fora and principal actors

In the area of human and medical genetics, the fora in which decisions are taken as to the development, application and use of genetic technology are dispersed. They operate at a sub-national level, within laboratories and the medical profession, at a national level, both within the internal bureaucracy of the health service and as statutory and non-statutory executive bodies, and at an international level. The diffuse and often opaque nature of the decision making structures and the partial nature of the regulation mean that access points are dispersed, and thus the categorisation of 'insiders' and 'outsiders' is often fluid and unclear. Again, in the absence of detailed empirical research, only published documents and guidelines can be used as witnesses to the perceptions which are held of the issues to be addressed.

Laboratory research is the subject of the GMO regulation outlined above. In addition, research programmes are reviewed by the relevant funding bodies for their ethical acceptability, and all research involving patients must be approved by local research ethics committees (LRECs) set up in each health authority. The terms of reference of the Human Genetics Advisory Commission (HGAC) include the review of scientific progress in human genetics. There are also separate regulatory fora relating to discrete areas of research. Research into gene therapy must be approved by the Gene Therapy Advisory Commission (GTAC),[59] which was set up to supplement the work of the LRECs. It must also be authorised by the Medicines Control Agency, which must be satisfied that it meets the required levels of safety, efficacy and quality.[60] Research which involves the use of human embryos requires approval from the Human Fertilisation and Embryology Authority (HFEA).[61] Pathology laboratories (which investigate the causes of disease) are accredited by the Clinical Pathology Accreditation (UK) Ltd which audits the standards of professional practice existing in the laboratories.

Further, a number of international conventions apply to genetic research, in particular to research into human cloning. In November 1996 the Council of Europe adopted a Convention for the protection of human rights in biomedicine and has agreed that protocols on, *inter alia*, genetics and medical research will be developed under it.[62] The Convention includes a moratorium for a minimum of

---

58   Given that there are gaps in the regulatory structure, this will in fact also include fora in which decisions as to the clinical deployment of genetic technology are made.

59   GTAC has issued two sets of guidance: *Guidance on Making Proposals to Conduct Gene Therapy Research on Human Subjects*, September 1994, and *Writing Information Leaflets for Patients Participating in Gene Therapy Research*, August 1995.

60   Under the Medicines Act 1968 and Directive 65/65/EEC, as subsequently modified.

61   Under the HFEA Act 1990.

62   Convention for the Protection of Human Rights and Dignity of the Human Being with regard to the Application of Biology and Medicine, adopted by the Committee of Ministers on 19 November 1996 (Doc DIR/JUR(96)14 — Legal Affairs Directorate of the Council of Europe).

five years on germ line gene therapy in humans. In November 1997 UNESCO adopted the Declaration on the Human Genome and Protection of Human Rights, which seeks to establish universal principles covering all research into the human genome and its application when it appears that it might conflict with human dignity and the rights of the individual.

The use of genetic technology in medical applications is also subject to regulation which derives from a number of different sources. The supply and manufacture of genetic tests is regulated by the Advisory Committee on Genetic Testing (ACGT), which has issued a voluntary code of practice on testing services which are supplied directly to the public rather than via the NHS.[63] A Directive on *in vitro* diagnostic tests, which would include genetic tests, is also being negotiated by the EC Council of Ministers.[64] Any product developed from genetic engineering which is intended for medical use has to be approved by the European Medicines Evaluation Agency before it can be marketed in the EU[65] or by the MCA for market authorisation in the UK,[66] and there are obligations to maintain records relating to medicinal products.[67]

Access

Such an array of regulatory bodies would appear to contradict Beck's contention that 'medicine possesses a *free pass* for the implementation and testing of its "innovations" '.[68] To a significant extent, however, the principal actors within these different regulatory and decision-making fora are medical professionals, and as noted, non-professionals enter principally in their capacity as patients. Their access is defined in terms of the medical norms of informed consent, and those norms determine what information they should receive, in what manner, and what principles of confidentiality should attach to that information.

Conceptualisations/definitions of the problems

The issues which genetic technology raises are to some extent seen as questions of risk, but to a large extent seen in terms of the ethics of patient care. In other words, how the advances in genetic technology should be passed onto the patient, rather than what those advances should be. There is one important exception, and that is with respect to the use of genetic technology in the reproductive context. The main

---

63 ACGT, *Code of Practice and Guidance on Human Genetic Testing Services Supplied Direct to the Public*, September 1997.

64 See further, ACGT, *Consultation Report on Genetic Testing for Late Onset Disorders* (November, 1997). The Directive would require all *in vitro* diagnostics (IVDs) to be CE marked in declaration of conformity with the essential requirements of the Directive in order to be placed on the market.

65 Established under Council Directive 87/22/EEC (OJ No L 15, 17.1.87, p 38) on the approximation of measures relating to the marketing of biotech medicinal products, following the procedure in Council Regulation 2309/93. Authorisation is given by the Committee for Proprietary Medicinal Products (part of the Agency), which takes into consideration the environmental safety requirements set out in the Deliberate Release Directive. EMEA operates in addition to the National Biological Standards Board, set up under the Biological Standards Act 1975, which manages the National Institute for Biological Standards and Control (NIBSC) which monitors the safety and quality of biological substances used in medicines such as vaccines, hormones, whose purity or potency cannot be adequately tested by chemical or physical means.

66 The MCA is supported by independent advisory committees, chiefly the Committee on the Safety of Medicines and the Medicines Commission (which also consider appeals).

67 EC Directive 91/507/EEC on updated standards and protocols for the testing of medicines for human use.

68 Beck, *Risk Society: Towards a New Modernity*, n 1 above, 207 (emphasis included).

areas of debate at present concern the activities of genetic testing, gene therapy and cloning, which are considered separately below.

Genetic testing

Genetic testing for some diseases is already part of established medical practice. Testing is used either for diagnostic purposes, to test for the causes of particular symptoms, or for predictive purposes. Predictive testing provides information as to whether a person has a genetic disorder which may lead to, or which may mean that they are susceptible to, particular diseases. Genetic testing can be of benefit both to an individual or couple, and to the overall gene pool of a particular group. Genetic testing of Ashkenazic Jews in the US has reduced the incidence of Tay-Sachs disease in the population by 90 per cent.[69] Testing may be carried out on adults or children (neo-natally or pre-natally). Since the 1950s, most babies in the UK have had blood tests to establish whether they have inherited the genetic defect responsible for PKU. More recently, it has become possible to test at various stages of pregnancy for genetic conditions responsible for Tay-Sachs disease, Huntington's disease, cystic fibrosis, Duchenne muscular dystrophy (DMD), and thalassaemia. Tests for genetic susceptibility to common diseases such as cancer, heart disease and diabetes are being developed, and it is reasonable to expect that an increasing range of tests will become available in the next few years.[70]

Most genetic testing in the UK is carried out within the NHS, and is based on regional genetics centres which serve groups of health authorities. Other genetic testing services may be provided by general practitioners, within particular medical specialisms such as oncology and haematology, and within research settings, often in collaboration with regional genetic centres.[71] There is also an increase in the sale of genetic tests developed in pharmaceutical companies directly to the public, bypassing the normal medical structures.[72] Direct services aside, the decisions as to when testing should be offered are made within the relatively diffuse and opaque decision structure of the NHS. Discussion and guidance on when testing should occur has come from a number of medical bodies, including the Royal College of Physicians,[73] the British Medical Association,[74] and from the Nuffield Council on Bioethics.[75] The consensus view of these organisations is that testing should be for therapeutic purposes only, and in particular only for serious diseases, that it should allow carriers for a given abnormal gene to make informed choices regarding reproduction, and/or go towards alleviating the anxieties of families and individuals faced with the prospect of serious genetic disease.[76] Regulation, however, is currently patchy.

Regulation of genetic testing is found principally in professional guidelines and in the single voluntary code which has thus far been issued by the Advisory Committee on Genetic Testing. Established in 1996 on the recommendation of the

---

69 BMA, *Our Genetic Future: The Science and Ethics of Genetic Technology* (Oxford: OUP, 1992) 192.
70 See ACGT, Consultative Report, n 64 above.
71 *ibid*; Chief Medical Officer and Chief Nursing Officer, *Population Needs and Genetic Services: An Outline Guide*, PL/CMO (95) 5 and PL/CNO (93) 4.
72 The subject of ACGT, *Code of Practice*, n 63 above.
73 Royal College of Physicians of London, *Ethical Issues in Clinical Genetics* (London: Royal College of Physicians, 1991).
74 n 69 above.
75 Nuffield Council on Bioethics, *Genetic Screening: Ethical Issues* (London: Nuffield Council on Bioethics, 1993).
76 *ibid* para 3.9.

Select Committee on Science and Technology,[77] the remit of the ACGT is to consider and advise health ministers on developments in genetic testing, the ethical, social and scientific aspects of testing and establish requirements to be met by suppliers of genetic tests. It considers tests in use in clinical practice and to be supplied to the public. Those which are to be supplied directly to the public have first to seek the approval of the ACGT,[78] although the Committee has no powers to proceed against those who do not seek its approval.

The ACGT has not sought to regulate the availability of tests in the clinical setting, and the decision making fora here are health authorities. It has sought to provide guidance on the procedures which should be followed in conducting certain types of tests, those for late onset disorders,[79] but not for other types of disease. This is otherwise the subject of NHS circulars and the professional ethics of patient care. The process of testing itself is subject to a fair degree of regulation from other sources aimed at ensuring the accuracy of the test results, and much of this will be put on a statutory footing when the IVD Directive is introduced.

Those inside and outside the profession and the regulatory fora appear generally to accept the view that genetic testing raises a wide range of issues. There is doubt as to the predictive reliability of the tests, particularly for late onset disorders and diseases which are not caused by a single gene. Tests are also not wholly accurate, or do not test for all forms of a disease.[80] The absence of treatment for a diagnosed disease and the uncertainty surrounding predictive testing mean that people may receive information the significance of which is uncertain and to which they cannot respond by taking preventative or curative action. Moreover, pre-symptomatic testing may have significant psychological implications.

At present, these issues are addressed in the context of the doctor-patient relationship, and by the doctrine of informed consent. It is considered essential to ensure that full consent to be tested has been given and that the information is imparted in an appropriate manner with full counselling and support. The need for such clinical support (and doubts as to the adequacy of its current provision) has been repeatedly emphasised by the Nuffield Council,[81] the BMA,[82] in the Select Committee's Third Report on Human Genetics,[83] and by the ACGT.[84] It is required by the ACGT's Code of Practice for those who supply tests directly to the public.[85]

Testing is thus seen essentially to be a matter of individual patient choice,[86] although there are particular issues where testing of children is concerned.

---

77 Select Committee on Science and Technology, Third Report, *Human Genetics: The Science and its Consequences* HC 1994/5, HC Paper 41.
78 ACGT, *Code of Practice*, n 63 above.
79 ACGT, *Consultation Report*, n 64 above.
80 For example, there are over eighty mutations of the CF gene; the current tests will identify only those which occur in around 85 per cent of the population, leaving the other 15 per cent undetected.
81 Nuffield Council, n 75 above, chapter 4, especially para 4.21.
82 BMA, n 69 above, 193–200.
83 SCST, Third Report, n 77 above, paras 72–106.
84 See the ACGT *Code of Practice*, n 63 above, and *Consultation Report*, n 64 above.
85 n 64 above, paras 5 and 6. Indeed, the unlikelihood of such support services being adequately given by such suppliers, as well as concerns about the accuracy of the tests, underlay the ACGT's recommendation that only certain tests should be supplied outside the clinical context. The ACGT's Code of Practice (para 3) provides that only tests for carrier status of recessive disorders, where such status carries no direct health implications for the individual (eg cystic fibrosis), should be provided directly to the public. They should not be provided for inherited dominant and X-linked disorders, chromosomal disorders (eg Downs syndrome), late onset disorders (eg Huntington's), or for the genetic component(s) of multifactorial diseases (eg heart disease or cancer). Genetic tests should not be provided over the counter for children.
86 See ACGT *Consultation Report*, n 64 above; *Population Needs*, n 71 above, Annex 3 para 3.

Concerns have been raised at the wider pressures that may be exerted on the patient affecting the way in which that choice is made, however.[87] For example, it has been suggested that pre-natal screening conveys a signal that a positive result justifies an abortion: why else offer the test pre-natally instead of, for example, neo-natally? There have moreover been reports that screening for Huntington's disease in some areas is only given on the basis that the pregnancy will be terminated if the test is positive.[88] Attitudes to pre-natal testing tend therefore to be linked to the position a person takes on abortion more generally. Experience with genetic testing has shown that pre-natal testing can however lead to societal pressure to abort. There is some evidence that in Sardinia, where there is routine pre-natal testing for thalassaemia, women who fail to abort a foetus diagnosed as having thalassaemia are stigmatized by the local community.[89] Testing is thus not simply a neutral technique and a private issue; it has significant social consequences. Mediating these concerns has not thus far been a significant feature of either regulation or medical decision making on the provision of testing services; there has recently been a citizens' jury held in Wales on the issue of the availability of genetic testing, but it is not clear what impact this will have in the relevant decision making fora.[90]

A somewhat different issue which is seen to be central to genetic testing is the confidentiality of the information which the test produces. Confidentiality issues arise in a number of forms. First, there is the issue of whether the person to whom the information relates has a right to receive that information. Where the person has requested and/or consented to a genetic test, then they should be told the result of that test. Difficulties arise where the test shows other information which was not the specific subject matter of the test (and can be particularly problematic if it relates to paternity), or where subsequent research on a person's DNA shows that he or she has a genetic abnormality the testing for which was not part of the original reason why the DNA was taken. Should the person be told of the results? At present, there is no specific regulation on the issue, although with respect to information obtained in the course of subsequent research the current practice is not to inform that person. On this issue, the ACGT's proposed solution is that samples should be anonymised, so as to prevent the situation arising, and in any event information should not be given to the individual unless a clear and specific arrrangement has been made at the outset.[91]

Secondly, there is the question of whether other family members should be made aware of the test results. As has been well observed, genetic testing may reveal information not only about those who have given their consent to testing, but about members of their families who have not.[92] Again, there is no specific regulation on the matter. After reviewing existing case law and professional guidelines, the Nuffield Council concluded that in certain circumstances that information could be revealed to other family members, without the patient's consent. In all cases individuals should be made aware that the test would reveal information that could

---

87 See further S. Shiloh, 'Decision-making in the Context of Genetic Risk' in T. Marteau and M. Richards (eds), *The Troubled Helix: Social and Psychological Implications of the New Human Genetics* (Cambridge: CUP, 1996).
88 See SCST Third Report, n 77 above, para 90.
89 Professor Sir David Weatherall, 'Genetic Science — Looking Ahead', paper given at the 21st Century Trust Conference on Genetics, Ethics and Identity, Oxford, 29 March–4 April 1998.
90 Welsh Institute for Health and Social Care, *Report of the Citizens' Jury on Genetic Testing for Common Disorders* (University of Glamorgan: WIHSC, 1998).
91 ACGT, *Consultation Report*, n 64 above, 24–25.
92 Nuffield Council, n 75 above, para 5.1.

be relevant to other family members, and should be encouraged to disclose the information to those people. However, if the individual refused, then if disclosure of that information might avoid grave damage to other family members it could be revealed. Although they recommended that the medical professional have a discretion to reveal that information, the Council was against the imposition of a legal duty to do so.[93] Here there is a noted difference of view between the profession and others. In particular, the Council's conclusion was categorically rejected on policy grounds by the Select Comittee on Science and Technology. In the Select Committee's view, the individual's decision to withold information should be paramount. It would place relatives in no worse position than they were already, and failure to respect individual privacy could discourage people from having tests done.[94]

Thirdly, there is the question of disclosure of genetic information to third parties who are not members of the family group, notably employers and insurance companies. The tension between the profession and those outside it is here even clearer. Insurance companies argue strongly that they should see the information; that disclosure is entirely consonant with the norms and practices of the insurance industry and the principle of *uberrimae fidei* which underlies all insurance contracts. In the employment context, employers could attempt to justify the requirement for the person to have a test or to disclose the results of tests on the basis of their duty to provide a safe system of work under the HSWA. Refusing to employ someone on the basis of the results of those genetic tests would not be unlawful, unless it also constituted sex or race discrimination. Dismissing someone on the basis of a test result would not necessarily constitute unfair dismissal.

Whether information should be disclosed is thus contentious. Some attempt has been made to negotiate a solution by the Nuffield Council and more directly by the HGAC. The Council appeared to conclude that information which bore a direct relation to the employment context could be disclosed. Such information would include that a person suffered from a disorder which would be exacerbated by the conditions in which he or she would be working, or a disorder that posed a particular and serious risk to others. The SCST agreed, although it is notable that its position on this issue is in conflict with its reasoning with respect to the disclosure of information to other family members. In that case, the SCST argued for non-disclosure on the grounds that the family members would be no worse off in their ignorance than they would have been before, even though that information could provide the basis for preventative action on their part. In the employment (and indeed insurance context), this argument was clearly rejected.

In the insurance context, in December 1997, prompted by the threat of statutory regulation, the ABI produced a code of practice on the use of genetic test information in the context of life insurance.[95] The code provides that insurance companies will not require tests or test results for life insurance of up to £100,000. In excess of that amount, they may require genetic tests before giving insurance. The HGAC has stated that a moratorium on the use of genetic test results in any insurance contract should be imposed, as serious doubts remain as to the accurate and valid use of such information.[96]

There are thus concerns expressed within the medical profession as to the context in which genetic testing occurs and the impacts which it can have, but it

---

93   *ibid* paras 5.7, 5.29.
94   SCST, Third Report, n 77 above, paras 227–228.
95   ABI, *Code of Practice on Genetics and Life Insurance* (London: ABI, 1997).
96   HGAC, *The Implications of Genetic Testing for Insurance* (London: HGAC, December 1997).

would seem testing continues unabated, and the resolution of the issues which are raised can be seen in large part to be decided by patients themselves within the context of the patient-medical professional relationship. On the other key issue of confidentiality, there is a clear conflict between the perceptions of employers and insurers, and those of the medical profession and patients themselves, and there has been some attempt at negotiation made by the HGAC in the insurance context.

Gene therapy

Gene therapy is a far more difficult technique than testing, and this difficulty has consequences for the focus and design of the regulation.[97] The regulation both anticipates and requires that gene therapy be conducted purely in a research context. This is not because the use of gene therapy in a medical context is deemed un-needing of regulation, but because gene therapy has not yet reached the stage in which it can be applied in that context. The nascent state of gene therapy techniques is of course in contrast to genetic testing or screening, where the relative scientific ease of the testing process means that the operational context is either a clinical one or one of direct supply to the public. The state of science thus dictates the regulatory focus. GTAC requires all proposals for gene therapy research to be submitted to it for approval and the regulation operates on an individual, case by case assessment of those protocols. Most of the research in the UK on single gene disorders has so far been directed at cystic fibrosis.[98] Gene therapy is also being investigated as a way of managing other diseases such as AIDS, some forms of cancer, and chronic forms of diabetes. Indeed GTAC has noted a continuing shift from gene therapy for single gene disorders towards strategies aimed particularly at tumour destruction in cancer patients.[99] Genetic modification carries certain risks, however. It might not work: there may just be no effect. Potentially worse, the correcting gene could be inserted into the wrong cell type, or be expressed either in the wrong amount or at the wrong time, or be inserted in such a way as to cause a new mutation, initiating a new genetic disease. It might also be 'infective', moving from the cells to other somatic or germ line cells.

The ethical issues arising out of gene therapy were the subject of a report by the Clothier Committee,[100] and that report has largely defined the approach taken in the regulation of gene therapy. The Committee took the view that gene therapy should be confined to somatic cells. On the grounds of risk and uncertainty, it recommended that gene therapy of germ line cells should not yet be permitted.[101] Too little was yet known about the possible consequences and hazards of gene therapy to permit genetic modification which would be deliberately designed to affect subsequent generations.[102] Moreover, given the uncertainties surrounding the safety and effectiveness of gene therapy, it should be limited to patients in whom the potential for benefit is greatest in relation to possible inadvertent harm. It should thus be restricted to disorders that were life threatening or caused

---

97 By January 1997 only 18 protocols had been approved, with 13 studies carried out involving 134 patients. GTAC, *Third Annual Report 1996* (London: GTAC, June 1997) para 2.1.

98 *ibid.*

99 *ibid.*

100 *Report of the Committee on the Ethics of Gene Therapy* (chair, Sir Cecil Clothier) Cm 1788 (London: HMSO, 1992).

101 Germ line cells provide sperm or ova, and so the genes carried by them may be transmitted to successive generations. Somatic cells carry genes which operate only in the body of the individual.

102 Clothier Committee, para 2.26, and Part 5.

serious handicap, and for which treatment was either unavailable or unsatisfactory.[103]

Whilst arguing that somatic gene therapy (alteration of the genes in the cells of particular individuals) raised no new ethical issues, the Committee suggested that given the risks arising and the technical competence which was necessary to assess those risks, it should be subject to regulation which went beyond the normal review given by local research ethics committees (LRECs).[104] Further, gene therapy was not sufficiently developed a technique to be considered part of medical practice, and rather should be treated as research on human subjects. It should therefore conform to the slightly higher ethical requirements which applied to such research. These required that the therapy be useful for biomedical knowledge; that it be conducted in a way that maintained ethical standards of practice, protected the subjects of research from harm, and preserved the subject's rights and liberties. Moreover, reassurance had to be provided to the professions, the public and Parliament that these standards were being upheld.[105]

As a consequence of the Report, GTAC was established in 1993 on a non-statutory basis.[106] GTAC's remit is to consider the scientific merits and potential risks of gene therapy, and it has not appeared to see it to be necessary to consider itself the wider social or ethical implications of interfering with genetic make-up. At least, if it has, it has not made its deliberations or their outcomes public. GTAC's Guidance maintains that its primary concern is to ensure that research proposals meet accepted ethical criteria for research on human subjects.[107] Ethical aspects are stated to include scientific merit and safety;[108] there is no requirement, in contrast to the Clothier Committee's recommendation, that a separate ethical assessment of the research proposed be given.[109]

GTAC perhaps takes the view that the wider issues raised by gene therapy were covered by the Clothier Committee. However, Clothier gave scant attention to these arguments. Whilst it noted that genetic modification might cause harmful or unacceptable genetic alterations or lead to social abuses[110] and stated that it was alert to 'the profound ethical issues that would arise were the aim of genetic modification ever to be directed to the enhancement of normal human traits',[111] it did not expand on these views. In particular, the objection to germ line therapy was that it was too risky, rather than being rooted in any deeper philosophical argument (although there was a nod towards human dignity).[112] Two paragraphs sufficed to dismiss the issue.[113]

It may also be that the nascent state of science in this area affects the regulatory agenda. There is perhaps seen to be little need to have a debate on, for example, the reasons why one should confine gene therapy to the treatment of diseases as given the present state of science and the cost of research no-one would wish to fund anything else. Or it may be that there is no point discussing wider ethics of genetic modification for non-human traits as such modification is just not possible. Or that GTAC feels that such debates are occurring elsewhere in the regulatory structures:

---

103   *ibid* para 4.3.
104   *ibid* para 4.8 and Part 6.
105   *ibid* para 8.3.
106   All trials do however have to gain approval from the statutory Medical Control Agency.
107   Guidance, Part I, para 11.
108   Guidance, Part I, para 6.
109   Clothier Committee, para 6.2.
110   *ibid* para 1.1.
111   *ibid* para 2.16.
112   *ibid* para 4.22.
113   *ibid* paras 5.1–5.2.

in LRECs, for example.[114] There is little public articulation on these matters. The issues raised by somatic cell gene therapy may well be adequately met in GTAC's current approach. Certainly its work has been praised as being 'sensible and effective'.[115] Germ line therapy raises quite fundamental issues, however, which have not been aired by any of the current regulatory bodies, or, as noted, by the Clothier Committee.[116] These include whether germ line manipulation should be permitted as a matter of individual choice, with only manipulation which is deliberately intended to cause harm being prohibited; or whether manipulation should be seen as an act which directly affects another, and so limited to improving the health of that person (with the inevitable problems in both cases of defining 'harm' or drawing the line between 'cure' and 'enhancement'); how, if at all, germ line manipulation affects the dignity of another human being; the psychological effects of germ line manipulation on parents and children; and the broader implications for genetic diversity and variability. There is a danger in adopting the attitude that there is no point in discussing these issues on the basis that such manipulation just would not happen. As has been stated:

> in science as in life it is important to distinguish between chastity and impotence. They both have the same effect and that is why every scientist that I know will put his hand to his heart and say that he will not conduct germ line therapy. He is not being chaste.[117]

Nevertheless, there is little sense that GTAC sees its role to be the discussion of these issues.[118] Moreover, it is not clear what contributions non-scientists are seen to be able to make to such a debate. The membership of GTAC is drawn widely, and includes a psychologist, a genetic counsellor, religious, legal and industry representatives. GTAC is beginning to show greater willingness to open up its proceedings, and is considering holding them in public. However, private hearings were considered to be essential initially as it was felt that lay members would have been inhibited from showing their ignorance of science by asking questions.[119] Further, whilst one does not want to read too much into these things, the title of GTAC's first workshop (held in 1996) shows some discounting of popular views of gene therapy: 'Myth and Reality: Hype and Practicality'. The criticism being levelled is not that GTAC is not careful in its assessment or that its procedures for considering individual cases are flawed, but of the apparent narrowness of its focus. Such narrowness would be partly excusable if there had already been a full consideration of the issues surrounding gene therapy; this was what Clothier was in part meant to provide, but failed to do so.

Cloning
Cloning provides perhaps one of the starkest examples of the fundamental differences in the way that genetic technology can be perceived. For a scientist, cloning is the production of genetically identical unicellular or multicellular

---

114 The MCA has no remit to consider ethical issues per se, rather its role is to approve products for marketing on the basis of their safety, quality and efficacy.

115 SCST, Third Report, n 77 above, para 110 and further para 108.

116 For discussion see for example, W. French Anderson, 'Human Gene Therapy: Scientific and Ethical Considerations', in R. Chadwick (ed), *Ethics, Reproduction and Genetic Control* (London: Routledge, 1990).

117 Evidence to the SCST, Third Report, n 77 above, para 116.

118 Although in its defence it could be argued that germ line therapy which involves the manipulation of embryonic cells is covered anyway by the HFEA, (though this does not cover genetic manipulation of the gametes or ovum) or that the HGAC is now the body which should air such issues.

119 See the comments of the then Chairman of GTAC, Dame June Lloyd, to the SCST: Third Report, n 77 above, para 110.

organisms by natural or assisted processes. For a non-scientist, cloning is the key to immortality, the 'resurrection' of dead loved or admired ones, the ultimate ego trip, Jurassic Park. These perceptions are fuelled by some scientists: in the US, Richard Seed recently announced that he was proposing to clone human beings.[120] There have even been reports of proposals to take DNA from the Turin shroud and clone it.[121]

The current debate was of course triggered by the birth of Dolly in February 1997. Dolly was the first example of an adult vertebrate cloned from another adult. The nucleus of a cell taken from the udder of a six year old Dorset Finn ewe was introduced into an unfertilised egg from which the nucleus had been removed. That egg was then placed in the uterus of another sheep, and Dolly was born.[122] Dolly is the exact genetic twin of her 'mother', the Dorset Finn. The purpose in cloning Dolly was to develop methods for the genetic improvement of livestock.[123] The technique could also be used for the production of transgenic livestock: animals which contain genes from other species. Instead of taking the nucleus from the cell of one sheep and introducing it as it is to the ennucleated egg of another sheep, a gene from another animal or human is inserted into that nucleus before it is introduced to the egg. It was through this process that Polly and her identical clones Holly, Molly and Olly (short for Olivia, not Oliver) were born in December 1997. Polly and her sisters are transgenic sheep: they carry a human gene for a blood clotting factor which is used for treating haemophilia.[124]

Human cloning is still some distance away in terms of scientific development.[125] Nevertheless, the birth of Dolly prompted a flurry of regulatory activity nationally and internationally.[126] There is no UK legislation specifically directed at human cloning, but current techniques which would be used in human cloning, in that they involve the introduction of DNA into an ennucleated oocyte, probably fall under the HFEA.[127] There are a number of international instruments banning cloning: in

---

120 *Nature Biotechnology*, vol 16, January 1998, 6. He would not be the first: in 1993 two scientists at George Washington University, Robert Stillman and Jerry Hall, announced they had cloned human embryos by splitting them (which replicates the natural process which occurs when identical twins are formed and is a quite different technique to that used to produce Dolly): *Nature* vol 365, 28 October 1993, 778.

121 'Today', BBC Radio 4, 31 March 1998.

122 In fact, Dolly was the only success from 277 attempts. The procedure was used on 277 eggs, only 29 of which were successfully reconstructed (ie the nucleus was successfully introduced). Of those 29 which were then implanted in surrogate ewes, only Dolly was born. See 'Viable Offspring Derived from Foetal and Adult Mammalian Cells', *Nature*, vol 385, 27 February 1997, 810, 811.

123 For discussion of the potential applications of the technique, see SCST, Fifth Report, *The Cloning of Animals from Adult Cells*, 1996–97 HC 373-I, paras 7–10; *Nature Biotechnology*, vol 15, April 1997, 306.

124 'Transgenic Sheep Expressing Human Factor IX', *Science*, 19 December 1997, 2130–2133.

125 Although the editorial of the issue of *Nature* in which the birth of Dolly was announced stated that cloning humans from adults' tissue is likely to be achievable 'any time from one to ten years from now': *Nature*, vol 385, 27 February 1997, 753.

126 Within days President Clinton called on the US National Bioethics Advisory Committee (NBAC) to investigate the ethics of cloning and gave instructions to the head of executive departments and agencies that no federal funds be given for the cloning of human beings. The NBAC report, published in June 1997, focused primarily on the risks involved and called for a five year moratorium on human cloning until the risks were better understood. It has been criticised for taking too narrow a view to the issue (see for example *Nature Biotechnology*, n 123 above), but following the report President Clinton introduced the Cloning Prohibition Bill into Congress, where it is currently being considered.

127 This is the view taken by the HFEA: HGAC and HFEA, *Cloning Issues in Reproduction Science and Medicine: A Consultation Document*, but the Select Committee on Science and Technology took the view that the position was more ambiguous: SCST, Fifth Report, n 123 above (January 1998) paras 23–33.

November 1997 UNESCO published the Universal Declaration on the Human Genome and Human Rights, clause 11 of which states that 'practices which are contrary to human dignity, such as reproductive cloning of human beings, shall not be permitted.' A protocol forbidding the cloning of human beings has been developed under the Council of Europe's Convention on Bioethics.[128] The recent Biotechnology Patents Directive forbids the issue of a patent on work leading to the deliberate cloning of human beings.[129] Human cloning of various forms was already banned, explicitly or implicitly in several different countries.[130]

The HGAC and HFEA have taken steps to negotiate a position on human cloning by producing a consultation paper which seeks to address a number of the ethical issues which this area of science raises.[131] The paper distinguished two different types of cloning. First, reproductive cloning, where the intention is to produce identical fetuses and babies, and second, what it termed 'therapeutic' cloning, which involved other applications of nuclear replacement technology. Those could include studying cell development or developing stem cell lines with a view to developing medical applications. The strategy would be to take cells donated by one patient, transfer the nucleus to an ennucleated oocyte,[132] then grow it in culture to generate stem cells, and transfer the stem cells to a patient.[133] Possible applications could be for Parkinson's disease or the treatment of blood diseases.

The paper deliberately seeks to address the far wider questions that human cloning raises. It asks whether the use of nuclear replacement techniques or embryo splitting to create embryos would raise any new issues with respect to the special status of the human embryo or what may ethically be done within the first fourteen days of the embryo's development. It asks whether there are any medical or scientific areas that might benefit from research involving the creation of a cloned embryo, and whether any of the potential applications of nuclear replacement that would not result in cloned fetuses or babies raise any new ethical concerns.[134] With respect to reproductive cloning, the consultation paper asks some fundamental questions. To what extent can a person be said to have a right to an individual genetic identity, particularly given that the experience of genetically identical twins suggests that a unique genetic identity is not essential for a human being to feel and to be an individual? Would the creation of a clone of a human being always be an ethically unacceptable act? Would it be beyond the limit of what is ethically acceptable to resolve a couple's infertility problem? Do the large 'wastage' rates and uncertainties about malformations of embryos which would be involved, certainly in the nascent stages of the technology, make experimentation in humans involving the implantation of cloned embryos ethically impossible? And finally, what ethical importance might be attached to the distinction between artificial technologies which have a counterpart in natural processes (IVF), and those which do not (nuclear replacement technology)?[135]

---

128 Council of Europe, Convention for the Protection of Human Rights and Dignity of the Human Being with Regard to the Application of Biology and Medicine 1996 (Strasbourg: ETS 164).

129 European Parliament and Council Directive on the Legal Protection of Biotechnological Inventions, COM (97) 446 final. Approved by the European Parliament on 12 May 1998.

130 For summaries of different countries' positions see HGAC and HFEA, *Consultation Document*, n 127 above, Annex D; Union for Europe Group, *Report on Cloning*, May 1997.

131 HGAC and HFEA, *Consultation Document*, n 127 above.

132 An egg mother cell.

133 Alan Colman, 'Dolly — the implications of cloning', paper presented to the 21st Century Trust seminars on Genetics, Ethics and Identity, 27 March–4 April 1998.

134 *Consultation Document*, n 127 above, Section 7.

135 *ibid* Section 8.

The approach taken by the HGAC and HFEA to the issue of human cloning is one which seeks to marry scientific knowledge with ethical concerns; to use the one to inform the other. It contrasts with the approach taken by the Clothier Committee which, as noted above, simply dismissed the consideration of germ line therapy in two paragraphs, and then principally on the basis of safety, and which did not seek to explore the wider social and ethical impacts of somatic cell therapy. The consultation paper is an attempt to pre-empt science by discussing the acceptability of human cloning before all aspects of it become scientifically possible. It is also an attempt to forestall a blanket ban on human cloning which could potentially lead to regulation which in fact inhibits the development of research which might not offend public ethics either at all or to the same degree as full reproductive cloning. Achieving a position in which science and ethics can develop a mutually reinforcing relationship is not an easy task; the consultation paper suggests that at least with respect to this issue the regulatory bodies are willing to try.

Rights to exploit genetic material

The final aspect of the regulation of genetics to be explored is the issue of the rights to exploit genetic material. Defined broadly, this embraces questions of the ownership of genetic material, in particular whether human tissue should be treated as property, and the ability to gain intellectual property rights over it. The first issue, although important, will not be explored here.[136] Instead discussion will focus on the second: the issue of intellectual property rights.

Regulatory fora and principal actors

At first glance, including intellectual property rights in a discussion of the regulation of genetic technology seems misplaced. The Patent Office is not a regulator of such technology. It does not prescribe what research should be done or how, nor is its approval necessary for the development and sale of genetic products or services. However the controversy surrounding the role of patents in genetic research and product development and the significant impact which patents can have on those activities mean that patent law is a significant forum in the genetic debate.

A patent is a monopoly right granted to a person to exploit an invention, and thus to exclude others from its exploitation.[137] Patents can be sought from national bodies (in the UK the Patent Office) or in Europe from the European Patent Office, set up under the European Patent Convention — a regional arrangement limited to European countries, although not solely to members of the EU. The EPO has the capacity to grant applicants patent rights in any number of signatory states nominated by the applicant. The requirements for the granting of a patent under the UK Patents Act 1977 and the EPC are similar.[138] They are novelty, inventiveness, industrial applicability and sufficiency of description. The EPC and the UK Act

---

136   The issue was the subject of an extensive report by the Nuffield Council on Bioethics, *Human Tissue: Ethical and Legal Issues* (London: Nuffield Council, 1995). On the question of ownership of human tissue see G. Dworkin and I. Kennedy, 'Human Tissue: Rights in the Body and its Parts' [1993] 1 *Medical Law Review* 291.

137   See generally, W.R. Cornish, *Intellectual Property* (London: Sweet and Maxwell, 3rd ed. 1996).

138   s 130(7) states that certain provisions of the 1977 Act, in particular those dealing with criteria for patentability, revocation and infringement, are 'so framed as to have, as nearly as practicable, the same effect in the UK as corresponding provisions in the EPC... have in the territories to which it applies.'

exclude from patentability mere discoveries, biological processes, animal or plant varieties and those things which are contrary to public order or morality.[139] A Directive on the patenting of biotechnological inventions has also recently been agreed which aims to harmonise the criteria for the patentability of genetic material across the EU Member States and to facilitate a uniform application of the immorality exclusion in all Member States.

The principal actors are thus the members of the patent offices, patent agents, patent lawyers, and those who are seeking patents: in this context biotechnology companies, universities, and other research institutions. They are thus lawyers, scientists and industry.

The internal conceptualisation of the issues

As noted, a patent is a monopoly right to exploit an invention, and thus to exclude others from its exploitation. It is the notion of a patent as an exclusionary right which tends to be most frequently emphasised by patent lawyers (and patent holders), particularly when defending the patent system.[140] Patents give no obligation to use: they simply allow the patentee to stop others using and making the invention. The classic justifications for granting that monopoly are that it thereby promotes dissemination of information about an invention, information which would otherwise not be disclosed and which would remain as a trade secret, and that it provides an incentive to invent and to exploit that invention.[141] It is the latter which has become the basis for the more recent justification for patents: viz that a strong patent system is a core aspect of commercial development and thus economic policy. The patents that a firm holds are seen by investors as the most important factor in deciding whether or not to invest in a company,[142] and a strong system of patent protection is frequently argued to be essential for a country's economic development and international competitiveness.[143]

Internal debates

The internal debates reflect the rationalities of the three principal groups of participants: those of law, science and economics. They are thus principally as to the appropriate application and development of legal terms to scientific practices, and as to whether the practices of the courts and patent offices adequately meet the economic goal of providing incentives for invention and commercial development.[144]

---

139 Article 53(a) EPC; the UK counterpart, s 1(3)(a) states that a patent will not be granted for 'an invention the publication or exploitation of which would be generally expected to encourage offensive, immoral or anti-social behaviour.'

140 See for example, BioIndustry Association, *Innovation from Nature: The Protection of Inventions in Biology* (London: BIA, undated).

141 See generally Cornish, n 137 above.

142 Ernst and Young, *European Biotech '97: A New Economy* (Frankfurt: Ernst and Young International, 1997) 36, figure 15.

143 Reflected in the recitals of the recent Directive on Biotechnology; E. Armitage, 'EU Industrial Property Policy: Priority for Patents' [1996] EIPR 555; J. Lerner, 'Patenting in the Shadow of Competitors' (1995) 35 *J Law & Econ* 463; A. McInerny, 'Biotechnology: *Biogen* v *Medeva* in the House of Lords' [1998] EIPR 14; these arguments are also loudly voiced in the context of TRIPS (the Agreement on Trade-related Intellectual Property Rights): see S.K. Verma, 'TRIPs and Plant Variety Protection in Developing Countries' [1995] EIPR 281; M. Blakeney, 'The Impact of the TRIPs Agreement in the Asian Pacific Region' [1996] EIPR 544.

144 Thus particular decisions have been criticised on the basis that they do not provide sufficient reward and incentives to patentees in biotechnology: for example R. Ebbnik, 'The Performance of Biotech Patents in the National Courts of Europe' [1995] *Patent World* 25; N. Jones, 'The New Biotechnology Directive' [1996] EIPR 363.

    The advent of biotechnology has posed significant challenges for patent law, and
many argue that patent law is struggling to meet that challenge.[145] The
requirements of novelty and inventiveness are those around which much of the
contention arises in deciding whether and when genes and gene technology are
patentable. The novelty requirement demands that the invention claimed has not
been made available anywhere in the world prior to the filing date.[146] The question,
therefore, is not whether what is claimed already exists, but whether its existence is
known. Thus where a product claim is in issue, it is arguable that even if an
identical substance to that which is claimed occurs in nature, it may be regarded as
novel when isolated and identified, or 'characterised' (eg by means of a DNA
sequence) for the first time. Alternatively, a claimed substance may satisfy the
novelty test if it is produced in a refined or purified form, ie a form that does not
occur naturally.[147] The inventiveness requirement, however, demands in addition
that the invention claimed be not obvious to a person ordinarily skilled in the
relevant art. Gene technology is not of itself regarded as inventive, and nor,
without more, are its products. Thus it will generally be regarded as obvious to
attempt to sequence a gene or to produce the substance for which it codes in a pure
form using standard recombinant DNA techniques.[148] The applicant will need to
point to a method which overcomes particular difficulties attendant upon these
techniques.[149] Further, the sufficiency requirement will ensure that broad claims,
extending to other recombinant methods than those actually invented by the
claimant, will be disallowed.[150]
    As in any legal system, there are areas of contention and uncertainty as to the
application of legal provisions to particular fact situations. In the context of gene
related patents, disputes arise as to the interpretation of the provision which
excludes plant and animal varieties from patentability,[151] as to the meaning of non-
obviousness and inventiveness in the biotechnological context,[152] and as to
whether patents are being granted which are too wide in their scope.[153] Concern is
also being expressed in the US over the recent decision of the US Patent Office to
grant patents for expressed sequence tags of no known utility on the basis that
patents are being granted to reward very little commercial or scientific outlay, and
in a way which will severely inhibit future research.[154]

---

145   See B. Sherman, 'Patent Law in a time of Change: Non-obviousness and Biotechnology' (1990) 10
      OJLS 278. For discussion of the application of patent law to biotechnology see further Nuffield
      Council, n 136 above; Cornish, n 137 above; G.T. Laurie, 'Biotechnology and Intellectual Property:
      A Marriage of Inconvenience?' in S. McLean (ed), *Contemporary Issues in Law, Medicine and
      Ethics* (Aldershot: Dartmouth, 1996). I am grateful to Anne Barron for her advice on this section.
146   In contrast to the US, where it is the date of publication rather than of filing which is critical.
147   Decision of the EPO in the Opposition to Patent No 112 149 in the name of the Howard Florey
      Institute of Experimental Physiology and Medicine, 18 January 1995 (the Relaxin Opposition)
      (1995) OJEPO 388, and in the UK see *Genentech*, which suggests that both genes and the substances
      for which they code are mere discoveries, and as such not patentable: [1989] RPC 147 (CA).
148   *Genentech Inc's Patent* [1989] RPC 147.
149   *Biogen Inc v Medeva plc* [1997] RPC 1 (HL).
150   *ibid.*
151   Article 53(b) EPC, discussed (despite the title) by D. Beyleveld and R. Brownsword, *Mice, Morality
      and Patents: The Onco-mouse Application and Article 53(a) of the European Patent Convention*
      (London: Common Law Institute of Intellectual Property, 1993).
152   For the most recent discussion of the issue in the UK context see *Biogen v Medeva*, n 149 above.
153   S. Crespi, 'Biotechnology, Broad Claims and the EPC' [1995] EIPR 371; T. Roberts, 'Broad Claims
      for Biotechnological Inventions' [1994] EIPR 371; *Biogen v Medeva*, n 149 above.
154   Human Genome Sciences has also recently filed an application with the EPO for patents on the
      genetic sequence of one of the bacteria which cause meningitis: *The Guardian*, 7 May 1998.

Outsider perspectives

These issues are of undoubted importance to the operation of the patent system, and they are sources of controversy both within and to an extent outside that system. However, the granting of patents to gene sequences in humans, plants or animals is opposed by many on more fundamental grounds. These are essentially that patents should not be granted over such material not because existing legal definitions are being wrongly applied (although those arguments are also made)[155] but because the granting of monopoly rights for its exploitation is simply inappropriate.

The inappropriateness argument takes a number of forms, not always distinguished or explicit. For these purposes three main versions can be identified. The first is that granting patents over genetic sequences amounts to the patenting and thus commodification of life.[156] The objection is rooted in concepts of property and ownership, and the appropriateness of the application of those concepts to the DNA particularly, although not uniquely, of humans. So in its opposition in the *Relaxin* case, which was an application for a patent of the DNA sequence which codes for the hormone relaxin, opponents argued that to patent human genes was to patent life, and that it amounted to slavery contrary to the fundamental human right to self determination.[157] The objection that patenting genes is tantamount to patenting life has also been put by a number of non-governmental organisations.[158] Further, the revised EU draft directive on patents in biotechnology provides that 'the human body, at various stages of its development, and the simple discovery of one of its elements including the sequence or partial sequence of a gene, cannot constitute patentable inventions.'[159]

The second type of objection to the granting of gene related patents is essentially directed not so much at the patent itself as at the process or substance which is being patented. Patents are being objected to on the grounds not that only *one* person should be able to conduct the activity for which the patent is sought, but that *no-one* should. Thus the recent EU directive on patents and biotechnology expressly provides that the following shall be considered unpatentable: the procedures for human reproductive cloning; processes for modifying the germ-line genetic identity of human beings; methods in which human embryos are used; and processes for modifying the genetic identity of animals which are likely to cause them suffering without any substantial medical benefit to man or animal and animals resulting from such processes.[160] This is not because such activities should be open to all to exploit; quite the opposite. It is because it is felt that these activities are morally insupportable. Opposing a patent on essentially moral

---

155 eg Beyleveld and Brownsword, n 151 above.

156 For a discussion see A. Wells, 'Patenting New Life Forms: An Ecological Perspective' [1994] EIPR 111.

157 *Relaxin* opposition, n 147 above.

158 See for example the campaigns of Jeremy Rifkin in the US; further, *The Case Against Patents in Genetic Engineering: A Special Report by the Genetics Forum* (London: The Genetics Forum, 1996), the 'No Patents on Life' campaign which the Forum co-ordinates in the UK, and the 'Blue Mountain Declaration' issued by NGOs in the US opposing patents on living organisms and their component parts.

159 Article 5, para 1. Note however that the Article also provides in para 2 that 'An element isolated from the human body or otherwise produced by means of a technical process including the sequence or partial sequence of a gene may constitute a patentable invention, even if the structure of that element is identical to the natural element.'

160 Amended Proposal for a European Parliament and Council Directive on the Legal Protection of Biotechnological Inventions, COM(97) 446 final, article 6, approved by the Parliament on 12 May 1998.

grounds is an attempt to prevent the activity altogether. It is an attempt which is not made through a direct ban on the activity however, but obliquely, by a withdrawal of the incentives to perform it.

The third form of objection is not so much to the activity per se, but to the commercial exploitation which patents facilitate, or indeed enable. It is an objection to the introduction of commercial norms in areas where many regard them as inappropriate. At its most extreme, it is an objection to the biotechnology industry itself. Thus the application for patents over expressed sequence tags generated in the course of the Human Genome Project which was filed by the US National Institutes of Health was widely condemned as violating the spirit of academic co-operation in which the Project had begun.[161] The claiming of patents over gene sequences obtained from indigenous peoples or plants has been strongly criticised as a form of 'bio-piracy', or as 'gene prospecting'.[162] The example of the agreement reached in 1991 between Merck and an agency of the Costa Rican government is often cited in this context. Merck paid US $1.2m for the right to inventory, test and commercialise plants, micro-organisms and insects from the rainforest. The agency would then receive five per cent of any royalties.[163] In the agricultural context, the granting of patents over genetically modified crops is resisted on the grounds that it will adversely affect farmers, plant and animal breeders and biodiversity.[164] The ethical code of the Human Genome Diversity Project now contains a provision that no patents will be sought on the basis of genetic material obtained as part of the project.

Access

Patent law tries hard to remain insulated from these arguments. However, they enter the patent arena directly through the gateway of article 53(a) of the EPC. Essentially dormant until the arrival of gene related patents,[165] article 53(a) provides that patents may not be granted for inventions the publication or exploitation of which would be contrary to *ordre public* or morality. Through this entry point have come arguments which are totally alien to the closed world of patents and the EPO has tried to narrow the gateway as far as possible.[166] The EPO Guidelines state that the test is whether the public in general would consider the invention to be 'so abhorrent that the grant of patent rights would be inconceiveable.' It has made it clear that its assessment of morality is essentially utilitarian in form. So creating a transgenic mouse which contained an activated gene for cancer, the Harvard onco-mouse, was found to be acceptable (although the case is still under consideration), but creating a transgenic mouse for the purposes of attempting to alleviate baldness (the Upjohn case) was not. Morality also seems

---

161 For an outline of the moves and countermoves involved see SCST, Third Report, n 77 above, paras 35–45; for an excellent discussion of the background to the HGP see T. Wilkie, *Perilous Knowledge* (Harmondsworth: Penguin, 1993).

162 See for example, D. Dickson, 'Whose Genes are they Anyway?' *Nature*, vol 381, 2 May 1996, 11; V. Shiva and R. Hollar-Bhar, 'Intellectual Privacy and the Neem Tree', *The Ecologist*, vol 23 no 6, November/December 1993.

163 See further Rural Advancement Foundation International (RAFI), *Communique*, Sept/Oct 1995, Ottawa, Canada.

164 See for example, the Genetics Forum, 1996.

165 L. Bentley and B. Sherman, 'The Ethics of Patenting: Towards a Transgenic Patent System' (1995) 3 *Medical Law Review* 275.

166 For discussions of, variously, the Onco-mouse case, *Greenpeace UK v Plant Genetic Systems NV*, the *Relaxin* case and the *Upjohn* case, see for example Beyleveld and Brownsword, n 151 above, Bentley and Sherman, n 165 above, Laurie, n 145 above.

to be an essentially risk-based assessment: Greenpeace's opposition to the Genentech patent for a herbicide resistant crop was rejected on the basis that the environmental risks had not been made out. Finally, the morality arguments are ultimately countered by technical ones in what often appears to be a dialogue of the deaf. Thus the claim in the *Relaxin* case that allowing patents of genes or gene fragments is 'patenting life' was rejected with the explanation, scientifically and legally correct, that what is being patented is a chemical substance which carries a genetic code to produce medically useful proteins.[167]

Attempts at negotiation

The EPO, practising patent lawyers, and biotechnology companies, are visibly frustrated at the attempts which are being made to use the morality clause to introduce arguments which they see to be completely inappropriate in the world of patents.[168] Again, the issues which outsiders see to be relevant to the administration of the regulatory regime, this time of intellectual property, are not those which that regime considers relevant to its operation. There is moreover a manifest tension between the perceptions of such 'insiders' of the patent system as to what patents are and the views of outsiders.

These arguments are articulated to varying degrees in a number of places, but can be analysed as follows. Essentially, insiders see patents as objective, technical and legal, and so in express contrast to ethics which are malleable, subjective and emotive. Outsiders implicitly or explicitly see patents as social privileges conferred on inventors which could be witheld or to the exercise of which certain conditions could be attached. The insiders retort that they have already paid for the privilege. In return for the patent they grant disclosure of the invention: the classic view of the exchange relationship which underlies patent law. However, the implicit rejoinder is either that this is not enough, or this is not the point. In certain instances society does not see any merit in granting the patent at all, regardless of the disclosure to which it may lead. This is not because it does not want that disclosure, but because it does not think that social privileges should be granted for its exploitation. In turn, to echo the arguments given above, this could either be because it does not think the invention should be exploited at all (as with germ line therapy or human cloning) or because it does not think that a monopoly should be given over that exploitation.

Some have suggested that these alternative perspectives should be introduced into the patent system through a change in the institutional structure of that system. A proposal put forward by the Nuffield Council and other commentators[169] is that the patent system should better equip itself to assess ethical issues by altering the membership of the Patent Office. Alternatively, or in addition, it should be given better guidance by the appropriate legislative body as to what types of things are considered to be contrary to morality, which it should then apply.

However, although altering the institutional structure of the regulation or its remit could perhaps go some way to ensuring that the patent system takes into account ethical issues in granting patents, it is not clear that this would really

---

167 *Relaxin* case, n 147 above.
168 See for example, S. Crespi, 'Biotechnology Patenting: The Wicked Animal Must Defend Itself' [1995] 9 EIPR 431; J. Woodley and G. Smith, 'Conflicts in Ethics/Patents in Gene R&D', *les Nouvelles*, September 1997, 119.
169 Nuffield Council on Bioethics, n 136 above; Beyleveld and Brownsword, n 155 above; Bentley and Sherman, n 151 above; Wells, n 156 above.

address the core issues. Withholding a patent on the grounds of morality may send a signal that wider societal approval for the activity will not be conferred and may remove the incentives for anyone to undertake the activity, but it does not prohibit it. As Laurie has commented, '[a]t best, the "morality" exception can draw attention to matters requiring attention and action. In reality, it demonstrates the inappropriateness and inadequacy of using such a system to regulate matters which are clearly outside its scope.'[170] The attempt to use patent law to prevent unwanted commercial exploitation is again simply to use an instrument which is badly fashioned for the task. If what is wanted is to regulate the biotechnology industry, then this has to be done through regulation specifically designed for that end.[171]

Nonetheless, patent law has been one of the central areas in which ethical and moral issues have been raised. It is suggested that one of the principal reasons why such a wide range of opponents are trying to use the immorality door to enter this forum is not (or not just) because they want to deny the implicit conferral of society's approval which the patent manifests. Rather it is because it is the only door available. It is the only point in the different fora in which decisions are made relating to the development and application of genetic technology at which widely based ethical and social objections to genetic engineering itself are given the opportunity to make a formal, and highly visible, appearance.

Facilitating regulation: towards negotiation and integration

There are thus a multitude of regulatory fora in which questions of the use and application of genetic regulation are determined. In each, there are different participants, different rationalities, and different criteria on which regulatory decisions are based. There are, however, tensions between the rationalities, the cognitions, of the different systems of science, academia, industry, government and between the rationalities of those systems and other sub-systems of society.[172] At a risk of caricature, scientists tend to see issues simply in terms of scientific feasibility and risk. Regulation is justified only when directed at particular risks, and debate as to what regulation should be is seen as irrelevant unless and until the scientific means exist for actually doing what it is which is discussed. Industry seeks regulation which is based in scientific assessments of risk, and which facilitates and protects its ability commercially to exploit genetic technology and which does not put it at a disadvantage with respect to international competitors. Academia's position is more complicated: on the one hand it seeks to engage in pure research and values collaboration and co-operation; on the other, it is fiercely competitive, with researchers competing nationally and internationally for reputation and for finance. It also seeks increasingly to exploit its research commercially. For government, the bio-industry's voice speaks loudly and there are a number of initiatives to encourage its development: bio-technology is arguably one of the new 'national champions'.[173] In 1992 the Biotechnology Industry Regulatory Advisory

---

170 Laurie, n 145 above, 255.
171 For one suggestion as to how this could be achieved see M. Llewelyn, 'The Legal Protection of Biotechnological Inventions: An Alternative Approach' [1997] 3 EIPR 115 (regulate the exercise of the right, not its grant).
172 Again, the focus is still on the way in which issues are viewed, rather than the interests which are pursued; the two are related, but this is not the occasion to explore the interaction between them. See further Black, n 7 above.
173 Industries deliberately supported and promoted by government as symbols of national success, traditionally those of heavy industry.

Group was set up by government to discuss the regulation of biotechnology,[174] and in 1995 a £17 million awareness programme, 'Biotechnology Means Business', was launched.[175] The programme includes funding for small companies and for joint ventures between academia and industry,[176] funding for academia to encourage it to develop patentable products,[177] the creation of business 'mentoring and incubation' services, and a finance advisory service.

The concerns which may loosely be attributed to the wider public, or those outside the individual regulatory fora, tend, as we have seen, to be broader than those which are recognised by those within the fora. Moreover, each forum has a different sense of its own purpose and rationale. The patent system in particular is striking in its closure and its resistance to external interventions. The other regulatory structures also operate with their own logics, however. Risk dominates regulation of laboratory work, and the research, development and marketing of genetically modified products. Risk is also a key aspect of the regulation of the direct supply of genetic testing and gene therapy. In both, risk is considered essentially to be a scientific and technical assessment. Considerations of medical ethics play a strong role in human and medical genetics, and wider social concerns are evident in the development of the policy with respect to cloning.

At present, non-scientists have limited access to the regulatory fora, and tend to be recognised by those fora in the capacity of either consumers or patients. As consumers, the regulatory emphasis is on their ability to exercise informed choice in their purchasing decisions, to which end product information is seen to be the key. In their capacity as patients, a different logic has prevailed. The context is that not of the market place but of the hospital; the norms of the medical profession have informed the way in which issues arising from genetic technology are defined and treated. The overriding concerns are for informed consent, counselling, communication and confidentiality. In both contexts the individual's participation is restricted, however, to the ability to say yes or no to what is offered, not to shape the choice.

There are, however, moves to open up the regulatory decision process. Various attempts have been made to broaden the views to which different systems have to respond: the wider membership of the HGAC, for example, or the role of the European Group on the Ethics in Science and New Technologies, which advises the EU Commission.[178] In addition, some industry associations (although not in the UK) have drawn up their own ethical codes,[179] and there have been some initiatives

174 The industrial representatives come from a range of biotechnology users, including pharmaceuticals, agriculture and food, and biotechnology-specific SMEs (small and medium enterprises). The regulatory departments represented are the DTI, the DOE, the HSE, MAFF, the Patent Office and the MCA.

175 For details see the DTI's Bioguide at http://www.dti.gov.uk/bioguide.htm#contents.

176 The SMART scheme helps SMEs and individuals to 'research, design and develop technologically innovative products and processes for the national benefit': Bioguide. It provides funding of 75 per cent of project costs, up to a maximum of £45,000 to assist in technical and commercial feasibility studies and 30 per cent to help the development of technological products. The LINK scheme aims to 'accelerate the exploitation of technology and to bridge the gap between science and the market place.' Government Departments and Research Councils provide up to 50 per cent of the eligible costs of a project with the balance coming from industry. So far over 120 projects have been supported.

177 Under the banner 'Biotechnology Exploitation Platforms', grants of up to £250,000 are available to encourage higher education institutions to develop exploitable patent portfolios, and identify commercial opportunities.

178 This was established in December 1997 and replaces the Group of Advisers on the Ethical Implications of Biotechnology, established in 1992.

179 In the US, the Bio Industry Organisation has issued a *Statement of Principles* (http://www.bio.org), and in Europe, EuropaBio has issued for consultation *Draft Core Ethical Values* (June 1997) (http://www.europa-bio.be).

in improving public understanding of genetics.[180] These include a Consensus Conference on plant biotechnology[181] and a Citizens' Jury on genetic testing.[182] Such initiatives appear to provide the structures in which the integration which is sought by the participatory or procedural models could be achieved. It would seem that they begin to meet the theoretical demands made from sociology, science, and law for the proceduralisation of regulation in the face of competing rationalities. But these initiatives seem often not so much to integrate different views as simply aggregate them, and in so aggregating them afford science a voice which is regarded as more authoritative, and indeed more legitimate, than that of others.[183]

The call that is being made here is not simply for the broadening of participation in regulation, however, but for regulators to adopt a different role: that of facilitators, of negotiators. For that, it is suggested, they need to take on the role of interpreters: of re-translating the views of different groups and putting them into a language that the others can understand. In order to develop regulation which truly aims to facilitate the integration of contending views, it is thus suggested, there has to be a focus on more than institutional design. There has to be a focus on status, on language and on understanding.

The warning, in other words, is that focusing on institutional design will not necessarily alter much. The mere existence of lay participants in the regulatory process may not in fact result in regulation which is very different from that which would have been formed by scientists alone. For example, in a context where the problem is defined solely in terms of risk, and in which scientific assessments are seen as rational and their risk assessments as assessments of 'real' risk, the inclusion of ethics committees or non-scientists in the decision making process will not necessarily achieve the integration sought simply because it is only the scientific view which is afforded legitimacy. Unless lay views are seen as equally valid, they will be marginalised and will therefore not be afforded full standing in the debate.[184]

In this context, regulation should seek to enable contending groups to arrive at an accepted decision or set of decisions. For this to occur, however, a number of pre-conditions have to be met. It has to be recognised that scientific approaches are not necessarily 'correct', nor can they claim a monopoly over rationality. In turn, it has to be accepted that lay views of science, and in particular of risk, are not necessarily incorrect nor irrational. The argument is thus that to facilitate the integration of scientific and non-scientific views, we need to remove the idea of scientific objectivity *versus* lay irrationality and to replace it with one which recognises different rationalities.

The task is a significant one, and its nature can be illustrated briefly by looking at the question of risk. As we have seen, risk is an important aspect of the debate surrounding genetic technology, and although not the sole aspect of that debate it is nonetheless one of the principal justifications that science would accept for regulation, analogous to the role that welfare economics plays for economists in

---

180 For example the establishment of the Committee on the Public Understanding of Science.
181 UK National Consensus Conference on Plant Biotechnology, Final Report (November 1994), available at ftp://ftp.open.gov.uk/pub/docs/sci_museum/consensus.txt.
182 WIHSC, n 90 above.
183 On integration and aggregation see further S. Krimsky and D. Golding, 'Reflections' in S. Krimsky and D. Golding (eds), *Social Theories of Risk* (New York: Praeger, 1992).
184 This is a point made by Beck, *Risk Society: Towards a New Modernity* n 1 above, and has been picked up and developed in some of the 'socio-scientific' literature: for a review see S. Eden, 'Public Participation in Environmental Policy: Considering Scientific, Counter-Scientific and Non-Scientific Contributions' (1996) 5 *Public Understanding of Science* 183.

justifying economic regulation.[185] By examining the debate which surrounds the definition and regulation of risk, we can begin to see the nature of the task which a facilitative, integrationist approach to regulation entails.

In the area of risk, the question of the relative roles of scientists and non-scientists in defining societal risk is a matter of considerable debate, both in academia and in government circles.[186] Few would deny individual patients or consumers the opportunity to determine the extent to which they expose themselves to risk through, for example, the principles of informed consent to medical treatment, or the provision of information to enable consumers to make purchasing decisions,[187] but the extent to which non-experts should be making decisions as to the degree of risk to which society should be exposed is a more contested question.

The shades and nuances in that debate are multifarious, but for our purposes we can distinguish between three broad propositions.[188] First, that scientific identification of hazards and determinations of risks should determine the regulatory response. This may be termed the technocratic view. The dominant language should be that of science. To the extent that it is seen to be a problem, the lack of public understanding of the scientific language, or of public acceptance of the scientific view (including the adequacy of its regulation), is to be met through public education. Until then the public is simply ill-equipped to participate in regulatory decision making, and indeed their participation could be positively harmful both to science and to the commercial exploitation of its activities.

This attitude is evident in the approach of government, science and industry to the issue of public understanding. Encouraging public understanding is essentially seen as encouraging public *appreciation* of science. It is an attitude to public understanding which is essentially one-way, based on the view that the public is currently ignorant, and that ignorance needs to be dispelled.[189] If it were, then there would be a greater chance of the public accepting genetic research and its outcomes. This would not only improve the public image of science, and so help secure public funding, it would also mean that the public would adopt a proper attitude towards science and its findings, by for example, adopting proper risk calculations.[190]

---

185 On which see generally, A. Ogus, *Regulation: Legal Form and Economic Theory* (Oxford: Clarendon Press, 1994).

186 eg O. Renn and D. Levine, 'Trust and Credibility' in H. Jungermann, R.E. Kasperson, P.M. Wiedemann (eds), *Risk Communication* (Julich: KPA, 1992); R.H. Phildes and C.R. Sunstein, 'Reinventing the Regulatory State' (1995) 62 *Univ Chicago LR* 1; A. Hutchinson, *Dwelling on the Threshold: Critical Essays on Modern Legal Thought* (London: Sweet and Maxwell, 1988); A. Ogus, 'Risk Management and "Rational" Social Regulation' in R. Baldwin (ed), *Law and Uncertainty: Risks and Legal Processes* (Berlin: Kluwer, 1997); D.J. Fiorino, 'Technical and Democratic Values in Risk Analysis' (1989) 9 *Risk Analysis* 293.

187 Although exactly what these principles require in any one circumstance can of course still be contested; witness, for example, the debate on the labelling of novel foods and food ingredients.

188 This characterisation of positions focuses simply on the assessment of risks posed by particular hazards; it does not include aspects of risk management, for example risk or cost benefit analysis. A number of other classifications are possible: for discussion see O. Renn, 'Concepts of Risk: A Classification' in Krimsky and Golding, n 183 above; R. Baldwin, 'Introduction – Risk: The Legal Contribution' in R. Baldwin (ed), *Law and Uncertainty: Risks and Legal Processes* (Berlin: Kluwer, 1997).

189 For a discussion of the different approaches to public understanding of science more generally see B. Wynne, 'Public Uptake of Science: A Case for Institutional Reflexivity' (1993) 3 *Public Understanding of Science* 321; 'Public Understanding of Science Research: New Horizons or Hall of Mirrors?' (1991) 1 *Public Understanding of Science* 37.

190 See for example the report of the Committee to Review the Contribution of Scientists and Engineers to the Public Understanding of Science, Engineering and Technology, November 1995 (the Wolfendale Report).

The need for public understanding initiatives to improve public appreciation of science is an explicit aim of the Committee on the Public Understanding of Science (COPUS), of the Wolfendale Committee,[191] and underlay the Select Committee's report on biotechnology.[192] Thus Walter Bodmer, chairman of COPUS, deplores the low levels of 'genetic literacy',[193] with individuals being unable, for example, to provide correct definitions of DNA.[194] The question is seen to be how science can go out to meet the public, not how the public comes in to science.[195] The assumption is that there is a knowledge deficit on the part of the public which it is the role of science to fill. Once filled, the public will see, and accept, the scientific light.

The scientific light in the field of genetics, at least as shone by the proponents of gene technology, is one which encourages support for that technology on a number of grounds. Those involved in genetic research, and indeed its commercial exploitation, emphasise that it has the potential to confer considerable benefits. These include medical applications (diagnosis and treatment), benefits for the environment (less use of herbicides and pesticides), for the farmer (greater yields, less expenditure on chemicals), and for the consumer (lower fat pork, tastier tomatoes).

Fears of genetic engineering are addressed by stressing that its development is evolutionary rather than revolutionary: it is simply a further step building on existing techniques. Analogies are drawn between genetic engineering and 'traditional' biotechnological techniques of fermentation in the production of wine, beer, or bread, or the traditional cross-breeding of plants and animals.[196] It is argued that genetic engineering poses no greater hazards than those which society already tolerates; that in fact it could pose fewer hazards as it is more precise than traditional methods.[197] Genetic engineering is sometimes termed 'precision genetics',[198] allowing specific traits to be introduced through the introduction of a single gene rather than a random mixing of thousands of genes from two parents as occurs in traditional cross-breeding techniques.[199] Such precision, it is stressed, means that it confers greater benefits for the plant breeder and for the animal[200] as well as in medicine.

---

191 Wolfendale Report, para 1.8.
192 n 44 above.
193 W. Bodmer and R. McKie, *The Book of Man* (London: Little Brown, 1994).
194 For further examples see J. Durant, A. Hansen and M. Bauer, 'Public Understanding of the New Genetics' in *The Troubled Helix*, n 87 above, 239.
195 For example the Wolfendale Committee recommended the linking of research grants to initiatives to disseminate results to the public, encouraging universities to give training in communication skills, linking success in promoting public understanding to an individual's appointment and promotion prospects, and through continuing education initiatives. It proposed that initiatives be assessed by counting the number of hours spent on doing 'popular lectures, interviews, popular articles etc' (para 4.2.1), with individuals keeping logs of activities and portfolios of the outcome, and using questionnaires or audience interviews to assess quality (presumably to test how much the person had 'learned').
196 See for example the SCST Report on Biotechnology, n 44 above, ch 2.
197 See for example, evidence of the then head of the ACGM to the SCST *ibid* (para 5.11), and of Sir Walter Bodmer, head of COPUS (para 5.14) concerning genetic engineering and animals; or that given with respect to genetically modified foods (para 5.24); see further the OECD 1992 report on food safety.
198 eg M. Cantley, 'On LMOs, Catch 220 and DNA, Editorial Overview' (1996) 7 *Current Opinion in Biotechnology* 259
199 *Genetically Modified Crops and Their Wild Relatives — a UK Perspective*, GMO Research Report No 1, DOE 1994, (i). See generally the scientific advice cited in the SCST Report on Biotechnology, n 44 above, paras 5.4–5.8; 5.15–5.18, and the Committee's endorsement of this view, at para 6.10.
200 G. Bulfield, 'Genetic Manipulation of Farm and Laboratory Animals', in P. Wheale and R. McNally (eds), *The Bio-Revolution: Cornucopia or Pandora's Box?* (London: Pluto Press, 1990).

Finally it is argued that the risks that do exist are controllable. The particular hazard posed can be identified, an assessment of the likelihood of harm occurring made, and the nature of the consequences posited. The aim of regulation should be to ensure the adequate control of risks; not necessarily to eliminate them, but to reduce them to an acceptable level.

On this view, therefore, regulation should be 'science-based, proportional to real risk and unclouded by other issues'.[201] Science should be the benchmark. Lay views are irrational deviations from that benchmark, which should be corrected by education and which, if they insist on remaining, should be first, negotiable items in determining policy and second, extrinsic to the real business of regulation. What is necessary is that the public needs to be educated in the language and methods of science. Once people are made aware of science and of the benefits that genetic engineering can bring, and of the relatively low risks involved, they will be more prepared to accept the technology itself and the fruits it can bear.

The second proposition is that there is a role for public participation, but that the public's role should be confined. This view is thus one which may be termed modified technocracy. The scientific view is still that which is seen as the true 'objective' view, but to the extent that public concern relating to particular risks is high, or the public would derive particular utility from a regulatory approach which recognised such concerns, some deviations from this objective view may be permitted. Such deviations would be justified either on economic grounds,[202] or for the more pragmatic reasons of political expediency and the need to maintain the acceptability of the regulation in the eyes of the public.

The third proposition is more radical. It involves the rejection of the authoritative position of science in regulatory decision making, giving it no stronger voice than any other. Science is not infallible and it is not neutral; lay perceptions, moreover, are not arbitrary or irrational but based on identifiable criteria, exhibit a systematic pattern, and are institutionally embedded. It is the acceptance of this proposition which has to underlie any system of regulation which seeks to facilitate full integration. Whether this acceptance can be achieved, both theoretically and in practice, has been a significant topic of debate in social science writings on risk and of parts of the scientific literature on the broader issue of the objectivity of science and on public understanding.

In this proposition, contesting the idea of the objectivity of science is a central part of the discussion. Indeed, that discussion has reached such a point that the idea that scientific risk analysis is not objective is the accepted point of departure, and not something which could seriously be questioned. There are two core operating premises: first, that objectivity is particularly absent in areas characterised by a high degree of uncertainty and so risk analysis can never be free from judgement; and secondly, that in making those judgements science and scientists are not immune from bias or from the impact of institutional and social norms which affect all other aspects of society.[203] Scientists' assessments cannot claim to be 'rational' in any universal sense, but only according to the norms which operate within the scientific system. Other views can be equally 'rational', in the sense of flowing logically from different sets of premises. There are simply competing constructions of risks, those of scientists and those of anybody else. As Shrader-Frechette argues,

---

201 BIA, 'The BIA Leads the Way in the UK', *Nature Biotechnology Supplement*, June 1997, 29.
202 A. Ogus, 'Risk Management and "Rational" Social Regulation' in Baldwin, n188 above.
203 See in particular, K.S. Shrader-Frechette, *Risk and Rationality: Philosophical Foundations for Populist Reforms* (Berkeley: UCLA Press, 1991).

'there is no distinction between perceived risks and actual risks because there are no risks except perceived risks',[204] experts have no 'magic window on reality'.[205]

With respect to the second, it has been repeatedly demonstrated that lay ideas or understandings of risk are based on fundamentally different criteria than those of scientists. Attitudes towards risk are not dependent on the narrow criteria of the rate of expected fatalities which scientists use in risk estimation or measurement. Scientists are frustrated that people will undertake higher risk activities but not lower risk ones and that they continually mistake the level of risks of activities. That frustration, however, fails to recognise the complex matrix of variables which comprise the risk decisions that individuals make. These include: the voluntary or involuntary nature of exposure; the degree of personal control over the outcomes; the degree of uncertainty over the probabilities or consequence of exposure; the familiarity of the risk; the immediacy or delay of exposure to the risk; the potential for catastrophic consequences; the distribution and visibility of benefits; and whether the risk is individual or societal.[206] Moreover, and critically for regulation, public trust in the institutional arrangements which exist to manage risk plays a key role in attitudes towards risks.[207]

Public attitudes towards genetic technology bear out a number of these findings. UK survey findings show that risk perceptions tend to focus on safety issues and on a perceived lack of control of the technology. They show a generally low estimation of the competence of regulatory agencies and their ability to effectively control the risks of technology.[208] They also show a lack of trust, with people feeling that the public was being kept in the dark about genetic engineering (for example, although 95 per cent felt the public should be told about releases of genetically engineered products only 25 per cent felt it would be). This low level of trust in government is echoed in the perceptions which are held of the relative trustworthiness of different sources of information about genetic engineering. Work by Martin and Tait on public perceptions of trust in different sources of information shows that the public on the whole rate special interest groups as the most trustworthy source, but government, together with industry and tabloid newspapers as the lowest.[209]

Psychometric studies show that perceptions are systematic: they can be mapped according to a range of variables. Lay perceptions of both the magnitude and acceptability of risk may thus be explicable, but are they 'rational'? There are a number of responses. Cultural theorists, for example, would argue that they are indeed rational, in that a person's perception of and attitude to risk is consistent with the rest of their understanding and approach to the world around them.[210] Others do not need to enter the world of grid/group analysis to suggest that

---

204 Shrader-Frechette, *ibid* 84.
205 *ibid.* See also J. Hunt, 'The Social Construction of Precaution' in O'Riordan and Cameron, n 38 above.
206 B. Fischoff, S. Lichtenstein, P. Slovic, D. Derby and R. Keeney, *Acceptable Risk* (Cambridge: CUP, 1981); H.J. Otway and D. von Winterfeldt, 'Beyond Acceptable Risk: On the Social Acceptability of Technologies' (1982) 14 *Policy Sciences* 247; Royal Society, *Risk: Analysis, Perception, Management* (London: Royal Society, 1992).
207 Royal Society, *ibid*; Wynne, n 189 above.
208 Ives, n 49 above.
209 S. Martin and J. Tait, 'Attitudes to Selected Public Groups in the UK to Biotechnology' in Durant (ed), n 49 above.
210 M. Douglas and A. Wildavsky, *Risk and Culture* (California: UCLA Press, 1982); M. Thompson, R. Ellis, A. Wildavsky, *Cultural Theory* (Boulder, Colorado: Westview Press, 1990); M. Schwartz and M. Thompson, *Divided we Stand: Redefining Politics, Technology and Social Choice* (Philadelphia: University of Pennsylvania Press, 1990).

attitudes to risk, and indeed to science, are indeed rational. Thus, drawing on a number of empirical studies conducted with workers in nuclear plants, Wynne argues that the technical ignorance which scientists lament as an intellectual vacuum and social defect is instead 'a complex "active" social construction': people decide what they need to know, based on their trust in regulations, and in operating processes.[211] Responses to risk and 'irrational' approaches are not 'irrational', but are rather understandings which are institutionally embedded.

Risk is only one example of how different approaches to the role of science in regulatory decision making can play out. As the above discussion shows, a conceptualisation of genetic technology as simply posing the problem of risk is itself too narrow to embrace the range of perceptions which exist. Nevertheless, it illustrates the point that an approach to regulation which aims to facilitate integration would require that these different conceptualisations, which are based on and expressed in very different languages to that of science, be included in any regulatory and decision making forum. For that inclusion to occur, regulators have to be able to understand the different cognitive structures which give rise to those different perceptions, and to explain to others what those perceptions are and why they are held in a language that others can understand.

Conclusions: facilitating integration and its implications

For technocrats, the integrationist model is a recipe for chaos: the replacement of regulation based on rigorous analysis with regulation based on public whim. A whim, moreover, which is shaped by the media portrayals of genetic technology, portrayals which prefer sensationalism to caution, black and white to shades of grey.[212] That attitude, although it pervades many of the current regulatory fora, has to be seriously challenged. For the technical, scientific definition of genetics simply misses the enormous emotive power of genetics: as Nelken and Lidden observe, the gene is more than a biological structure, 'it has become a cultural icon, a symbol, an almost magical force'.[213] This power alone means that debates over the appropriate course of genetic research, its uses and applications cannot remain a closed issue, defined in ostensibly technical language by experts. The myth of the gene is not the only reason why non-scientists demand a voice, however. There is a much more fundamental reason, and justification for that voice. It is that despite many scientists' assertions to the contrary, science is not neutral, just as law is not neutral. It shapes society's expectations, and provides it with choices which it did not otherwise have.[214] Indeed, it is the dislocation of the 'chance/choice' boundary which genetic technology provides, the opportunities to exercise choices where previously matters were left to chance, which Dworkin rightly identifies as being the explanation for the current, confused reactions to that technology.[215] In so shaping choices and expectations, science has a structuring role which extends far beyond the confines of a laboratory.

---

211 Wynne, n 189 above (1991), (1993) and 'Risk and social learning: reification to engagement' in Krimsky and Golding, n 183 above.

212 On the role of the media in portraying genetic technology see in particular F. Neidhart, 'The Public as a Communication System' (1993) 2 *Public Understanding of Science* 339; Durant, Hansen and Bauer, n 194 above; and more generally D. Nelkin and S. Lidden, *The DNA Mystique: The Gene as a Cultural Icon* (New York: W.H. Freeman & Co, 1995).

213 D. Nelkin and S. Lidden, *ibid* 2.

214 See for example Beck, n 1 above.

215 R. Dworkin, 'Justice and Fate', paper presented to the 21st Century Trust seminar on Genetics, Identity and Justice, Oxford, 27 March–4 April 1998.

The facilitation of the integrationist approach which is being suggested here may itself have significant implications for science, and they are ones which technocrats fiercely resist. Nevertheless, the constructivist approach to science on which it draws finds a chord in some scientists' own reflections on their activity and rationality, reflections which have strong resonance in the genetics context.[216] The problems which science faces, it has been suggested, are more fundamental than those which it has traditionally faced. In order to address them, science has to shift from the traditional scientific methods to those of what Funtowicz and Ravetz term 'post normal' science.[217] The move to post normal science, they suggest, is necessary for two reasons. First, the conditions of extreme uncertainty in which science now operates pose a critical challenge for science. It has to recognise that in these conditions the traditional, Kuhnian approach to science as problem solving is impossible. Second, science-based technology has created moral complexities. Science simply cannot maintain the stance that it is neutral: that it simply provides information or capacities to society, and it is for society to decide what to do with them (and, moreover, that it is not the fault of science if society chooses badly). Science can thus no longer be a process of routine puzzle-solving conducted in ignorance of the wider methodological, societal and ethical issues which are raised by scientific activity and its products. It can no longer ignore the debate about itself. It cannot in effect borrow and adapt the slogan, 'science doesn't kill, people do'. Despite the continual assertion of this closure of science, it has to be abandoned, for where the decision stakes are high, no scientific argument can be logically conclusive.[218]

The move from the traditional model of scientific objectivity to one which recognises the limits of that objectivity does not however necessarily entail an ineluctable slide into subjectivity. It is maintained by these writers that it is still possible for there to be objectivity in science, but that it has to be one which is defined not simply by the current scientific methodology. What they seek is not de-objectification but re-objectification. Critical assessment of scientific claims is essential, but has to be undertaken by an extended peer community, whose roots and affiliations lie outside those who create the problems which it is sought to address.[219]

Those who advocate such a re-conceptualisation of science's own rationality urge science to adopt this reflexivity, this questioning of itself, if it is to maintain its legitimacy and credibility amongst non-scientists.[220] The public is no longer

---

216 See in particular A. Chalmers, *Science and its Fabrication* (Milton Keynes: Open University Press, 1990).

217 S.O. Funtowicz and J.R. Ravetz, 'Three Types of Risk Assessment and the Emergence of Post-Normal Science' in Golding and Krimsky, n 183 above, and 'Risk Assessment, Post-Normal Science, and Extended Peer Communities' in C. Hood and D. Jones (eds), *Accident and Design: Contemporary Debates in Risk Management* (London: UCL Press, 1996). For similar arguments on the role of science in risk management see K. Lee, *Compass and the Gyroscope: Integrating Science and Politics for the Environment* (New York: Island Press, 1993); O'Riordan, n 4 above.

218 Funtowicz and Ravetz, n 217 above.

219 *ibid*; see also Shrader-Frechette's model of 'scientific proceduralism', n 203 above, especially 169–196; H. Nowotny, 'Socially Distributed Knowledge: Five Spaces for Science to Meet the Public' (1993) 2 *Public Understanding of Science* 307; Wynne, n 189 above. Nevertheless it is still feared that there is a danger of moving from a position in which the core set of 'experts' is too narrowly defined, to one in which it is too extended, where 'inexperienced and untrained outsiders assume and are granted the right to communicate authoritatively on scientific matters': Nowotny, *ibid* 317; H. Collins, 'Public experiments and displays of virtuosity: the core set revisited' (1988) 18 *Social Studies of Science* 725.

220 See for example, Wynne, n 189 above (1993), who disputes the argument that science is the quintessential reflexive system and argues that '[i]n eschewing an automatic assumption of authority

content to observe science and accept its products, or indeed its definitions. Rather, it has been suggested, the boundaries separating science and the public are becoming more fluid.[221] Science has to recognise the role that non-scientific factors play in shaping responses to it. Otherwise it will continue to be bemused and frustrated by those responses, and unable to engage in debate with them simply because the language in which they occur is one which is alien. If it continues simply to discount those concerns, however, and not to accept its own fallibility or its own limitations, it is liable to lose its authority and trustworthiness.[222]

What are the implications of a facilitative, integrationist approach to regulation for the role of science in regulatory decisions? Is science, for example, simply to be discounted as just another social construct? To an extent, this is a debate for science; in so far as regulation relies on science to determine its content, however, it becomes one for regulation. If regulation sees science as simply one voice amongst many, which in part is what is sought, then the debate is not so central to regulation's own validity. With respect to many issues science is the dominant language, however, frequently manifested in the adoption of risk as the organising principle of regulation. The debate about science then has a correspondingly greater significance. But science and scientific definitions of the issues should not be the only ones which are relevant for regulation, no more than should those of medicine, law or business. As the above discussion suggests, however, facilitating the wider negotiation of regulatory norms is far from a simple task.

To start, diluting the connection between regulation and science is difficult, largely because the voices of science and of industry are those which tend to be heard loudest. It may be that the first step is to move away from the dominant regulatory model of scientific-bureaucratic decision making to one in which opposing views are publicly debated; to develop a forum in which a wide range of groups can participate simultaneously, debating directly and in public.[223] Making changes along the structural dimension of regulation is a proposal which has already been advanced by many commentators in many disciplines. It is not the occasion to pursue this proposal here, but it is perhaps worth emphasising that the debate need not become stuck in the rut of statutory vs non-statutory, legal vs non-legal: many different institutional structures are possible, with many different combinations possible of regulatory instruments which derive from a range of sources and which can or can not have formal legal validity. Moreover, although the structural aspect of this model may have some feasibility in the context of policy formation, difficulties of ensuring participation may well remain in the day to day conversations which will inevitably occur between regulator and regulated.[224]

But as has been stressed throughout, facilitating integration is not simply a question of institutional design. Institutional design is an important aspect, but it is not a panacea for all regulatory ills. Simply introducing the public to the regulatory

---

to a canonical model of science, and allowing greater problematization of its own founding commitments, science would trade in its presumptions of control for greater public identification and uptake, hence "understanding" ': *ibid*, at 335.

221 See further Nowotny, n 219 above.

222 A point forcefully made in much of the socio-scientific literature; see for example, Wynne, n 189 above; Funtowicz and Ravetz, n 217 above.

223 What Hood calls the 'shark' approach: C. Hood, 'Where Extremes Meet: "SPRAT" versus "SHARK" in Public Risk Management' in Hood and Jones, n 217 above, drawing on Dunsire's model of collibration: A. Dunsire, 'Holistic Governance' (1990) 5(1) *Public Policy and Administration* 4; 'Modes of Governance' in J. Kooiman (ed), *Modern Governance* (London: Sage, 1992).

224 J. Black, 'Talking about Regulation' [1998] *Public Law* 77.

fora will have no effect if it is the scientific language which remains dominant, and only the scientific voice which is recognised as valid. The more interesting challenges thus lie, it is suggested, in the other two dimensions: the cognitive and the communicative. In cognitive terms, there has to be a change in the terms of the debate: a re-definition of the 'problem' posed based on a recognition of others' understandings and identification of the issues which are raised and how they need to be addressed.

On the communicative dimension, then as the discussion above demonstrates, there still remains a more fundamental problem which the facilitation of integration faces. That is that participants in the debate simply speak different languages. The languages of science, of commerce, of ethics, of ecology, of law are foreign to each other; each can hardly understand what the other is saying, let alone why they should be saying it. As we have seen, for each, the others' view simply misses the point. Addressing this problem of mutual incomprehension is fundamental to facilitating integration in any form. In so doing, it has been suggested, there is a need not for a common language, which is unattainable. Nor is there a need for an 'official' language, for that would be a denial of the philosophy underlying the integrationist model. Rather, it has been suggested, there is a need for translators, for interpreters. By acting as interpreters, regulators can then facilitate the negotiation of regulation and the integration which is sought. It is how to perform this interpretive and facilitative function which the controversies surrounding genetic technology show to be one of the central challenges facing its regulation.

Human Dignity, Human Rights, and Human Genetics

Deryck Beyleveld and Roger Brownsword[*]

According to an emerging international consensus, the practice of human genetics should respect both human dignity and human rights.[1] In the Preamble to the Council of Europe's Convention on Human Rights and Biomedicine,[2] for example, the signatories resolve 'to take such measures as are necessary to safeguard human dignity and the fundamental rights and freedoms of the individual with regard to the application of biology and medicine'; and, similarly, in the Preamble to UNESCO's recently adopted Universal Declaration on the Human Genome and Human Rights[3] — an instrument peppered with references to human dignity and human rights — it is emphasised that research on the human genome 'should fully respect human dignity, freedom and human rights'.

Yet, how should we interpret this commitment, particularly the commitment to respect for *human dignity*? Even if we do not dismiss '[a]ppeals to human dignity ... [as] comprehensively vague',[4] we can scarcely deny that they need some unpacking. As Mohammed Bedjaoui has remarked:

> [A] legal framework for potential new practices or those already engaged in which concern the human body is absolutely essential in that it protects man in his freedom and dignity. But it is by no means an easy task. . . .
>
> Take, for example, the concept of ... 'human dignity'. It is an expression which seems simple: one immediately apprehends its prospective import, if not its exact meaning. But, paradoxically, it is also an expression full of fragility, for in the name of the same argument of 'human dignity' some refute [sic] the legitimacy of euthanasia, whilst others claim it as the ultimate right of those who wish to 'die in dignity'![5]

---

* Sheffield Institute of Biotechnological Law and Ethics.

Drafts of this paper, or parts of the paper, were presented to Biomed 2 sponsored seminars at Sheffield (April 1997) and Utrecht (November 1997), to staff seminars at the Universities of Leicester (December 1997), Hull (March 1998), and London (QMWC) (March 1998), and at the MLR pre-publication conference in Cambridge (April 1998). For assistance with the concept of dignity in French and German law, our thanks to Irma Arnoux and Sabine Michalowski.

1 See, eg, *Proceedings of the Third Session of the International Bioethics Committee of UNESCO, September 1995: Volume 1,* at 120, where Philippe Séguin, referring to the three French Acts on bioethics of July 1994, said:

> It is therefore fortunate and encouraging that a number of countries have, like France, set out over the last decade to equip themselves with bioethics laws. This trend illustrates a growing awareness around the world that legislators must, despite the difficulties, act to ensure that *science develops with respect for human dignity and fundamental human rights,* and in line with national democratic traditions. (Our emphasis).

2 Council of Europe, *Convention for the Protection of Human Rights and Dignity of the Human Being with regard to the Application of Biology and Medicine: Convention on Human Rights and Biomedicine* (DIR/JUR (96) 14) (Strasbourg: Directorate of Legal Affairs, November 1996).
3 This Declaration, adopted unanimously by the General Conference on 11 November 1997, is the result of more than four years work by UNESCO's International Bioethics Committee.
4 John Harris, *Clones, Genes, and Immortality* (Oxford: Oxford University Press, 1998) 31.
5 n 1 above, 144.

Euthanasia apart, such fragility is all too evident where it is argued that the right to adopt a particular life-style (claimed on the basis of human dignity) should be limited for the sake of human dignity — witness, for example, both the German *Peep-Show Decision*,[6] where the Federal Administrative Tribunal denied a licence for a mechanical peep-show on the ground that the performance would violate Article 1(1) of the Basic Law (according to which, the dignity of man is inviolable), and the Conseil d'Etat ruling that dwarf-throwing ('lancer de nain') is incompatible with 'ordre public',[7] because the dwarfs compromise human dignity by allowing themselves to be used as mere things.[8] Fragility leads to paradox as agents (peep-show performers and dwarfs) are rescued from one situation where (as the FAT and the Conseil interpret it) human dignity is violated only to be placed in a situation where (as the consenting agents interpret it) the basis for human dignity is even more seriously undermined. How, then, should we understand human dignity; how does it relate to human rights; and is it a concept that is rightly seen as central to deliberations about the legitimate scope of human genetics?

Our paper has five parts. First, we review the protean employment of the idea of human dignity in international human rights instruments. Secondly, we isolate two seminal notions of human dignity, one the idea that human beings, having intrinsic value, must not be treated simply as a means, the other the idea that dignified conduct is a virtue. Thirdly, we analyse these core ideas from a duty-led perspective (of the kind associated with Kantian moral theory) before, fourthly, interpreting these same ideas from a rights-led perspective (specifically that associated with the moral theory of Alan Gewirth).[9] Finally, we consider how far our (Gewirthian) analysis supports the widely held view that respect for human dignity requires prohibitions on commercialisation of the human genome, on human germ-line (and positive) interventions, and on human reproductive cloning.[10] Our conclusion is that the concept of human dignity has a legitimate place in debates about human genetics. However, it is something of a loose cannon, open to abuse and misinterpretation; it can oversimplify complex questions; and it can encourage a paternalism that is incompatible with the spirit of self-determination that informs the mainstream of human rights thinking.

---

6   BVerwGE 64, 274 (1981); and see Shayana Kadidal, 'Obscenity in the Age of Mechanical Reproduction' (1996) 44 *American Journal of Comparative Law* 353.

7   Conseil d'Etat (October 27, 1995) req nos 136–727 (Commune de Morsang-sur-Orge) and 143–578 (Ville d'Aix-en-Provence).

8   See Marie-Christine Roualt's note on the two decisions, *Les Petites Affiches* (January 24, 1996: No 11) 30, at 32; and, Bernard Edelman, 'La Dignité de la Personne Humaine, un Concept Nouveau' Recueil Dalloz 1997, 23e Cahier, Chronique, 185, 187–188.

9   See Alan Gewirth, *Reason and Morality* (Chicago: University of Chicago Press, 1978).

10 See Articles 4 (commerce), 11 (cloning), and 24 (germ-line interventions) of the *Universal Declaration on the Human Genome and Human Rights*; Articles 13 (germ-line interventions) and 21 (commerce) of the *Convention on Human Rights and Biomedicine*, together with the draft Protocol prohibiting human cloning (see n 18 below); Article 6(2) of the Directive on the Legal Protection of Biotechnological Inventions, in which 'processes for cloning human beings' and 'processes for modifying the germ-line genetic identity of human beings' are excluded from patentability (see further n 12 below); and the HGAC and HFEA Consultation Document, *Cloning Issues in Reproduction, Science and Medicine* (London: Human Genetics Advisory Commission, January 1998) which discusses whether cloning 'raises new questions about more abstract concepts such as individuality and human dignity' (4).

Human dignity and international human rights instruments

What do the leading post-War human rights instruments tell us about the idea of human dignity? In general, where reliance on human dignity is explicit — in the case of the European Convention on Human Rights, for example, reliance is merely implicit[11] — it is largely foundational, declaratory, and undefined.[12] Thus, the Preamble to each of the constituent instruments comprising the 'International Bill of Rights' — the Universal Declaration of Human Rights, 1948 (UDHR), the International Covenant on Economic, Social and Cultural Rights, 1966 (ICESCR), and the International Covenant on Civil and Political Rights, 1966 (ICCPR) — provides that 'recognition of the inherent dignity and of the equal and inalienable rights of all members of the human family is the foundation of freedom, justice and peace in the world'; and Article 1 of the UDHR proclaims that 'All human beings are born free and equal in dignity and rights.' However, only twice thereafter do the drafters of the UDHR draw explicitly on the concept of dignity — first, in Article 22 (concerning the right to social security and the economic, social and cultural rights indispensable for dignity and the free development of personality) and then in Article 23(3) (concerning the right to just and favourable remuneration such as to ensure an existence worthy of human dignity). Similarly, there are just two further references to human dignity in ICESCR and ICCPR: in Article 13 of the former (where it is agreed that 'education shall be directed to the full development of the human personality and the sense of its dignity'), and in Article 10 of the latter (to the effect that 'All persons deprived of their liberty shall be treated with humanity and with respect for the inherent dignity of the human person').

At first blush, the pattern of the Convention on Human Rights and Biomedicine is not unlike that of the UDHR; for, having recited 'the importance of ensuring the dignity of the human being' in the Preamble, and having declared in Article 1 that the parties 'shall protect the dignity and identity of all human beings', the drafters do not make any further explicit reference to human dignity. However, the Explanatory Report accompanying the Convention emphasises that 'human dignity ... constitutes the essential value to be upheld ... [and] is at the basis of most of the values emphasised in the Convention';[13] that all Articles must be interpreted in the light of the aim of the Convention 'which is to protect human rights and dignity';[14] and that the principle of respect for human dignity is central to Articles 15 (the general rule with regard to scientific research),[15] 17 (protection of persons not able to consent to research),[16] and 21 (which provides that 'The human body and its parts shall not, as such, give rise to financial gain').[17] Moreover, the draft Protocol

---

11 See, especially, Article 3 of the ECHR (concerning torture, inhuman, or degrading treatment or punishment); and cf eg Clare Dyer, 'Euro court lets Aids victim die "with dignity" ' *The Guardian* 3 May 1997.

12 Whilst not directly an international human rights instrument, Directive 98/44/EC on the Legal Protection of Biotechnological Inventions (OJ L 213, 30.7.1998, p. 13) fits this description. The need for patent law to respect dignity is mentioned twice in the Preamble (in Recitals 16 and 38) but not in the Articles.

13 Council of Europe, *Explanatory Report to the Convention for the Protection of Human Rights and Dignity of the Human Being with regard to the Application of Biology and Medicine: Convention on Human Rights and Biomedicine* (DIR/JUR (97) 1) (Strasbourg: Directorate of Legal Affairs, January 1997) para 9.

14 *ibid* para 22.

15 *ibid* para 96.

16 *ibid* paras 106 and 111.

17 *ibid* para 131.

(to the Convention) dealing with the cloning of human beings,[18] is guided by the consideration that 'the instrumentalisation of human beings through the deliberate creation of genetically identical human beings is contrary to human dignity and thus constitutes a misuse of biology and medicine.'[19]

The Explanatory Report also highlights another aspect of dignity. Article 1 of the Convention distinguishes between 'everyone' (viz, the undefined bearers of human rights under the ECHR) and 'all human beings' (viz, those whose dignity and identity is to be protected). Given that some signatories might take the view that embryos and fetuses do not have human rights (because they are not included within 'everyone'), but given, too, that 'it was a generally accepted principle that human dignity and the identity of the human being had to be respected as soon as life began',[20] Article 1 purports to protect such potential life in terms of the dignity and identity of human beings. Although this drafting device is designed primarily to contain divisive questions concerning the regulation of abortion, it indicates how some might seek to deploy the concept of human dignity to protect human life forms that are not yet eligible for human rights protections.

When we turn to the Universal Declaration on the Human Genome and Human Rights — an instrument already described as 'the first international text to bring the question of human dignity face to face with the problems raised by scientific progress'[21] — reliance on human dignity is unmistakably explicit and pervasive. Following a number of preambular references, including the significant recognition that respect for human dignity must take precedence over the progress promised by research on the human genome and its applications, the first four Articles (comprising Part A of the Declaration)[22] are grouped under the heading 'Human Dignity and the Human Genome'. The key prescription in this Part of the Universal Declaration is in Article 2,[23] according to which:

> (a) Everyone has a right to respect for their dignity and for their rights regardless of their genetic characteristics.
>
> (b) That dignity makes it imperative not to reduce individuals to their genetic characteristics and to respect their uniqueness and diversity.

Thereafter, dignity is explicitly referred to in seven Articles.[24] These Articles prohibit 'discrimination based on genetic characteristics' such as would infringe

---

18 Council of Europe, *Additional Protocol to the Convention on Human Rights and Dignity of the Human Being with regard to the Application of Biology and Medicine, on the prohibition of cloning human beings* (DIR/JUR (97) 14).

19 *ibid* Preamble. Similarly, see Section 8 of the HGAC and HFEA Consultation Document, *Cloning Issues in Reproduction, Science and Medicine* (n 10 above) where human reproductive cloning is said to raise 'serious ethical issues, concerned with human responsibility and instrumentalisation of human beings' (16). And, then, it is observed: 'There are moral arguments to support the claim that human dignity forbids the use of human beings only as a "means", holding that they are to be treated as an "end" in their own right' (18). For discussion, see text below.

20 n 13 above, paras 16–19.

21 See *Proceedings of the Fourth Session of the International Bioethics Committee of UNESCO, October 1996: Volume 1*, at 46 (Chantal Ralaimihoatra reporting the speech by Noëlle Lenoir, President of the IBC).

22 The Declaration comprises 25 Articles divided into seven Parts, namely: A. Human Dignity and the Human Genome; B. Rights of the Person Concerned; C. Research on the Human Genome; D. Conditions for the Exercise of Scientific Activity; E. Solidarity and International Co-operation; F. Promotion of the Principles set out in the Declaration; and G. Implementation of the Declaration.

23 Article 4, providing that 'The human genome in its natural state shall not give rise to financial gains', is also an important prescription in this Part of the Universal Declaration.

24 This was no last-minute conversion to the importance of respect for human dignity. In the draft leading to the final version of the Universal Declaration, dignity appeared explicitly six times in the first twelve Articles, see Articles 1, 2(c), 4(b), 5, 7, and 12 (as they then were).

human dignity (Article 6), 'research or research applications concerning the human genome' that fail to respect human dignity (Article 10), and 'practices' that are 'contrary to human dignity' (such as reproductive cloning of human beings) (Article 11); they require parties to make available to all 'advances in biology, genetics and medicine' but 'with due regard for the dignity ... of each individual' (Article 12), to 'take appropriate steps to provide the framework for the free exercise of research on the human genome' but in such a way as to 'safeguard respect for ... human dignity' (Article 15), and to take steps to raise awareness of 'responsibilities regarding the fundamental issues relating to the defence of human dignity' arising from research in human genetics and the like (Article 21); and, finally, the International Bioethics Committee is required, *inter alia*, to 'give advice concerning the follow-up of this Declaration, in particular regarding the identification of practices that could be contrary to human dignity, such as germ-line interventions' (Article 24).

What are we to make of all this? Sometimes, human dignity is equated with human beings having value or worth which grounds their having rights — for example, in ICESCR, and ICCPR, the equal and inalienable rights of human beings are said to 'derive from the inherent dignity of the human person'.[25] The logic of this view is that any violation of human rights *implicitly* violates human dignity. In some cases, however, respect for human dignity moves out of the background to underline its association with particular human rights. We might detect such a movement, for example, where human dignity is referred to in the context of the basic conditions for working people and for those who have been deprived of their liberty, as well as in several of the Articles of the Universal Declaration on the Human Genome and Human Rights.[26] In the instruments specifically concerned with biomedicine and genetics, however, we also glimpse the idea that the key to the protection of embryonic and potential human life might be human dignity rather than human rights, as well as the idea (signalled most clearly by the prohibition on commercialisation of the human body) that dignity might be compromised by our own (self-regarding) actions as much as by the unwilled interferences of others.

In sum, human dignity appears in various guises, sometimes as the source of human rights, at other times as itself a species of human right (particularly concerned with the conditions of self-respect); sometimes defining the subjects of human rights, at other times defining the objects to be protected; and, sometimes re-inforcing, at other times limiting, rights of individual autonomy and self-determination.

Two concepts of human dignity

We should not be surprised that international human rights instruments offer no clear lead on the concept of human dignity. After all, this is a concept with a long history, employed in both religious and secular traditions; and, as Ronald Dworkin has remarked, the notion of a 'right to dignity' has been used in many senses by

---

25   cf the Preamble to the African Charter on Human and Peoples' Rights, 1981, where fundamental human rights are said to 'stem from the attributes of human beings'; and, similarly, the Preamble to the American Convention on Human Rights, 1969, which states that 'the essential rights of man ... are based upon attributes of the human personality'.
26   See, eg, Articles 2(a), 6, 10, 12, and 15.

moral and political philosophers.[27] How, then, are we to proceed? We propose to take our bearings from two reference points. First, there is the idea — embedded in human rights' thinking, and commonly articulated in debates about human genetics in the form of an injunction against 'instrumentalisation' — that dignity relates to the intrinsic value of persons (such that it is wrong to treat persons as mere things rather than as autonomous ends or agents).[28] Secondly, there is the idea — less obviously relevant perhaps to debates about human genetics — that dignified conduct is a special kind of virtue.[29]

The first idea finds its classic expression in Kant's second formulation of the Categorical Imperative, the so-called Formula of the End in Itself:

> Act in such a way that you always treat humanity, whether in your own person or in the person of any other, never simply as a means, but always at the same time as an end.[30]

According to Kant, in the Kingdom of Ends, everything has either a price (in which case something else can be put in its place as an equivalent) or a dignity (in which case it has intrinsic value and is beyond price).[31] Because 'morality is the only condition under which a rational being can be an end in himself' — because only in this way is it possible to be a law-making member in a Kingdom of Ends — then it follows that 'morality, and humanity so far as it is capable of morality, is the only thing which has dignity.'[32] In other words, 'the dignity of man consists precisely in his capacity to make universal law, although only on condition of being himself also subject to the law he makes.'[33] Thus, Kant says:

> Every human being has a legitimate claim to respect from his fellow human beings and is *in turn* bound to respect every other. Humanity itself is a dignity; for a human being cannot be used merely as a means by any human being ... but must always be used at the same time as an end. It is just in this that his dignity (personality) consists, by which he raises himself above all other beings in the world that are not human beings and yet can be used, and so over all *things*.[34]

In contrast with the idea that *all* humans have dignity, another view (also current at the time of the Enlightenment) was that dignity referred 'to a rank within a

---

27 See Ronald Dworkin, *Life's Dominion* (London: HarperCollins, 1993) esp at 233–237 (for Dworkin's distinction between a right to dignity and a right not to suffer indignity). And, on the latter, see the recent BMA consultation paper, *Withdrawing and Withholding Treatment* (London, July 1998) para 2.9.5.

28 Here, nothing turns on whether 'persons' are identified (as in the Kantian view) with rational beings with a will, or end-setters, or (as in the Gewirthian view) prospective purposive agents. Generally, when we use the term 'agent', we use it in the Gewirthian sense of beings having the capacity for free and purposive action. It should be noted that agency is not co-extensive with human life. Some forms of human life (biologically defined) do not have the relevant capacity; and, in principle, other species might have the capacity.

29 Whilst we do not claim that these two ideas cover all the discourses of dignity, we take it that, as two of the seminal ideas that have come through from the Enlightenment to the present day, they offer a reasonable starting point for reflection upon the nature of a commitment to human dignity; cf Michael J. Meyer, 'Introduction', in Michael J. Meyer and William A. Parent (eds) *The Constitution of Rights* (Ithaca and London: Cornell University Press, 1992) 1.

30 See H.J. Paton, *The Moral Law* (Kant's *Groundwork of the Metaphysic of Morals*: first published, 1785) (London: Hutchinson, 1948) 91. It should be emphasised that the Kantian duty is *not* that we should never treat others as a means — this would be an argument against all manner of co-operative interactions. The duty is that we should never treat others *simply* as a means but *always at the same time as an end*. See further n 45 below.

31 *ibid* 96.

32 *ibid* 96–97.

33 *ibid* 101.

34 Immanuel Kant, *The Metaphysics of Morals* (translated and edited by Mary Gregor) (Cambridge: Cambridge University Press, 1996) (first published 1797) 209.

recognized and established social hierarchy — for example, the dignity of a king, of a noble, or of a bishop'; hence a person's dignity 'was simply a function, or a sign, of an individual's elevated social rank.'[35] However, the idea of the dignity of the nobles, understood as the virtue of dignified conduct, can be applied beyond the boundaries of the elite classes (who, then, simply serve as role models for all classes). In this broader application, dignity is equated not so much with social grace and presentation (neither of which is a guarantor of respect for others)[36] as with the (dignified) manner in which individuals (from Socrates to Nelson Mandela) handle adversity. To adopt William Parent's language, our second core idea of dignity is one that is grounded on an agent's 'empirical understanding of himself and of his natural powers, limitations, and aspirations' — that is, 'a view of dignity that doesn't demean but instead elevates the status of beings who are struggling to cope in the natural world.'[37]

Anticipating two issues for the next part of our discussion, how might intrinsic human dignity and dignified conduct relate to one another;[38] and, in a *rights*-led regime, might the former serve to re-inforce an agent's control over its selection of ends while, in a *duty*-led regime, it limits the range of ends available to each agent?

Human dignity: a duty-led interpretation

In a duty-led framework (such as Kantian morality), human dignity might be taken to generate both duties to others and duties to oneself. In this light, we can consider, first, the idea of dignity as intrinsic human value and then the idea of dignified conduct.

The duty not to compromise the dignity (intrinsic value) of others

If we should not treat others only as a means or as a mere thing, there is a broad sense in which *every* wrong that we do to others compromises their dignity. We might, however, employ the idea of compromising the dignity of others more sparingly. For example, we might reserve it for cases where there is a failure to recognise others as having the capacity for self-governance;[39] or treating them in a way that undermines their conditions of self-respect.[40] In specifying the latter duty, a critical question is whether 'the conditions of self-respect' are given a 'subjective

---

35   n 29 above, 4.
36   cf William A. Parent, 'Constitutional Values and Human Dignity' in Michael J. Meyer and William A. Parent (eds) n 29 above, 47, 55: '[E]vil men like Hitler often displayed ... presentational dignity, at least in their public behaviour. And so, for that matter, do Mafia hit men. So from a moral standpoint, this conception of dignity is wholly bankrupt.'
37   *ibid.*
38   See, eg, Alan Gewirth, *Human Rights* (Chicago: University of Chicago Press, 1982) 27–28.
39   See, eg, Victor Frankl, *Man's Search for Meaning* (New York: Washington Square, 1984) 43 (recalling an incident when a Nazi guard threw a stone at him as he rested from his work on a railroad track). Such a duty of recognition might be specified in several ways. On the one side, the relevance of the non-recogniser's *intent* (and *knowledge*) must be determined; and, on the other side, the relevance of the *effect* upon the non-recognised must be settled; cf Stephen R. Munzer, 'An Uneasy Case Against Property Rights in Body Parts' in Ellen Frankel Paul, Fred D. Miller Jr, and Jeffrey Paul (eds) *Property Rights* (Cambridge: Cambridge University Press, 1994) 259, 274: 'If I have an unconditioned and incomparable worth, and if you insult that worth by treating me as a repository of body parts, you have offended my dignity even if I have the strength to resist your impositions.'
40   As with the duty of recognition, this duty can be developed along both an axis of intent and an axis of effect; see n 39 above.

(experiential)' or an 'objective (non-experiential)' interpretation. On the former reading, the duty relates to those (contingent) conditions that seem to be material if agents are to enjoy a sense of self-respect (particularly concerning experience of inhumane, demeaning, and degrading treatment). Interpreted in an objective way, however, the conditions of self-respect take on a different meaning. Divorced from any actual experience of loss of self-respect, the claim is that certain conditions quite simply are the basis of self-respect — thus opening the way to arguing that human dignity is violated even though the transgressor has no intention to demean another and even though the transgressed actually experiences no reduction in self-esteem.

The duty not to compromise one's own dignity (intrinsic value)

In principle, a duty-led regime may prescribe duties that are designed to protect agents, not against others, but against the risk that they compromise their own dignity. Thus, according to Kant, human beings cannot give themselves away for a price, otherwise they would violate their duty of self-esteem[41] — a line of reasoning, as we have seen, that underpins the rulings in the French case of the circus dwarfs as well as in the German *Peep-Show Decision*. Similarly, in the context of commerce in one's own body parts, the Warnock Committee noted that some oppose surrogacy on the ground that 'it is inconsistent with human dignity that a woman should use her uterus for financial profit and treat it as an incubator for someone else's child';[42] and, extending this logic, the prevailing view seems to be that respect for one's own dignity militates against gene-selling and financial gain.[43]

On the face of it, the duty not to compromise one's own dignity (not to instrumentalise oneself) imposes significant limits on an agent's power of self-determination. The extent of these limits will vary, however, depending upon the precise specification of the duty and the manner (and effectiveness) of its enforcement.

With regard to the specification of the duty, one key question is whether or not the conditions of self-respect are given an experiential (subjective) interpretation; and another is whether the duty, so to speak, 'black-lists' or 'grey-lists' conduct, in the former case prohibiting certain actions without reservation, in the latter case prohibiting certain actions unless the agent's own dignity has been fully taken into consideration.[44] In the ordinary course of things, an agent's power of self-determination will be restricted more by a black-list version of the duty than by a grey-list, and more by a duty specified in terms of a metaphysical rather than an experiential constitution of dignity.

An agent's power of self-determination is also affected by the way in which the duty is enforced. If A's breach of duty involves a violation of B's correlative right, we might expect B (or B's representatives) to hold A to account (at least, in the first instance). However, where A's breach is simply of a duty owed to A, how is A

---

41   n 34 above, 209.
42   *Report of the Committee of Inquiry into Human Fertilisation and Embryology* (London: HMSO, 1984) para 8.10.
43   See n 10 above.
44   See, eg, Munzer, n 39 above, 271 for the (grey-listing) suggestion that sellers might compromise their own dignity 'if the strength of the reason for selling is insufficient in relation to the nature of the part sold.' Munzer's theory of sufficiency turns on biological factors such as the renewability and vitality of particular parts as well as on the necessity for the use of body parts and whether the part retains a close personal link with the seller: *ibid* 275–277.

to be held to account? In some duty-led communities, the view might be that duties are to be self-enforced; but, in others, public measures will be taken to prevent and discourage agents from compromising their own dignity and a range of sanctions will be in place for duty violations. Significantly, where the latter context obtains, dignity's demand that agents must not treat themselves as mere things can take on a paternalistic role, potentially restricting the free choices of circus dwarfs, peep-show performers, surrogates, gene sellers, and the like, even though none of the agents involved actually experiences any loss of self-respect.[45]

The duty to conduct oneself in a dignified manner

In a duty-led regime, a duty to conduct oneself in a dignified manner might be understood as an end in itself (dignified conduct being valued for its own sake) or as indirectly supportive of other duties. On the former reading, the duty would not relate closely to the duty not to compromise the dignity of *others*; rather, it would complement the duty not to compromise *one's own* dignity (or it would pick out a specific aspect of the general duty not to compromise one's own dignity). On the latter reading, the argument would be that those who violate the duty, by attempting to put themselves outside the conditions of human finitude (undignified conduct), are more likely to compromise the dignity of themselves or others (ie, to treat themselves or others as mere things).[46]

Human dignity: a rights-led (Gewirthian) interpretation

Next, we can analyse human dignity from a rights-led moral perspective, tackling this in three stages: first, sketching why the particular rights-led analysis associated with the moral theory of Alan Gewirth[47] must be adopted; secondly, contrasting a (Gewirthian) rights-led analysis of dignity with the duty-led view that we have just considered; and, thirdly, relating dignity to the status of potential agents.

The Gewirthian approach

The central contention in Gewirthian moral theory is that agents — conceived as those who (prospectively at least) have the capacity freely to select and act for purposes[48] — are categorically bound by the 'Principle of Generic Consistency' (the *PGC*). Under the *PGC*, agents have reciprocal rights and duties to respect one another's freedom and well-being. Although the interests protected by the *PGC* are hierarchically ordered (relative to the needs of agency), the substance of Gewirthian morality is not dissimilar to that of many modern rights-driven moralities (eg, Rawlsian and Dworkinian). What marks out Gewirthianism as distinctive and controversial amongst modern liberal moral theories is its claim that any agent, no matter what that particular agent's practical viewpoint, is logically committed to acceptance of the *PGC*. The dual significance of this claim is that the *PGC* is binding not only on agents who are disposed to take a moral

---

45 Kant might be read as supporting such paternalism. However, if treating humanity as an end amounts to an injunction to respect the autonomy of persons, then this militates against paternalism; cf n 30 above.

46 cf n 30 and n 45 above.

47 Seminally, see Alan Gewirth, *Reason and Morality* (Chicago: University of Chicago Press, 1978).

48 cf n 28 above.

viewpoint of some kind, but on agents *as such*, simply by virtue of their taking anything at all to be a reason for their action. In this respect, the Gewirthian project runs parallel to Kant's attempt to establish the categorical imperative via a transcendental argument.

Gewirth's strategy in defending this bold claim is to demonstrate (by what he calls the dialectically necessary method) that an agent would contradict its status as an agent if it did not accept that it was bound by the *PGC*. Put shortly, the argument takes an agent through three stages of progressive self-reflection on its interests and responsibilities as an agent. At the first stage, the argument is that an agent must value its chosen purposes and, in consequence, value the generic conditions (designated by Gewirth as its 'freedom and well-being') that must obtain for any of its purposive activity, as being instrumental to these purposes, whatever they may be. At the second stage, the argument is that, since the agent values its chosen purposes in a way sufficient to motivate it to pursue them, the agent must consider that it ought to act for its freedom and well-being as instrumental to its purposes (whatever they may be), from which it follows that the agent must consider that others ought not to interfere with its freedom and well-being *against its will* (and that others ought to assist it to have its freedom and well-being if it cannot secure these for itself and *wishes such assistance*), correlative to which the agent must consider that it has both negative and positive rights to its freedom and well-being. Finally, at the third stage, this claim to the generic rights is universalised. From the fact that the agent would contradict that it is an agent if it did not consider that it has the generic rights, it follows logically that the agent would contradict that it is an agent if it did not consider that the sufficient reason why it has the generic rights is that it is an agent.[49] Logical universalisation then requires the agent to accept that all agents have the generic rights.

The fact that the agent's rights-claim derives from the categorical instrumental value that it must attach to its freedom and well-being and that nothing in the argument shows that, or presumes that, the agent has to value its freedom and well-being for their own sakes, has the consequence that the *PGC* not only grounds what is essentially an ethics of rights rather than an ethics of duty, but that the generic rights are rights according to the will (or choice) theory of rights, rather than according to the interest theory.[50] This, as we will later see, is of central significance in contrasting Gewirth's view of human dignity with Kant's.

Alongside his dialectically necessary method, Gewirth contrasts what he calls a dialectically contingent method. Whereas the former purports to hold good against any practical standpoint, the latter operates only on a particular optional practical standpoint. Given Gewirth's philosophical ambitions, any concession of optionality is fatal and, thus, dialectically contingent forms of argument are of little interest to him. For our purposes, however, at least one such argument is significant: namely that, where human rights are accepted, then the *PGC* is (dialectically contingently) presupposed. There are two threads to this argument.[51] First, since one who accepts any human right must also accept that there is a right to the conditions that are necessary for the exercise of any human right (where the

---

49   This is demonstrated by Gewirth's Argument from the Sufficiency of Agency (ASA). See Gewirth, n 47 above, esp at 110–112, and 115–119.

50   See, further, Deryck Beyleveld, *The Dialectical Necessity of Morality: An Analysis and Defense of Alan Gewirth's Argument to the Principle of Generic Consistency* (Chicago: University of Chicago Press, 1991) esp at 26–27, and 32–33.

51   See Deryck Beyleveld, 'Legal Theory and Dialectically Contingent Justifications for the Principle of Generic Consistency' (1996) 9 *Ratio Juris* 15.

exercise of a right is understood in terms of claiming, waiving, or operating the right), and since the *PGC* confers a right to the generic conditions of purposive action (including the exercise of a human right), acceptance of any human right entails acceptance of the *PGC*. Secondly, assuming that human rights are conceived of as claims to benefits that rights-holders can waive (which, typically, we take to be the case), then such rights-holders are more accurately equated with agents than with humans.[52] Combining these two threads, our second-best position is that, in a culture of human rights, the *PGC* is (dialectically contingently) presupposed.

Human dignity from a Gewirthian perspective

Having so declared our moral hand, how do the two core ideas of human dignity stand when viewed in a Gewirthian rights-led framework?

A right that other agents do not compromise our dignity (intrinsic value)
Gewirth treats dignity as 'the ground or antecedent of [human] rights',[53] arguing that an agent's 'attribution of worth to himself derives not only from the goodness he attributes to his particular actions but also from the general purposiveness that characterizes all his actions and himself qua agent.'[54] It follows that, in a broad sense (paralleling that in the duty-led approach), all violations of the rights of others compromise their dignity. Put more narrowly, Gewirthians might equate compromising the dignity of others with cases where there is a failure to recognise one with the capacities for agency as an agent, or where an agent's conditions of self-respect are damaged.

The parallel with a duty-led approach, however, is not perfect. In a Gewirthian framework, a right that others do not compromise one's dignity, by damaging one's conditions of self-respect, must be specified in a way that is compatible with an agent's autonomy-based rights. Crucially, what matters is whether the agent freely invites the 'compromising' conduct of others, not whether a loss of self-respect is experienced, even less whether dignity in some metaphysical sense is compromised. Thus, if two (or more) agents freely embark upon some supposedly 'demeaning' or 'deviant' course of conduct, the dignity of neither is compromised; indeed, where agents freely interact and transact with one another, it is precisely respect for dignity that demands that there should be no interference — for, to interefere with such agents would be to treat them as mere things.

A right that other agents should not compromise their own dignity (intrinsic value)
An agent's right of self-determination (autonomy) is fundamental to the Gewirthian moral regime. So long as no harm is done to the *PGC*-protected rights of other agents, an agent can do no wrong in its acts of self-authorship.

Consider, for example, the case of suicide. Against Kant, who argued that an act of suicide would violate human dignity, modern liberal rights-theorists emphasise

---

52   As we have indicated in the text (above), in Gewirth's dialectically *necessary* argument, an agent may (without contradiction) will purpose-specific interference with its freedom and well-being and, thus, waive the ordinary benefit of the protective rights flowing from the *PGC*.

53   Alan Gewirth, 'Human Dignity as the Basis of Rights' in Michael J. Meyer and William A. Parent (eds) n 29 above, 10, 14.

54   *ibid* 22; and see, too, Alan Gewirth, *The Community of Rights* (Chicago: University of Chicago Press, 1996) 66.

the individual's right to autonomy.[55] In line with this view, Gewirthians see no contradiction in an agent freely choosing to terminate its life, nor for that matter freely choosing to inflict lesser degrees of self-harm. Thus:

> What does the *PGC* require in cases where persons fulfill the cognitive and emotional conditions for voluntary consent and yet refuse to consent to interferences with their self-destructive or other projects whereby they intend to inflict basic harms on themselves? Such projects include suicide, selling oneself into slavery, ingesting harmful drugs, and the like
> . . . .
>   [W]hen it is clear that the conditions of voluntariness have been met by the projected self-harmer, further interference with him must be discontinued.[56]

The import of these remarks is clear: agents who voluntarily choose to harm themselves, whether by restricting their future freedom or by damaging their well-being (including undermining their own basis for self-respect), breach the generic rights of neither themselves nor others.[57] Granted, agents might live to regret their actions but, in this sense, Gewirthians accept that dignity-based autonomy can come at a price.

Surely, though, self-harming agents must breach a duty to themselves?[58] We think not. First, in a rights-led moral regime, the idea of a duty to oneself (performance of which, as the correlative rights-holder, one might waive)[59] is something of a contradiction in terms. Of course, insofar as the supposed duties to oneself relate either to the avoidance of qualities that militate against, or to the inculcation of qualities that conduce towards, the fulfilment of one's responsibilities towards others, then there is no such contradiction: we are dealing *indirectly* with an agent's duties to others. Secondly, Gewirth allows for what he calls 'a more analogical' form of duties to oneself,[60] where we might speak of an agent being unfair to or demeaning itself. To the extent that we mean that a particular agent, A's, immediate actions are antithetical to A's long-term purposes, this is relatively unproblematic: A remains free to choose its purposes and any criticism of A's short-term action is by reference to A's own established preferences and purposes. Thirdly, however, Gewirth extends this analogical use to an agent's long-term desires or ends, suggesting that the analogy might be pursued either in terms of equilibrium (in which model, no one of the agent's interests should dominate the others) or hierarchy (in which model, the agent's 'higher interests' should control its 'lower interests'). Where we speak of a person degrading himself, Gewirth says that it is the model of hierarchy that is invoked.[61] To the extent that such analogical uses are simply seeking to impose some kind of unity or order on the agent's preferences, there is no great problem. What respect for the *PGC* demands, however, is that we do not allow the analogical duty not to violate one's own dignity to become an excuse for others to restrict the range of purposes that agents may otherwise freely choose.

A right that other agents should conduct themselves in a dignified manner
Do other agents have a right that we develop a dignified character (accepting the limits of human finitude)? One thing is clear. Agents have responsibilities, both

---

55   See, eg, Max Charlesworth, *Bioethics in a Liberal Society* (Cambridge, Cambridge University Press, 1993) ch 3.
56   n 47 above, 264–265.
57   *ibid* 266.
58   For Gewirth's own discussion of duties to oneself, see *ibid* 333–338.
59   cf text above at 670.
60   *ibid* 335–338.
61   *ibid* 337.

negative and positive, in relation to one another. If the practical consequence of agents becoming obsessed with pushing back the limitations of human finitude is that they neglect their responsibilities to one another, then the development of a dignified character has much to commend it. Contrasting this with the model that we encounter in Ernest Becker's work, where a human is said to be 'most "dignified" when he shows a certain obliviousness to his fate ...; who is most "free" when he lives in secure dependency on powers around him, when he is least in possession of himself',[62] agents need not be oblivious to their fate; they should be self-driven and in possession of themselves. Pushing back the limitations of human finitude is permissible, even desirable, but only so long as this is compatible with discharging one's responsibilities to other agents. If dignified conduct indirectly promotes respect for the generic rights of other agents, then it is a virtue that other agents are entitled to have us cultivate.[63]

Dignity, rights-holders and potential agents

In Gewirthian (as in Kantian) theory, dignity relates to capacities that qualify agents (rational beings with a will) as rights-holders (duty-bearers).[64] The logic of the theory is that those who lack the relevant capacity are not agents and cannot be rights-holders. It is a moot point, however, whether non-agents have protected interests of some kind. For our purposes, the most important category of non-agents is that of potential human agents (covering embryos, fetuses, and neonates). There are several ways of arguing that agents have some responsibilities in relation to such non-agents — Gewirth himself relies on principles of proportionality and potentiality,[65] and elsewhere we have sketched a number of other lines of argument that might merit consideration.[66] It would be a mistake, however, to add to our list the view (as per Article 1 of the Convention on Human Rights and Biomedicine) that human dignity is the reason why potential humans (or potential agents) should be respected. To equate human dignity with any human life form (from the point of conception), is certainly to invite the objection of 'speciesism'; more importantly, from a Gewirthian (or Kantian) perspective, it simply begs the question why human life has intrinsic value such as to ground a regime of reciprocal rights and duties. Human life, without more, simply will not serve; and, in this context, appeals to human dignity threaten to operate as unhelpful 'conversation stoppers'.[67]

---

62 Ernest Becker, *The Denial of Death* (New York: The Free Press, 1973) 24.
63 Might it also be argued that acceptance of the limitations of human finitude is implicit in agency? Given that an agent is one who has the capacity to freely act for purposes (or who is logically committed to positively valuing its own generic features of action; or who is committed to respecting the generic features of fellow agents), the thought is that, if agency presupposes the possibility of unwilled interferences with one's freedom and well-being (ie, a context of limited resources and options), and if viewing oneself as an agent commits one to accepting the limitations of such a context, then to deny such limitations (by trying to put oneself beyond them) is to contradict one's own agency. If we say that such a denial is 'undignified', then there is a sense in which agents can violate their own dignity.
64 cf n 28 above.
65 Alan Gewirth, n 47 above, esp at 121–124 and 141–144.
66 Deryck Beyleveld and Roger Brownsword, 'Legal Argumentation in Biolaw' (paper presented at first international conference on bioethics and biolaw, Danish Parliament, Copenhagen, June 1996) (on file with authors).
67 cf Dieter Birnbacher, 'Do Modern Reproductive Technologies Violate Human Dignity?' in Elisabeth Hildt and Dietmar Mieth (eds) *In Vitro Fertilisation in the 1990s: Towards a Medical, Social and Ethical Evaluation* (Aldershot: Ashgate Publishing, 1998) 325; and Deryck Beyleveld, 'Some Observations on Human Dignity and Human Rights', *ibid* 335.

Rights, dignity and human genetics

In the final part of our paper, we consider briefly how our analysis would bear on three issues in human genetics where dignity is currently seen as an important limiting consideration. These are the issues of the commercialisation of human genes; interventions in the human genome; and human reproductive cloning.

The commercialisation of human genes

Article 21 of the Convention, together with Article 4 of the Universal Declaration, imply that a market in human genes would violate human dignity; but would it?[68] This question is entangled with some complex debates about property in body parts.[69] However, if we grant the possibility of a market in human genes, would 'primary transaction' commerce (in which one agent sells a sample of its own genome to another agent) violate human dignity? Possibly some buyers might compromise the dignity of sellers, treating them as no more than repositories of DNA — in the language of Article 2(b) of the Universal Declaration, some buyers might reduce sellers to their genetic characteristics. However, those buyers who related to sellers in this way would be disposed to take what they could without negotiating a price. The market, in other words, would not be the problem. Another possibility, albeit remote, is that buyers might use the market intentionally to demean sellers (experientially); but such an outside chance of abuse scarcely warrants prohibiting primary transaction commerce. As John Harris has tellingly remarked in another context:

> To ban cloning on the grounds that it might be used for racist purposes is tantamount to saying that sexual intercourse should be prohibited because it permits the possibility of rape.[70]

Thus, unless this is one of those cases where a rational regulatory approach requires a general prohibition, the most that we have is an argument for targeted restriction. Perhaps a more likely scenario is that sellers suffer an after-sale loss of self-respect. However, provided that sellers freely enter the market, any subsequent loss of self-esteem, whilst unfortunate, involves no violation of rights. No doubt, it will be said that dignity militates against a market in human genes, because gene-traders (by putting a price on their own bodies) undermine their own self-esteem; but this is precisely the line of thinking that must be rejected as incompatible with Gewirthian principles. Finally, commerce in human genes might encourage some undignified trading, in the sense that some buyers and sellers might be tempted to shirk their responsibilities. However, markets are full of temptations and it is not immediately obvious that a market in human genes would be any more likely to encourage such conduct than any other kind of market.[71]

---

68 For some sceptical remarks about appeals to dignity in the context of commerce in body parts, see Neil Duxbury, 'Do Markets Degrade?' (1996) 59 MLR 331.

69 See, eg, J.W. Harris, 'Who Owns My Body?' (1996) 16 *Oxford Journal of Legal Studies* 55.

70 John Harris, *Clones, Genes, and Immortality* (Oxford: Oxford University Press, 1998) 32.

71 Objections based on dignity commonly fall away once we turn to 'secondary transactions' (ie, where the seller is not trading in his own genetic material). To the extent that the objection is based on the Kantian duty of self-esteem, this is perhaps to be expected. However, from a Gewirthian perspective, there is no sharp distinction between primary and secondary transactions. In principle, if dignity-based rights might be violated by commerce in human genes, this can be at any point in the chain of transactions.

Commercialisation also involves the question of patentability. As is well-known, from the early 1990s, when applications were filed for sequences of DNA taken from brain cells,[72] the patenting of human gene sequences has developed rapidly (albeit controversially).[73] Whereas objections to the early applications centred on whether it was appropriate to patent gene sequences whose function in the human body was unknown and where potential use or benefit was not yet identified, the more recent objections insist that the patenting of human gene sequences is immoral as violating human dignity. Thus, in the *Relaxin* opposition,[74] the leading case on this point at the European Patent Office,[75] it was argued *inter alia* that the 'isolation of the DNA relaxin gene from tissue taken from a pregnant woman is immoral, in that it constitutes an offence against human dignity to make use of a particular female condition (pregnancy) for a technical process oriented towards profit'.[76] Rejecting this argument, the Opposition Division pointed out that those who had donated the tissue (that made it possible to isolate the gene) had done so consensually; and, moreover, there was no reason to doubt the morality of procedures of this kind (for many life-saving substances, such as blood-clotting factors, had been developed in this way).

Addressing the matter specifically in Gewirthian terms, what might the opponents of the patent have argued? Could it be argued that such a patent, or the research and development of the product, compromised anyone's dignity? Certainly, there was no evidence that the researchers failed to acknowledge that they were dealing with fellow agents; and it is hard to imagine how the grant of the patent would threaten such a right. Similarly, it is unclear how rights relating to self-respect might be threatened by such a patent. It will not do to argue that the researchers violated such rights in relation to the pregnant women who supplied the tissue (at any rate, not so long as the transactions were freely entered into). Nor, of course, will it do to argue that the pregnant women compromised their own dignity — and, to this extent at least, the Opposition Division was surely correct in dismissing the opposition.[77]

72 See Gerald Dworkin, 'Ethics of Human Genome Analysis. Intellectual Property and Ownership of Data' in Hille Haker, Richard Hearn, and Klaus Steigleder (eds) *Ethics of Human Genome Analysis* (Tübingen: Attempto Verlag Tübingen, 1993) 175, 176–177.

73 See S.M. Thomas, A.R.W. Davies, N.J. Birtwistle, S.M. Crowther, and J.F. Burke, 'Ownership of the Human Genome' 380 *Nature* (4 April 1996) 387.

74 *OJ EPO* 6/1995, 388. See, too, the opposition to the patent granted to the Biocyte Corporation over umbilical blood as a further expression of outrage at the use of the patent system for the commercialisation of the human body. See Kate Watson-Smyth, 'Doctors to fight charge for blood' *The Guardian* 14 April 1997.

75 The opposition was based on Article 53(a) of the European Patent Convention which, so far as is material, provides that European patents shall not be granted for 'inventions the publication or exploitation of which would be contrary to "ordre public" or morality. . . .' For extended analysis of this provision, see Deryck Beyleveld and Roger Brownsword, *Mice, Morality and Patents* (London: Common Law Institute of Intellectual Property, 1993); and, contra, see Edward Armitage and Ivor Davis, *Patents and Morality in Perspective* (London: Common Law Institute of Intellectual Property, 1994).

76 See para 6.1 of the Decision. It was also argued (*ibid*) that such patenting 'amounts to a form of modern slavery since it involves the dismemberment of women and their piecemeal sale to commercial enterprises throughout the world' — thereby infringing 'the human right to self-determination'; and, that the 'patenting of human genes means that human life is being patented', which is 'intrinsically immoral.' Clearly, though, it would be contradictory for Kantians or Gewirthians (who equate dignity with purposivity and end-setting) to claim that a patent on human genes amounts to a patent on life and, thus, violates human dignity.

77 But for criticism of the EPO's general approach under Article 53(a), see Deryck Beyleveld and Roger Brownsword 'Patenting Human Genes: Legality, Morality and Human Rights' in J.W. Harris (ed) *Property Problems — From Genes to Pension Funds* (London: Kluwer, 1997) 9; and, more generally, *Mice, Morality and Patents* (London: Common Law Institute of Intellectual Property, 1993).

Nevertheless, we have two concerns about commercialisation. First, if commerce in human genes is to be conducted on the basis of free choice — the only legitimate basis for trade — then how do we regulate in those many contexts where there are significant asymmetries of information and bargaining strength between the parties?[78] Recognising that informed consent procedures are no guarantor of autonomy, we might seek ways of strengthening such procedures or we might advocate a general prohibition on gene commerce (as the lesser of two evils, and for the sake of protecting the interests of vulnerable agents).[79] There is no reason to think, however, that the emerging reliance on human dignity points the way towards either a more effective or a more rational regulatory regime. Secondly, as the notorious John Moore case highlights,[80] the conjunction of prohibitions on primary transaction commerce, with permissions in the patent system, unjustifiably licenses entrepreneurs to take the whole profit from their exploitation of the human genome — but opportunistic use of the concept of human dignity is part of the problem here, not a potential solution.[81]

Interventions in the human genome

In 1982, the Parliamentary Assembly of the Council of Europe, concerned that interventions in the human genome should be limited by the rights to life and dignity, recommended that there should be a 'right to inherit a genetic pattern that has not been artificially changed.'[82] Reflecting this earlier concern, Article 13 of the Convention restricts interventions in the human genome to 'preventive, diagnostic or therapeutic purposes'; and, it proscribes attempts 'to introduce any modification in the genome of any descendants.'[83] The drafting of the Universal Declaration has also evinced concerns about 'eugenics';[84] and, although the provisions in Article 5(a) for 'research, treatment or diagnosis affecting an individual's genome' do not explicitly limit such interventions by reference to respect for human dignity, we can take it that such a limitation is to be implied. As for germ-line interventions, these are specifically singled out by Article 24 as one of the practices that could be contrary to human dignity.

Two widely held assumptions are evident here: first, that germ-line interventions are incompatible with human dignity; and, secondly, that 'negative' interventions

---

78   Obvious instances are patients who require treatment, gene sources in the Third World, and prisoners (see, eg, 'Death-row organs "for sale in US"' *The Guardian* 25 February 1998. See, generally, the discussion in Alain Pottage, 'The Inscription of Life in Law: Genes, Patents, and Bio-politics' (in this volume).

79   cf the reasoning of the majority of the Canadian Supreme Court in *Re Rodriguez and Attorney-General of British Columbia* (1993) 107 DLR 4th 342.

80   *Moore* v *Regents of the University of California* (1990) 793 P2d 479.

81   cf James Boyle, *Shamans, Software, and Spleens* (Cambridge, Mass: Harvard University Press, 1996) esp at 21–24, and 99–107; and Deryck Beyleveld and Roger Brownsword, 'Articles 21 and 22 of the Convention on Human Rights and Biomedicine: Property and Consent, Commerce and Dignity' in Peter Kemp (ed) *Research Projects on Basic Ethical Principles in Bioethics and Biolaw* (papers from the Utrecht meeting, November 1997) (Copenhagen: Centre for Ethics and Law, 1998).

82   See Noëlle Lenoir, 'Respect for Life and the Law of the Living' in Denis Noble and Jean-Didier Vincent (eds) *The Ethics of Life* (Paris: UNESCO, 1997) 165, 185 (discussing Council of Europe Recommendation No 934 on genetic engineering (1982)).

83   According to the Explanatory Report, n 13 above, para 89, 'intentional modification of the human genome so as to produce individuals or entire groups endowed with particular characteristics and required qualities' is the 'ultimate fear'.

84   See, eg, n 21 above, 49 and 50; also, Hille Haker, 'Human Genome Analysis and Eugenics' in Hille Haker, Richard Hearn, and Klaus Steigleder (eds) n 72 above, 290.

designed to avoid suffering are less threatening to human dignity than 'positive' interventions designed to promote 'desirable' or 'beneficial' properties.[85] Yet, are these assumptions, which raise complex philosophical questions about human identity,[86] plausible?

Consider, first, the case of germ-line intervention. Whilst there are grounds for precaution if we are not sure about the down-stream consequences of germ-line intervention,[87] is there any sense in which germ-line manipulation directly jeopardises human dignity? Perhaps practitioners of germ-line intervention might lose sight of the fact that they are dealing with agents — literally treating their agent subjects as guinea-pigs; or some might set out to demean those whom they treat (or the latter might experience a diminution in their sense of self-respect). There is no reason, though, to think that germ-line intervention per se involves distinctive hazards of this kind. An alternative approach is to look for the threat to dignity in future agents who are the progeny of those agents whose germ-line has been manipulated. Do we really believe that this class of agents might be regarded as inferior, leading to them valuing themselves less than those whose genome has not been so manipulated? If so, dignity is an issue here but the basis of the belief needs to be elaborated before we can take it seriously.

Secondly, for the sake of argument, let us suppose not only that we can draw a bright line between negative and positive interventions but also that the former are compatible with human dignity.[88] Why, then, should we think that positive interventions are not so compatible? Suppose, for example, that the interventions in question were designed to promote intelligence in our children: might we not agree with John Harris that to eschew such interventions would be akin to 'inventing antibiotics but declining to put them into production'?[89] In response, one argument might be that, whilst we can be reasonably confident that negative interventions will alleviate suffering, we cannot be sure that positive interventions will have such a benign outcome. With positive interventions, we have to place our bets; and, even with the safest bet, there is a risk that it will misfire, producing at some future time engineered agents who lack self-respect. This, it has to be conceded, is a possibility. However, unless those who procure positive interventions are unusually bad at reading the runes, there is no reason to think that the outcomes following from intervention will be worse relative to dignity than the outcomes that would have followed from non-intervention.

85 cf the discussion of sex selection in Ruth Deech, 'Family Law and Genetics' (in this volume) for the parallel distinction between 'medical' and 'social' reasons. Following a public consultation, the HFEA concluded that sex selection for social reasons was unacceptable, *inter alia*, because children might be seen as commodities.

86 See, eg. David Heyd, *Genethics: Moral Issues in the Creation of People* (Berkeley: University of California Press, 1992) esp ch 6.

87 Where a particular technology is thought to be unsafe or risky relative to the *PGC*-protected interests of agents, a precautionary principle is an important element of Gewirthian thinking. However, this is a principle that needs sensitive application from case to case, the importance of the interests at risk (discounted by the degree of risk) being set against the importance of the interests that would be promoted by the use of the technology.

88 But nb, insofar as a (negative) therapeutic purpose is conceived of as replacing 'bad' or 'abnormal' genes with 'good' or 'normal' genes, the line between theraputic and non-therapeutic purposes will be relative to judgments of badness and abnormality; cf Robert Schwartz, 'Genetic Knowledge: Some Legal and Ethical Questions' in David C. Thomasma and Thomasine Kushner (eds) *Birth to Death: Science and Bioethics* (Cambridge: Cambridge University Press, 1996) 21, esp at 24–26.

89 John Harris, *The Value of Life* (London: Routledge, 1985) 150.

Another argument is that positive interventions might abuse dignity by producing 'designer children', pre-disposed to have particular talents that enable them to excel at their designers' favoured conception of the good.[90] Yet, if respect for human dignity demands a neutral approach towards the reproduction and rearing of children (ie, an approach that is in no sense geared towards the parents' favoured conception of the good), then present practices of selective mating and environmental conditioning apparently observe this principle in the breach. Moreover, if we tie the objection specifically to (supposedly) abusive manipulation of the genome, we do not have an argument for prohibiting positive interventions; rather, what we have is an argument that smacks of genetic reductionism — which certainly cannot stand with the (non-reductionist) reasoning informing both the Kantian and the Gewirthian view of the intrinsic dignity of persons[91] — and, at most, an argument for targeted restriction.[92]

There is, of course, one other argument: where the manipulated genome is that of a *potential* agent, it might be objected that dignity is violated precisely because we are tampering with a potential agent. However, as we have said, to place a question mark against the treatment of potential agents is one thing; it is quite another matter to stipulate a meaning for human dignity that has no logical purchase on practical reflection but that nevertheless purports to be the reason why respect for embryonic life is required.

Human reproductive cloning

Article 11 of the Universal Declaration prohibits '[p]ractices which are contrary to human dignity, such as reproductive cloning of human beings ... .' We might think that no such prohibition is necessary; for, as David Heyd comments, many will find such a prospect 'horrifying' and will 'have no interest in exact mirror-images or in indistinguishable copies.'[93] On the other hand, the joint HGAC and HFEA Consultation Document on cloning, suggests a number of scenarios in which copies might appeal. For example, parents might wish to 'replace' an aborted fetus, dead baby, or child killed in an accident; or parents might wish to have a cloned sibling to provide a compatible organ for a child dying of kidney failure; or someone might wish to have a clone of themselves as a way, as that individual sees it, of cheating death.[94] Is Article 11 right in treating reproductive human cloning as contrary to human dignity?

Initially, we should distinguish between the technology of cloning itself, and the purposes that agents might have in seeking to employ cloning technology. If the technology itself is said to violate human dignity, this will probably prove to be a 'conversation stopper'. However, in current debates, the thrust of the objection to

---

90   cf Bruce A. Ackerman, *Social Justice in the Liberal State* (New Haven and London: Yale University Press, 1980) esp ch 4 (for various dialogues arising from the awesome powers of the Master Geneticist).
91   cf n 76 above.
92   There are, of course, many instances where, for prophylactic or evidential reasons, regulation is rightly given a broader sweep than the mischief at which it is aimed. Whether positive interventions in the human genome call for such a regulatory approach remains to be debated; and one of the questions to be addressed is whether different considerations are raised where positive interventions reflect (a) the various individual preferences of commissioning parents or (b) some larger public scheme of population design and control.
93   David Heyd, n 86 above, 217.
94   *Cloning Issues in Reproduction, Science and Medicine* (London: Human Genetics Advisory Commission, January 1998) para 8.3.

cloning is not so much that the technology per se violates dignity but that it might be used in a way that instrumentalises others.[95]

Consider the two examples of 'other-cloning' given in the Consultation Paper, where the parents wish to copy their children. Do the parents (A) instrumentalise their children (either the clone source (B) or the cloned product (C)) in these cases? Assuming that the parents who wish to clone another child as a would-be kidney donor have the consent of the clone source (B), are they instrumentalising the cloned product (C) (the would-be donor)? If so, it is hardly the cloning that involves such instrumentalisation. For, quite apart from the fact that the parents might have faced the same accusation had they tried to produce a sibling donor by natural reproduction, the objection only takes hold when pressure is applied to C to act as a kidney donor (only then is C treated as a mere thing). In the example of the parents who want to replace a lost child, it is unclear that they are instrumentalising the cloned product (C). Might they be accused, however, of instrumentalising the clone source (B)? Given that the clone source is already dead (as an ex-agent or as an ex-potential agent) the accusation of instrumentalisation is, to say the least, problematic. In both examples, however, we might try another tack, arguing that clones might experience a loss of self-respect, rather like that experienced by adopted children, when they realise that in a certain sense they were not wanted. For example, in the case of the parents who want a replacement child, the cloned product (C) might feel of reduced value because the parents would not have wanted the clone if the clone source (B) had survived. Yet, this might apply equally if C had been born by natural reproductive processes; moreover, a clone in particular might take a more upbeat view of things — far from being not wanted, the clone might reason that it was *just* what its parents wanted. On the face of it, there is no short-cut to the conclusion that other-cloning is dignity-threatening in itself; at most, the objection is that it might offer new opportunities for instrumentalising reasoning around the reproductive process and its results.[96]

Turning to 'self-cloning', if the intention is to cheat death, then this seems misguided, foolish, and bound to disappoint.[97] Does it, though, involve a violation of dignity? With regard to instrumentalisation, we can assume that the clone source consents to self-cloning. Accordingly, the focus for the instrumentalisation objection is the cloned product; and, in this respect, the issues raised by self-cloning seem comparable to those raised by other-cloning. Self-cloning, however, perhaps involves an additional element, in the sense that it exemplifies precisely the kind of conduct which we might condemn as undignified. By this, we mean that self-cloners, like agents who make extraordinary attempts to prolong their lives or to retain their youthful looks, are engaging in conduct that might be symptomatic of a lack of responsibility (relative to their duties, as agents, to their fellow agents). If cloning were to damage the culture of human rights, reversing agents' prioritisation of morality over mortality, there would be legitimate concerns for human dignity.[98]

---

95 According to the Explanatory Report accompanying the draft cloning Protocol, n 18 above, para 3: '[E]thical reasoning for a prohibition to clone human beings is based first and foremost on human dignity which is endangered by instrumentalisation through artificial human cloning.' Similarly, see the HGAC and HFEA Consultation Paper at 18.

96 cf the arguments against cloning raised by Ruth Deech, n 85 above (eg, that cloned children might become the butt of jibes, or might be discriminated against, or might be exploited by the media).

97 cf Ernest Becker, *The Denial of Death* (New York: The Free Press, 1973), esp at 266–267.

98 cf Daniel Callahan, 'The Genetic Revolution' in David C. Thomasma and Thomasine Kushner (eds) n 88 above, 13.

Conclusion

Recalling our opening question, what are we to make of human dignity in debates about the legitimacy of human genetics? First, from any perspective that values rational debate about human genetics, it is an abuse of the concept of human dignity to operate it as a veto on any practice that is intuitively disliked. Secondly, human dignity, whether viewed from a Kantian duty-led or a Gewirthian rights-led moral perspective, is rightly appealed to as requiring that agents should be treated as ends (not as mere things). It may also be appealed to in the form of the practical virtue of dignified conduct, this indirectly supporting respect for human rights and responsibilities. Thirdly, however, from both a Kantian and a Gewirthian perspective, it is improper to attach dignity to species-specific characteristics that have no practical relevance. Finally, as between Kantian duty-led and Gewirthian rights-led approaches, the central issue is the relationship between dignity and autonomy.[99] From a Gewirthian standpoint, respect for human dignity involves treating agents as autonomous ends; it is, thus, complementary to the fundamental right of agents that their freedom and well-being should not be interfered with *against their own will*. If agents freely choose 'to die with dignity', or to participate in dwarf-throwing or peep-shows, or to sell their genes, they have at least a prima facie right to do so; and, any duty-led claim that agents so compromise their own dignity must be rejected as misguided paternalism.[100]

---

99   But nb the caveats about the best reading of Kant in n 30 and n 45 above.
100 cf n 21 above, 49: 'Some speakers pointed out that ... this principle in the text [dignity] is designed essentially to serve as a political and moral signal so that its assertion may not give rise to liberticide interpretations' (Chantal Ralaimihoatra reporting the General Discussion of the draft Universal Declaration). We endorse such a reading.

Interventions in the Human Genome

Sheila A.M. McLean*

It is trite, but true, to say that few medical advances have been greeted with such public and media interest as has the so-called genetic revolution. Even before the cloning of Dolly, people's imagination was gripped by the literature, academic and fictional, that surrounds this subject. The possibility of genetic modification and enhancement, fears about the creation of communities of drones or totalitarian dictators, the recent eugenic excesses of the twentieth century and the brave new world held out by the imminent completion of the Human Genome Project provide rich and fertile ground for speculation, debate and sometimes concern. On the other hand, genetics offers the capacity to identify disorders and hopefully in the future to cure them. As Wilkie says, 'the new genetical anatomy will transform medicine and mitigate suffering in the twenty-first century.'[1]

Watson and Crick's discovery in 1953 of the structure of DNA — the key discovery on which the Human Genome Project rests — was probably one of the most remarkable scientific achievements of this century, and has led to the most ambitious scientific project since the space race. Its significance lies in the growing capacity to identify the molecular structures which make us who we are, at least physically. As Bodmer and McKie have said: 'DNA is the true chemical of life, for it is the essential component from which our genes are made. In it is encoded the genetic language that controls our destinies. And an astonishingly powerful lexicon it is. Just six million millionths of a gram of DNA carries as much information as ten volumes of the Complete Oxford English Dictionary.'[2]

Clearly the potential of being able to unravel and translate this lexicon in both depth and detail is of enormous fascination to science. Even if not all of the information ultimately discovered is of immediate interest or applicability (so-called 'junk DNA'[3]), much of what is discovered will be of theoretical and/or practical value. The capacity to identify rogue genes which cause disease or disability may lead to medical advances as yet unimagined. And the toll of genetic disorder should not be underestimated. Wexler suggests that '[i]t is now estimated that gene defects underlie 3,000 to 4,000 different diseases, and this is before one considers polygenic etiologies in which there is interaction between genes and environment.'[4]

---

* School of Law, University of Glasgow.

1   T. Wilkie, *Perilous Knowledge: the Human Genome Project and its Implications* (London: Faber and Faber, 1993) 1.

2   W. Bodmer and R. McKie, *The Book of Man: The Quest to Discover our Genetic Heritage* (London: Little, Brown and Company, 1994) 10.

3   The debate as to whether or not there is such a thing as 'junk DNA' is not resolved; cf BMA, *Our Genetic Future: the Science and Ethics of Genetic Technology* (Oxford: Oxford University Press, 1992) 215: 'Not all scientists ... accept the hypothesis implicit in the concept of junk DNA. For example, Gilbert has suggested that any characterization of some DNA as "junk" might merely be a reflection of our current ignorance about their true function.'

4   N.S. Wexler, 'Disease Gene Identification: Ethical Considerations' *Hospital Practice*, October 15 1991, 145, 145.

Manifestly, if such a major contributor to morbidity and mortality can be exorcised from society, this would represent a major advance in general health. However, it is by no means clear that the result of the identification of genetic disorders will be the hoped-for therapy.[5] The current gap between diagnostic and therapeutic capacity continues to cause problems of both a clinical and an ethical nature. For the moment, then, there is reason to be somewhat sceptical about the claims made for genetics.

Whether we adopt a positive or a negative view of genetic intervention will likely depend both on our understanding of what genetics can actually achieve and on the mechanisms in place to minimise the potential for abuse which undoubtedly exists. And no matter on which side we fall, it must be borne in mind that one result of the completion of the Human Genome Project will be that we are 'genetically laid bare as never before'.[6] This phrase encapsulates neatly the vulnerability which can flow from genetic knowledge. Although there is much to be welcomed in the so-called genetic revolution, it is perhaps unsurprising that much of the debate and discussion surrounding it has been what one commentator described as 'portentous, laden with apprehension and distrust'.[7] Without encouraging people into becoming scientific Luddites, there are genuine reasons for concern about the present and the future of genetics. As Kevles says, 'Given that changes in individual attitudes inevitably affect the scope of institutional action, both public and private, history surely teaches that serious attention is owed the warnings, however shrill they may sometimes be, of the dissenters from the eugenic revival.'[8]

For some, the outcome of the Genome Project is merely knowledge — often regarded as value-neutral. For example, Brenner says, '[w]hat is most important about the enterprise is the scientific knowledge that it will generate, and the insights it will give us into our structure, function and origins.'[9] Others, however, hold that it would be naïve in the extreme either to believe that knowledge is value-free or to imagine that, once gained, it will not be used.[10] It is the latter perspective which excites most controversy and has engendered considerable debate.

This is not the first medical miracle to generate concerns. Assisted reproduction also spawned a wealth of literature, much of it critical, generally from those not involved in the enterprise.[11] Charlesworth draws a parallel here, noting that 'Feminist critics of the new reproductive technologies have shown how difficult it is to divorce these technologies from their ideological contexts, and the same is true of genetics and genetic technologies.'[12] Thus, it is essential that the *drive* for

---

5   cf T. Friedmann, 'Opinion: The Human Genome Project — Some Implications of Extensive "Reverse Genetic" Medicine' (1990) 46 *Am J Hum Genet* 408, 411: '... there remains a serious gap between disease characterization and treatment.'

6   J.C. Fletcher and D.C. Wertz, 'An International Code of Ethics in Medical Genetics Before the Human Genome is Mapped', in Z. Bankowski and A. Capron (eds), *Genetics, Ethics and Human Values: Human Genome Mapping, Genetic Screening and Therapy*, xxiv CIOMS Round Table Conference, 1991, 97.

7   J. Maddox, 'New Genetics Means No New Ethics', *Nature*, Vol. 364, 8 July 1993, 97, 97.

8   D. Kevles, *In the Name of Eugenics: Genetics and The Uses of Human Heredity* (Harmondsworth: Penguin, 1985) 299.

9   S. Brenner, 'The Human Genome: the Nature of the Enterprise', in *Human Genetic Information: Science, Law and Ethics*, Ciba Foundation Symposium 149 (Chichester: John Wiley & Sons, 1990) 6.

10 S.A.M. McLean, 'Mapping the Human Genome — Friend or Foe?' (1994) 39(9) *Soc Sci Med* 1221.

11 cf G. Corea, *The Mother Machine: Reproductive Technologies From Artificial Insemination to Artificial Wombs* (London: The Women's Press, 1988).

12 M. Charlesworth, 'Human Genome Analysis and the Concept of Human Nature' in Ciba Foundation, n 9 above, 188.

knowledge is analysed as thoroughly as is its *outcome*. Even an apparently beneficial result may perpetuate or generate dubious ethical values. The critics of assisted reproduction have one thing in common — each of them identifies the extent to which the reproduction revolution serves to perpetuate a particular view of women — one which, for them, is unhealthy. Helping the infertile to reproduce has resulted, they would claim, in reinforcement of the view of women as mothers first and foremost, slaves to their biology, and has strengthened a male dominated view of the 'proper' shape of society. In addition, it can be argued that the promise that assisted reproduction holds out choice can all too easily become a metaphor for compulsion; that the existence of the option to reproduce can easily degenerate into a pressure to do so.

Genetic knowledge may plausibly have similar results, not least in that the availability of information might lead to a perceived obligation to access it. The range of topics discussed in this volume shows the extent to which the mere holding, never mind use, of genetic information has the capacity to pose profound ethical and legal problems. From the ethical perspective it is often suggested that these dilemmas are not new, as if this in some way makes them easier to resolve. Murray, for example, says:

> From the standpoint of bioethics, research on the human genome presents no completely novel ethical questions, at least for now. That is partly because of the nature of new ethical questions, which typically are variants of ethical questions that scholars and others have wrestled with before. This embeddedness of questions in experience with analogous questions means that we do not have to invent every response totally anew, but rather can draw on the history of scholarly analysis that has come before.[13]

However, even if true, this is little comfort given the history of societies which have failed so consistently either to solve ethical riddles or to act upon answers once identified.

The drive to find genetic causes and correlations for behavioural and medical characteristics is one which surely cannot be stopped. However, if knowledge translated into practice is not to pose a serious threat to at least some individuals and groups within communities, it is essential that fundamental questions are addressed. The identification of the values which inform a civilised world will be necessary if we are to control and adequately regulate the use of genetic knowledge.

Of course, it may well be argued that control is unnecessary; that we are and should be free to use knowledge as we choose, and that the only reasons for dissension from this position have their roots in paternalism or ignorance. Individuals, it may be said, are demeaned by any attempt to control what they know or can know, and those who seek control are merely interfering in the liberty of others. In an ideal world this view has much to commend it. However, in the real world, recent history has shown how foolish we would be to act upon it.

No matter the political structure, no matter the checks and balances which exist, no community can be complacent about its ability to neutralise all potential harm. Countries which appear wedded to civil liberties and which seem to guarantee individual freedoms and control of abuse by the State are not necessarily resistant to ideologies with the opposite effect. In the early part of this century, for example, elementary genetic knowledge was used in countries like the United States to support and encourage programmes of compulsory sterilisation, and to tighten immigration and other laws to the disadvantage of individuals and groups seen as

---

13   T.H. Murray, 'Ethical Issues in Human Genome Research' (1991) 5 *The FASEB Journal* 55, 55.

being 'undesirable'.[14] Cases such as *Buck* v *Bell*[15] found the Supreme Court backing non-consensual sterilisation in the alleged interests of the State and to the detriment of individual liberty. The well-documented pogroms of the Nazi era were not all new, but rather followed on the heels of coercive and demeaning behaviour in so-called liberal western democracies, who made the basic mistake of equating genetic inheritance with fundamental human worth.

It is the recreation of this misconception that initially poses the greatest possibility for misuse of genetics. In a culture dominated by the scientific, it may well be tempting to assume that scientific respectability implies moral and ethical neutrality, yet to do so would not merely be inappropriately to divest ourselves of responsibility for ourselves and others but would open the door to wholesale reductionism; to a denial of what it is to be human and to the discarding of what it is that makes humans worthy of respect. While it is true that '[h]umanity cannot be cut adrift from its own biology ... ',[16] it must also be remembered that '... neither is it enchained by it.'[17]

A preliminary to any assessment of the impact of intervention in the human genome must, therefore, be consideration of what genetics actually tells us about ourselves and others. This enquiry must be conducted in an atmosphere of healthy scepticism but free from the excesses of rhetoric which blunt the edges of the issues and lead to the triumph of the superficial over the thoughtful.

But this enquiry is intriguingly hard to formulate and generally difficult to evaluate. The reason for this lies in a number of factors, all of which taken together render the search for answers extremely difficult. Indeed, we may not even know the questions. But this does not mean that we are disenfranchised, nor is it solely a consequence of our limited knowledge of molecular biology. Rather it is a challenge to our sophistication — intellectual and ethical — and a consequence of the complexity of the issues. But it is this enquiry which will ultimately form the basis of any considered approach to the future of genetics and its impact on individuals and their communities.

Whether or not one views the genetic revolution as benign, evil or neutral, one thing is clear: there is a perceived need to master and control the Leviathan which genetic science is creating.[18] Equally, attempts to regulate genetic knowledge and techniques to maximise the benefits and minimise the potential harms must take place in an atmosphere, and from a perspective, which show balance and intellectual rigour. As has been said:

> We must be aware of the possible uses and misuses that may be made of biotechnology in the future ... but it distorts our thinking about the moral or human implications of genetic therapy and other forms of biotechnology if we always discuss them in terms of extreme and unreal possibilities. These exaggerated scenarios make imaginative science fiction and sensational journalism and exciting polemic, but they do not help to advance the truth.[19]

Of fundamental concern is the extent to which genetics may threaten expressed common goals of equality and non-discrimination. Our recent past, already

---

14   For discussion, see S.A.M. McLean, 'The Right to Reproduce', in T. Campbell *et al* (eds), *Human Rights: From Rhetoric to Reality* (Oxford: Basil Blackwell, 1986).
15   *Buck* v *Bell* (1927) US 200.
16   S. Rose, L. Kamin, R. Lewontin, *Not in Our Genes: Biology, Ideology and Human Nature* (Harmondsworth: Penguin, 1984) 10.
17   *ibid.*
18   cf L. Skene, n 5 above; S.A.M. McLean, n 10 above; S.A.M. McLean and D. Giesen, 'Legal and Ethical Considerations of the Human Genome Project' (1994) 1 *Medical Law International* 159.
19   M. Charlesworth, n 12 above.

referred to, has shown the extent to which genetic knowledge has been used as a political tool to disbar members of communities from equality before the law. It is the potential challenge to the inherent respect to which we are all entitled that underpins the occasionally apprehensive way in which we address genetics. However, some would disregard this fear, claiming that, '[t]he reality of the use of a detailed knowledge of the human genome in discrimination between people is ... almost certainly more distant than the fear.'[20] Comforting, if true, but certainly not susceptible of proof. Rather more resonance may be found in Murray's analysis: '[t]he sciences of inequality, with genetics at the forefront, will force us to reinterpret what equal treatment and equal regard mean in an enormous range of contexts.'[21] The outcome of this reinterpretation need not be bad, but it will present a real challenge.

This problem, of course, may arguably exist in all instances of ill-health or disability. The individual who becomes ill or who is disabled may well be the subject of discrimination, whether or not because of the nature of their condition (for example, HIV and AIDS) or because of the mere fact of its existence. However, genetic diagnoses postulate the potential for discrimination and disenfranchisement much more acutely, perhaps because they are less well understood or because they are more intimate to how we perceive ourselves. The Danish Council of Ethics[22] identified the kind of problems which can result from genetic, as opposed to other health related, information. They say:

> Just as people found through screening to have a particular gene or chromosome composition may happen to feel abnormal or outright ill ... so may others react to the persons involved by giving them a wide berth. The detection of certain genetic traits can thus form the basis for branding certain persons and groups among the population, with the possibility of discrimination proper as a result.[23]

This postulates two disabling consequences. The first is the adoption of the sick role, perhaps based on ignorance of the meaning of the genetic information. This may be especially true for those who are carriers of a genetic condition. These people do not suffer from the condition and their only genetic risk in life is that, should they choose to procreate with another carrier, they run a statistical risk that their children will suffer from the particular condition. Yet there is widespread ignorance of this fact. Skene notes that, 'In a pilot screening project in Greece, carriers of the gene that causes sickle cell disease were stigmatised by their community and considered ineligible for marriage, except to other carriers.'[24] Of course, the outcome of this would have not have been protective, but would rather have *raised* the risk to children of being born with that condition.

Secondly, there emerges again the general concept of discrimination — what the Danish Council of Ethics called 'branding'. Only a true understanding of what genetic information tells us will assist in ensuring that discrimination does not follow genetic diagnosis. This, in large part, is the responsibility of the scientists themselves.

Interestingly, virtually every report which has been issued in recent years on the subject of genetics has emphasised the importance of education — not to try to make us all experts in molecular biology but rather to ensure that the ethical and

---

20 J. Maddox, 'The Case for the Human Genome' *Nature* Vol 352, 4 July 1991, 11, 11.
21 Murray, n 13 above, 60.
22 *Ethics and Mapping of the Human Genome*, Copenhagen, 1993.
23 *ibid* 60.
24 n 18 above, 238.

scientific issues are exposed and where possible clarified and understood.[25] Scientists will play a major role in achieving this. As Davis says: '[t]o promote a healthy relationship between scientists and the rest of society it is important for scientists to try to educate the public on the limits, as well as the dazzling promise, of our new power to manipulate genes.'[26] This general view is echoed by the British Medical Association which puts it this way:

> ...[w]e believe that ... fears are largely unfounded, but combating them by adopting a paternalistic or secretive approach is not the answer. Instead, the scientific community, both in academia and commerce, has a duty to inform the general public of new developments in the application of genetic information in a manner comprehensible to lay people.[27]

But even if public education is undertaken, there remain fundamental concerns about the ideology of genetics, and of the industries which will control it. The Genome Project has the potential to pit individual against individual and community against community. At a community level this is most acutely seen in the control over genetic exploration which is held by the rich world. Perhaps inevitably this is a Project dominated by that world. It is not unreasonable, therefore, to speculate that the knowledge gained from mapping the human genome will be skewed towards its concerns. These concerns may be economic or social, but they may result in the further distancing of rich world from poor. For example, confronted with the whole genetic map, it may be tempting to concentrate energies — in terms of searching for therapies — on the preoccupations of the rich, at the expense of the poor, who represent a market not yet sufficiently wealthy to provide adequate returns for the industries which will market and exploit the science. Yet, it must also be noted that, '[e]asily 75% of the human genome is in the possession of those inhabitants of this globe who live in developing countries. It seems evident that these peoples and the nations to which they belong have a stake in the human genome project.'[28]

Rich pickings are to be had from the products which ride on the back of the genetic revolution. As Gannon *et al* have said: 'It is estimated that by the year 2010 products derived from the genome project may account for drug sales of $60 billion p.a.; half the international pharmaceutical industry's sales for 1992. Those who control such sales stand to secure considerable financial returns in the decades after the work of the project has been completed.'[29] However philanthropic the intention of scientists may be, the profit motive cannot be ignored and the BMA amongst others has expressed its concern that the enormous commercial benefits of genetics and in particular genetic therapies, may threaten or dissipate the collaborative nature of scientific research.[30] Moreover, scientists may be driven by financial considerations which are unrelated to personal profit but which rather stem from the non-availability or limited availability of research funding. As has been said:

---

25   BMA, n 3 above; *Ethical Issues in Clinical Genetics*, Royal College of Physicians of London, 1991; Nuffield Council on Bioethics, *Genetic Screening: Ethical Issues*, London 1993.

26   B.D. Davis, 'Limits to Genetic Intervention in Humans: Somatic and Germline' in Ciba Foundation Symposium, n 9 above, 81, 86.

27   BMA, n 3 above, 227–228.

28   V.A. McCusick, 'First South-North Human Genome Conference', (1992) 14 *Genomics* 1121, 1121.

29   P. Gannon, T. Guthrie and G. Laurie, 'Patents, Morality and DNA: Should there be intellectual property protection of the Human Genome Project?' (1995) 1 *Medical Law International* 321, 322.

30   BMA, n 3 above, 172: 'The accelerating transformation of scientific and technological research and knowledge into marketable commodities, not just in genetic modification but in other fields too, is undermining many of the traditional and desirable aspects of scientific work and collaboration.'

... if the government permits, and even provokes by lack of funding, a situation where basic research, including genetic research, is undertaken in commercially oriented laboratories, this can result in knowledge of the human genome being owned partially, and at least temporarily, by private individuals. Such circumstances are potentially dangerous because knowledge is closely associated with power and because ... knowledge and the power associated with it are uncontrollable.[31]

In addition, of course, for some, profit-making from the very essence of our humanity strikes a somewhat sour note.

In particular, the Human Genome Diversity Project has raised profound ethical concerns about what it tells us of the Western World's attitude to ethnic minorities. Describing this project, Wilkie says: '[t]he idea is to create a global map of human genetic variation, by analysing and comparing thousands of DNA samples from more than 500 different ethnic groups, including many ... that are on the verge of extinction.'[32] Doubtless an interesting scientific venture, but as Wilkie also notes, one which has become 'mired in controversy'.[33] As he says: 'Many of these peoples face physical or cultural extinction. Yet the scientists are not flying in to save human beings, merely to take DNA samples for preservation in laboratories in the USA and Europe.'[34]

The Diversity Project is a form of genetic archaeology, with the difference that the subjects are alive in the present day. Indeed the entire human genome project can be described in this way. For Bodmer and McKie, for example, '[s]tandard archaeology is a process for dealing with the dead and the fossilized. The startling feature about its genetic equivalent is that it deals very much with the living, with the very DNA that controls the behaviour of each of our cells. In other words, instead of using the fossilized past as a window on the present, genetics allows us to use the living present to understand the past.'[35] Clearly, this is an exciting prospect and one which has considerable support from within and outside of the scientific community. However, the Diversity Project, arguably, shows up the harsh side of this archaeology and may yet become what Wilkie describes as '... the latest episode in a long history of cultural imperialism and exploitation.'[36]

But it is not only these peoples who may find that genetics is a double-edged sword. Even for those in the rich world, it is clear that everything from basic survival to status may be affected by genetic knowledge. Our genetic inheritance may predict whether we are conceived, implanted or carried to term. It may also predict how we live our lives, how we view ourselves, our relationships with family and many others, and affect how we make decisions at the end of our lives. Employers, insurers, the state and our siblings, children and parents all have an interest in whatever genetic knowledge we may hold about ourselves, whilst we may equally wish to claim an interest in genetic privacy or even a right not to know genetic information. The tensions which emerge from these potentially irreconcilable interests have the potential to pit individual rights and interests against those of others. For example, as Suter notes, '... when genetic testing of one person can benefit another family member, privacy and autonomy interests of

---

31 J. Schmidtke, 'Who Owns the Human Genome? Ethical and Legal Aspects' *J Pharm Pharmacol* 44 (Suppl 1) 205, 205–206.
32 T. Wilkie, 'Gene Hunters' Channel 4, 26 February 1995, published by Channel 4 Television, London, 8.
33 *ibid* 8.
34 *ibid*.
35 n 2 above, 161–162.
36 n 32 above, 11.

the former may collide with the relative's interests in protecting her health or planning her future.'[37]

Fears about the uses or misuses of genetic information will recede as scientific enquiry leads to therapeutic options. But it would be naïve to assume that they will (or should) entirely disappear. It may always be realistic to view these advances with a healthy scepticism given that they have such enormous potential to challenge previous attitudes to personal integrity, liberty and respect for persons. Most acutely, the potential for misuse or abuse can be seen in the area of reproductive choice. For more than a century, reproductive liberty has been a central platform of the women's movement in particular, but of all libertarians in general.[38] From the early struggles of women to obtain legal access to contraception, through some landmark rulings in the Supreme Court of the United States, to the 'pro-choice' lobby in the abortion debate, the right to make uncoerced, mature, responsible and private decisions about when or whether to reproduce has been critical to the place of women in their community. Yet women are also vulnerable biologically and psychologically to the sometimes competing interests they may hold in the welfare of future children or actual embryos/ foetuses. In addition, they may also be subject to external pressures to discover otherwise unwanted information. As Berg says:

> ... choosing not to know [genetic status] would be ethically questionable if the choice to remain ignorant could have serious consequences for a third party such as the spouse or prospective spouse. Nobody should be brought into a situation where they unknowingly give birth to offspring with a very high risk of contracting a serious disease, if full information and options such as prenatal diagnosis could have been made available.[39]

Genetic information has the potential to affect reproductive choice before pregnancy is even embarked upon. This may be for the good, in that it can assist prospective parents to make an informed decision about whether to reproduce, or whether to take advantage of screening programmes in the course of an established pregnancy. However, it may also encourage the discarding of the less than perfect, leading to the fear that only 'designer babies' will be welcomed. It is, of course, entirely intelligible that intending parents seek to achieve the best possible quality of health for their future children. Few would deliberately choose to have a child suffering from a disabling or life-threatening condition. Accidents of nature, in the form of unexpected illness, may be unavoidable, but the transmission of genetic disorders is not. As scientists are able with greater accuracy to pinpoint the gene which expresses for a particular condition, intending parents may be offered the opportunity to avoid the birth of a child suffering from such a potential disability. This can be done at various stages using pre-implantation diagnosis or pre-natal screening.

Assisted reproductive techniques which can create embryos in a petri dish, can and do provide the opportunity for selection of embryos before they are implanted in the womb. The more we can identify genetic disorders, the more apparent choice we can give to couples involved in IVF programmes. And as the success rate of IVF improves, some genetically at risk but otherwise fertile couples may choose this as an option when they have reason to be concerned about their genetic inheritance.

---

37 S.M. Suter, 'Whose Genes Are These Anyway? Familial Conflicts over Access to Genetic Information' (1993) 91 *Michigan Law Review* 1854, 1855.

38 S.A.M. McLean, n 14 above.

39 K. Berg, 'Confidentiality Issues in Medical Genetics: The Need for Laws, Rules and Good Practices to Secure Optimal Disease Control' Council of Europe, CDBI-SY-SP(93)3, Strasbourg, 5 October 1993, 5.

At one level this seems unproblematic. Why should not people have the maximum available information on which to base their reproductive choices? Might it not be seen as irresponsible not to take advantage of the fullest possible set of facts before embarking on a pregnancy? And surely, it is folly not to use knowledge when it is or could be there? Buried in these questions are, of course, a number of presumptions which require consideration. It would be counter-intuitive to argue that there is some value in withholding relevant information from people embarking on a pregnancy, yet the quality of that information is also important, although this point is often ignored. Genetics can tell us something about the likelihood of the development of certain conditions, but it is seldom able to do so with complete accuracy. The scientific certainty which comes from genetic knowledge may well be exaggerated, yet it is doubtful if those apparently exercising a choice are adequately informed as to this possibility. Even in single gene disorders, where the future person will inevitably contract the condition if they have the gene, the mere fact that this is so tells us nothing about the timing or severity of onset. Thus, a decision not to implant an embryo which carries the gene for Huntington's Disease can be open to ethical question, particularly as this is a late-onset condition for which therapy may have become available by the time the child-to-be ever begins to suffer from it. Equally, many genetic conditions are multi-factorial, meaning that the emergence of the condition is considerably less certain. In receiving and utilising this kind of information, individuals are required to undertake a complex calculation of risk, for which they may be as yet inadequately prepared. Yet the consequence of these decisions may be the destruction of one or more embryos.

Clearly, selection at this stage is likely to be less contentious than the abortion of an embryo after implantation but it can scarcely be said to be morally neutral. Indeed, the moral quality of this decision may in part depend on the extent to which it was taken by individuals who understand the information provided. Clearly, the individual doctor cannot be expected to guarantee understanding, but this point reinforces the need for education and raises once again doubts about the value of offering choices which are not in fact real. Yet, driven by the imperative to know, science continues to throw up information which may ultimately confuse rather than enlighten. When moral decisions of such import are made on the back of this, there is reason for concern. It must be said, however, that this is not an argument for not disclosing information — rather it is a caution about seeking information in the first place, and about taking care that it is appropriately disseminated. Indeed, in this as in many other areas of medical practice, it may be that this is an argument for greater communication of information so long as those imparting it have the skills necessary to do so. Genetics on this view may serve positively to reinforce the individual's rights by re-emphasising the need for effective, full and intelligible disclosure.[40]

Other issues arise when the condition is not late-onset — that is, where the problems will manifest themselves on birth. Whereas the issues raised by decisions about late-onset disorders relate in large part to the full understanding of the likelihood of suffering from the condition, and the potentially full life which may be denied by the decision not to proceed with a pregnancy, here the ethical question relates more to whether or not by permitting embryo destruction on this

---

40 For discussion of the need to make full disclosure, see S.A.M. McLean, *Information Disclosure, the Doctor and the Law* (Aldershot: Dartmouth Publishing, 1989); J.K. Mason and R.A. McCall Smith, *Law and Medical Ethics* (4th ed) (London: Butterworths, 1994).

basis we are indirectly or directly making a value-laden statement about those who are already alive and have the condition. This is a peculiarly difficult conundrum to resolve.

It may be argued that we disvalue born sufferers of a condition if we are ready to discard similarly affected potential people, and for some — perhaps particularly those already afflicted — it may be felt that the relative ease with which we can dispose of an affected embryo makes a clear statement about their own lack of worth. Clearly, this is a real risk and has enormous emotional and societal overtones. On the other hand, it could equally be argued that we are actually saying *nothing* about these people when making decisions not to proceed with an affected pregnancy. Rather, we are simply expanding choice — a value which is weightier than an amorphous fear that we will hurt other people's feelings. In addition, it might be thought wrong to over-emphasise the concern that we are disvaluing others if the outcome is that prospective parents are not offered this choice. Resolution of this issue requires that the values involved are adequately identified and weighted. If choice trumps potential discrimination, then it will be necessary to live with the consequences for actual sufferers of the specific condition. However, this merely reinforces the need for the choice to be properly informed.

Additional problems are, however, posed when the information about genetic disorder comes to light in the course of an established pregnancy. What has been described as an 'evangelistic fervour'[41] for screening is likely to be enhanced by the possibility of detecting ever more genetic disorders pre-natally, with the anticipated outcome that an affected pregnancy will be terminated. One US example serves to illustrate the potential problems here.[42] A woman whose foetus was found to have the gene for cystic fibrosis was informed by her Health Management Organisation (essentially her health insurers) that they would pay out on her policy for the costs of a termination but would not pay for health care costs associated with continuing the pregnancy. Only the threat of litigation forced them to back down. Clearly, the funding of health care is different in the US from much of health care provision in the United Kingdom, but the interest lies not in the economics of the situation, but rather in the assumptions underpinning the HMO's attitude and the coercive nature of their response. In this case, genetic information could be said to have served to reduce rather than enhance reproductive liberty. In another example, it is reported that some women in the United States are terminating pregnancies '... because physicians have diagnosed a chromosomal irregularity, even though no one can say whether this irregularity would have noticeable effects.'[43]

Nor can it be assumed that these will necessarily be isolated incidents. When information is available, it may be felt that there is an obligation to use it in a particular way. Already, pre-natal screening programmes have at their core the expectation that a 'bad' result will lead to termination of the affected pregnancy. Where women will not countenance abortion, they may not be offered the tests in the first place. Genetics will be able to pinpoint potential problems with increased regularity, potentially resulting in an increase in abortion decisions. Whilst it is not the intention here to argue for restriction of the freedoms women have to make such a decision, it must be seen that the increased capacity to detect 'problems' pre-natally adds to the dilemmas facing pregnant women, for whom abortion is

41 D. Stone and S. Stewart (eds), *Towards a Screening Strategy for Scotland* (Glasgow: Scottish Forum for Public Health Medicine, 1994) 45.

42 P. Elmer-Dewitt, 'The Genetic Revolution' *Time* January 17 1994, No 3, 39.

43 R. Hubbard and E. Wald, *Exploding the Gene Myth* (Boston: Beacon Press, 1993) 30.

seldom morally or ethically a clear-cut and painless decision. However, again it might be argued that this information is enhancing liberty and as such it is a 'good' thing. Certainly, women (and their partners) may have very good reasons to avoid the birth of a child suffering (or likely to suffer) from a particular condition and this is a matter of personal and private choice. But the real concern here is not that more embryos or foetuses will be aborted as a result of the lawful decision of a woman, but rather that pressure may come to be placed on women to make a *particular* choice.

Just as it has been noted that existing pre-natal screening programmes have at their base the expectation that abortion will follow an adverse result, so too it is easy to see the extent to which this may become an obligation rather than an expectation. The mind-set behind screening may impose private obligations which become part of public policy. Thus, it is increasingly plausible to argue that knowledge imposes obligations, and these obligations may well be defined so as yet again to reduce choice. As Whittaker points out '[w]ith the availability of genetic tests, bringing an affected child into the world could be construed by some as reproductive irresponsibility.'[44] This irresponsibility may be in respect of the child if born, or in respect of the community whose scarce resources will be used to support that child through its disability.

However, not only might those who choose to proceed with an affected pregnancy find themselves accused of being irresponsible, either to their child or to the community as a whole, their behaviour may be seen to contravene another emerging concept, that of intergenerational justice. As Fletcher and Wertz put it: '[t]he completion of the human genome project will provide a basis for acting on a moral obligation for *future* generations, a claim that has appeared weak in the past. A generation *with* such knowledge who neglected to use it to minimize the risks in reproduction could hardly be said to respect the requirements of intergenerational justice.'[45] Yet what is this concept actually telling us? Essentially, its core message is that you may not choose to want or have a child with disabilities; that you are harming either that child or your community by bringing it into the world and allowing it to perpetuate its genetic inheritance throughout future generations. As the Nuffield Council on Bioethics has said: '[i]t has been argued that the availability of prenatal screening and diagnosis, together with the termination of seriously affected pregnancies, both reflect and reinforce the negative attitudes of our society towards those with disabilities. Indeed, medical genetics may add a new dimension if genetic disorder came to be seen as a matter of choice rather than of fate.'[46]

Of course, the pressure to make certain reproductive choices may also be an entirely personal one. As has already been said, few people, if any, would prefer to have a child who may have a short or unhappy life. This is not necessarily about the search for the perfect baby but rather the natural desire of prospective parents to secure the best future for themselves and their children. But it may also serve to add public pressure to this most private of decisions. As in the United States in the early part of this century, and in other countries also, '[p]rivate decision-making in the realm of genetic disorder and disease may ultimately lead to public consequences, and thus to demands for public regulation of reproductive

---

44 L.A. Whittaker, 'The Implications of the Human Genome Project for Family Practice' *Journal of Family Practice* Vol 35, no 3, 294, 296.
45 n 6 above, 103.
46 n 25 above, 77, para 8.11.

behaviour. A sizeable number of people may argue that the right to have genetically diseased children, or even to transmit deleterious genes to future generations, must be limited or denied.'[47] Not only does this inhibit reproductive liberty in ways which may seem ethically dubious, but it also creates a future society in which the gene pool has been deliberately manipulated with unforeseen and unforeseeable consequences.

The ability to diagnose is, for the moment, very much greater than is the ability to treat. As genetic science advances, and clinical skills improve, it may well be that the rationale for screening changes from selecting out affected embryos/ foetuses to identifying those for whom therapy before or after birth is needed. The latter raises few obvious problems — genetic therapy may well become the treatment of choice in the future and it is in any event virtually indistinguishable from any other form of medical intervention, so long as it is somatic and not germ-line; that is, so long as it affects only the individual concerned and the immediate condition and is not affecting the reproductive cells. For the moment, the latter is generally outlawed, whilst the former is accepted. Although there is some debate on this distinction, consideration of it here is not essential. What is important here is the consequences of the development of foetal therapy.

Yet again, there are two distinct approaches to this issue which cannot readily be reconciled. On the one hand, there is much reason to welcome the development of foetal therapy. It may, for example, be the case that in some conditions the timing of the therapeutic intervention is crucial to the outcome. The capacity to treat before birth may save considerable potential suffering, both emotional and physical, for the future child and its parents. In addition, Kand says: '[t]he possibility of treatment would spare many women (who might otherwise have contemplated the possibility of abortion) the agonising choice between going through the ordeal of having an abortion and loosing [sic] a child or giving birth to a child facing a life, the length and quality of which would be affected by illness and suffering.'[48] Assuming foetal therapy to be successful, most prospective parents would, therefore, probably choose it.

However, the other dimension to the availability of foetal therapy cannot be ignored. Inevitably, intervention in the foetus requires intervention in the woman. There is no alternative in treating the foetus but that the woman's body is invaded. For many, if not most, women, this will be unproblematic. For others, however, it will be unacceptable. Moreover, the capacity to treat in the womb poses stark ethical questions for doctors who may take themselves to have two patients (woman and foetus) rather than simply one (woman). As Mattingley says: '... elevation of the fetus to patient status has occurred not because of any change in the fetus or in the maternal-fetal relationship but because of a change in physicians — in how they think about and relate to their patients during pregnancy ... .'[49] Once again, the capacities of modern diagnostics and therapeutics raise dilemmas whose resolution is far from simple.

These problems are generally encapsulated within the concept of maternal/foetal conflict, a term which suggests, perhaps misleadingly, some hostility between the parties — presumably, therefore, hostility from the woman to the foetus, since the

47   D. Kevles, n 8 above, 300.
48   A.S.F. Kand, 'The New Gene Technology and the Difference Between Getting Rid of Illness and Altering People' *Eur J Gen Soc* 1995 Vol 1m, No 1, 12, 12.
49   S.S. Mattingley, 'The Maternal-Fetal Dyad: Exploring the Two-Patient Obstetric Model' 22, *Hastings Center Report*, 13.

foetus is incapable of such emotions.[50] Yet women may have many reasons, rational or otherwise for refusing medical intervention in their bodies, even for the benefit of the foetus. Indeed, it is clear that no individual, male or female, will generally be expected to undergo treatment on behalf of a third party, even where that person is born. The US case of *McFall* v *Shimp*[51] makes this perfectly clear. Morally, we may disapprove of the person who refuses to take a risk to assist another, but legally we should be most reluctant to force them to do so. There is as yet no legal imperative to rescue another. And, of course, in the instant case, there is in any event no other legal person to whom a duty might be owed. Whilst the embryo/foetus of the human species may, as the Committee of Inquiry into Human Fertilisation and Embryology (Warnock Report)[52] put it, be worthy of some respect, this somewhat vague assertion is as far as we can go. Certainly, it is clear in law that foetuses have no rights until live birth.[53] Yet, recent court decisions in the UK and elsewhere have shown that there is an increasing tendency to elevate the foetus from a non-legal person with no rights to an entity which has interests if not rights — interests which may be used to defeat the choice of a woman who would otherwise be deemed competent to make her own decisions.

There are many reasons for concern at this development in the law, many of which have been rehearsed elsewhere, but they nonetheless merit some reappraisal in the light of the new genetics. It has already been suggested that the genetic revolution, which has the undoubted potential to enhance reproductive choice by informing intending couples of potential hazards, also has the capacity to reduce it. In part, this is because of the pressure — social, emotional or clinical — which may be put on a woman to make a *particular* choice rather than necessarily the one which she might make otherwise. And, as has been noted, the obligation of intergenerational justice may also be used here as a rationale for emotionally (or even physically) coercing a woman into accepting treatment on behalf of her foetus.

Naturally, for many women, this will be unproblematic. It has already been conceded that the desire to have a healthy child is entirely intelligible, and many women will seek to achieve this both for their own sakes and for those of their potential children. However, this may not be universally the case, as has already been seen in other situations. Cases such as *Re S*,[54] *Re MB*[55] and *Re AC*[56] show all too clearly that for some women the choice of foetus over self is not always self-evident. The last case, a United States decision, perhaps shows most acutely the poignancy which often accompanies the choice which faces some, mercifully few, women.

In this case, a young woman (Angela Carder) was terminally ill with leukaemia and pregnant. Initially, she was prepared to sacrifice her own comfort for the well-being of the foetus, on the understanding that the foetus might have a chance of survival if the pregnancy continued for another few weeks. Ultimately, the doctors concluded that foetal survival (albeit with little real hope of achieving this)

---

50 For further discussion, see S.A.M. McLean, 'Moral Status (Who or What Counts?)', in S. Bewley and R. Humphry Ward (eds), *Ethics in Obstetrics and Gynaecology* (London: RCOG Press, 1994); L.B. McCullough and F.A. Chervenak, *Ethics in Obstetrics and Gynaecology* (Oxford: Oxford University Press, 1994).

51 *McFall* v *Shimp* 10 Pa D & C 3d (Allegheny County Ct 1978).

52 Cmnd 9314 (London: HMSO, 1984).

53 cf *Hamilton* v *Fife Health Board* 1993 SLT 624; (1993) 4 Med L R 201.

54 *Re S (Adult: Refusal of Medical Treatment)* [1992] 4 All ER 671.

55 *Re MB* (1997) 38 BMLR 175 (CA); [1997] Fam. Law 542.

56 *Re AC* 533 A 2d 611 (DC, 1987); *Re AC* 573 A 2d 1235 (DC, 1990).

depended on Mrs Carder agreeing to undergo a caesarian section. This she expressed herself unwilling to do. The response to this dying woman's competently expressed refusal was to obtain a court order forcing the caesarian upon her. Neither she nor the foetus survived. On appeal, it was held that such intervention should not have been undertaken, but the desire to do this, and the willingness of the first judge to authorise it, show the extent to which the potential interests of the foetus were taken as being of primary concern, rather than prioritising the rights of the woman. The recent decision in *Re S*[57] in the UK has taken a similar approach. Even though this is to be welcomed, it nonetheless follows on a number of cases, some of which have already been referred to, where the opposite conclusion was reached. Whether or not we approve of women's refusal to act in the perceived interests of their foetus, it is a fact of life that — in some of these cases — the question was unhappily resolved by the heavy-handed application of a legal process determined to protect the unborn at the expense of the born. Although obviously this is not a problem peculiar to genetics, it is one which the genetic revolution may exacerbate.

There are, of course, more general concerns which have been alluded to here, but which merit restatement. Outside of reproductive choice there is the concern that emphasis on genetics will reduce humanity to a mere collection of cells; that the nature/nurture debate will be resolved conclusively in favour of nature. Whilst it is undoubtedly important that we are aware of what it is that draws the template of what we are, the fear is that over-emphasis on that template ignores the reality of what it is to be a human being. One possible result of ignoring the other factors which shape us, of failing to consider personality, spirituality, environment or experience, is that we may simply give up a sense of responsibility for ourselves and for others. If we cannot change what we are because it is genetically programmed, why would we strive to be different or better? And why should we invest in programmes to rehabilitate others from, for example, anti-social behaviour if they too cannot change their behavioural patterns?

Identifying genes which predict disorders need not, of course, lead to the conclusion that there is nothing about people which can be changed, and indeed the search for therapies is designed, and has the capacity, to liberate people from the chains in which genetic conditions may otherwise ensnare them. However, disease characterisation is but one facet of the genetic revolution. Increasingly, other characteristics are being given genetic labels. Thus, behavioural patterns such as criminality, alcoholism and so on may be seen as genetically programmed, with all of the implications this may have for the status of the human being. As Murray says '... both scientists and the public may become too eager to embrace genetic explanations for a vast range of ethically significant phenomena.'[58] The dangers of this are obvious — not only would genetics reduce people to pre-ordained automata, but reproductive choices may also be used to screen out people thought to be undesirable in an unfortunate mimicry of the eugenic abuses of the earlier part of this century.

In effect, concern must remain that genetic information will be used or misused to construct a theory of what it is to be human which radically alters our perceptions of free will and human dignity. It is generally held to be the capacity for rationality and freedom of choice which marks human beings out as distinct from other species on the planet. The conclusion that people are defined by their

---

57   *R* v *Collins & Others, ex p S* Times Law Reports, 8 May 1998.
58   n 13 above, 59.

genes would require a radical revision of our successes as well as our failures. Moreover, it would reduce humanity to a set of predetermined and unchallengeable characteristics, removing spirit and adventure from our lives. And, of course, the drive would then be on to find ways of modifying or enhancing these people with all of the concerns which have already been expressed being multiplied by the fact that it is no longer disease but rather humanity itself that we are seeking to change.

This may not be a negative thing, but it does change the emphasis of science and medicine from therapy to enhancement. However, even if permissible, we must be cautious. As Engelhardt says, '...there is nothing sacrosanct about human nature ... we persons are free to refashion it, so long as we do so prudently....'[59] However, as he also points out, '...the radical refashioning of human nature is likely to change the content of the virtues that mark human life.'[60] These concerns have also troubled commentators such as Max Charlesworth who offers this caution:

> All attempts to erect theories of morality or theories of human nature on the basis of pure reason must fail because human beings are animals and not disembodied angels. Equally, attempts to construct a theory of human nature on the basis of biology and genetics must also fail, because human beings are meaning-making animals who use their biological and genetic endowments for their own purposes.[61]

From the legal perspective, of course, one major issue is whether regulation of genetics can or should be undertaken, and if so, in what form. The problems pointed to in this and other papers show that a legal response will not be easy. Yet, as Diana Brahams has said: '[s]ociety will expect the law to protect its wider ideals and, in particular, the individual citizen, from the excesses of over-enthusiastic doctors and scientists, greedy corporations and immoral profiteers and manipulators. The law will have to balance the need for future research against the need to protect society from its dangers and evils.'[62]

But this begs the question of the nature of the legal response. For some, like the British Medical Association, the law's relevance is in being reactive rather than proactive.[63] This, they consider, is more likely to produce responses which are relevant to advances, and which do not become too readily outmoded in the light of scientific progress and expanding knowledge. There is much sense in this, of course. However, this approach also presumes that the law should or will respond only in a piecemeal, even draconian, fashion. Lawmaking can come in a variety of forms which need not be inflexibly detailed. An appropriate regime might be one which establishes structures within which flexibility is possible, thus on the one hand providing the ability to monitor, police and license while on the other accommodating changing knowledge and capacity.

In conclusion, we must not underestimate the ethical and legal concerns which we are now facing, nor should we presume that they will be easily dealt with. Equally, we should not allow ourselves to drown under their weight. The pace of science is fast, yet to date our response to the dilemmas it poses has been slow to develop. The imminent completion of the Human Genome Project, and the rapidity with which spin-off developments are occurring, leave little time for mature debate, yet debate is necessary. For debate to be valuable it must be firmly based in

---

59 H.T. Engelhardt, *The Foundations of Bioethics* (New York: OUP, 1986) 381.
60 *ibid.*
61 n 12 above, 188.
62 D. Brahams, 'Human Genetic Information: the Legal Implications', in Ciba Foundation Symposium, n 9 above, 111, 117.
63 BMA, n 3 above.

knowledge and understanding, engaged in without prejudice, removed from the parochialism which may obliterate or obfuscate the concerns of the poorer world, mindful of other species on the planet and driven by strength not fear. But we must also remember that '[t]he ability to manipulate genes could eventually change everything: what we eat, what we wear, how we live, how we die and how we see ourselves in relation to our fate.'[64] A great responsibility falls on the shoulders of those who create and manipulate the techniques and technologies which produce these effects, but one also falls on the community to engage with them in a manner which is informed and mature. After all, '[s]cientists are at least no better and no worse than the society of which they are a part ....'[65]

In the end, it must be borne in mind that scientists will generally only do what the community facilitates or permits. As the US Congress, House of Representatives Committee on Government Operations puts it:

> [t]he routine availability of identifiable genetic information about individuals may have effects that reach far beyond the provision of medical care. As the amount of detailed genetic information grows, society may be required to re-examine the basic principles of health and life insurance, review the rules that govern employment and hiring, reconsider the confidentiality rules that are part of the doctor-patient relationship, and in general re-assess the way in which individuals are categorised and treated in a variety of social and economic relationships.[66]

The examples in this discussion and elsewhere in this volume have shown the extent to which the juggernaut is already rolling down the hill. Mature ethical and legal responses are urgently needed if the good that genetics offers is not to be outweighed by the bad.

---

64 P. Elmer-Dewitt, n 42 above, 34.
65 J. Schmidtke, n 31 above, 205.
66 US Congress, House of Representatives, Committee on Government Operations, *Designing Genetic Information Policy: The Need for an Independent Policy Review of the Ethical, Legal, and Social Implications of the Human Genome Project* (Washington DC: Government Printing Office, 1992) 2.

Family Law and Genetics

Ruth Deech*

Historically, family law has been constructed around a core of assumptions, for example, that the husband is the father; that upbringing shapes the destiny of the children; and that nothing is known about the health and reproductive future of the couple and their children. At the end of this century, however, given the pervasiveness of interest in genetics and knowledge about our genetic make-up, we may be moving to a culture of family law based on genetic evidence and not on behaviour/responsibility. Every week we are informed by news stories that another gene has been discovered that controls some aspect of human personality. It is expected that the entire sequence of the human genome will be mapped by 2005, identifying 100,000 separate genes.[1] The impact of the knowledge that this will bring is already being felt, and not only in family law. It is plain that the insurance industry is refusing to close its eyes to the genetic knowledge given by tests. Testing for cystic fibrosis (a debilitating respiratory condition affecting one in 1,000 children) carriers may already be taken 'over the counter' for around £100. If both partners carry the gene, their offspring have a 25 per cent chance of being born with the disease. The spread of tests and the impact of their results are unlikely to be rejected. The Human Genetics Advisory Commission's suggestion in 1998 of a two-year moratorium on tests to indicate the risks of hereditary disease or illness was promptly rejected by the insurance industry.[2] The insurance industry's impact on the use and spread of such testing cannot be over-estimated; one should recall that for many years AIDS testing was avoided, even for the most neutral of reasons, because it was a fact that the majority of insurers would refuse to insure a person who had taken a test, regardless of the reason and the outcome. The insurance industry's insistence on receiving the results of any genetic tests taken may well inhibit their use for a while to come.

In the area of family law, genetic knowledge impacts in many ways, of which only a few can be examined here. For example, an early embryo may be examined before implantation to discover whether it has certain genetic disorders. This 'pre-implantation genetic diagnosis'[3] (PGD) is carried out as a part of *in vitro* fertilisation (IVF) treatment for those who are at risk of passing on a serious inherited disorder to their children. The egg of the woman and the sperm of the man are brought together *in vitro* and if the egg is successfully fertilised and becomes an embryo, it is examined when it has reached the stage of eight cells.

* St Anne's College, Oxford.
This article is written entirely in a personal capacity and does not reflect the views of the Human Fertilisation and Embryology Authority (of which the author is Chairman). The author is grateful to Sarah Deech BSc for scientific advice, and to Mrs Suzanne McCarthy, Chief Executive, HFEA.

1 F. Collins, 'Sequencing the human genome' (1997) 32(1) *Hosp Pract* (Off Ed) 35–43; K. Uddhav et al. 'Advances in the human genome project' (1998) 25(1) *Mol Biol Rep* 27–43.
2 *The Implications of Genetic Testing for Insurance* (London, December 1997).
3 W. Lissens and K. Sermon, 'Preimplantation genetic diagnosis: current status and new developments' (1997) 12(8) *Hum Reprod* 1756–1761.

One or two cells may be removed at that stage without damage to the entire embryo. Once tested, the embryo may then be implanted in the would-be mother, although it should be noted that the chances of fertilisation in IVF and the chances of the woman becoming pregnant are relatively low, only about 15 per cent.[4] (This is known as the 'take home baby rate'.) Clearly, it is a procedure to be resorted to only by those who are very anxious indeed about the future health of their embryo and prepared to risk a much lower chance of becoming pregnant than would occur naturally, in order to avoid an inheritable disease. The genetically testable disorders known about at the moment include Lesch-Nyhan Syndrome, Beta-Thalassaemia, Sickle Cell Anaemia, and Cystic Fibrosis.[5] It is reported, although unconfirmed, that there are genetic links in dyslexia, asthma and diabetes. The same technique of PGD could be used to ensure that the resulting baby, if any, was of the chosen sex.

Family lawyers are already familiar with the use of DNA testing to prove paternity.[6] They will now have to become familiar with the possibilities of choosing or avoiding the birth of certain children; cloning; and various problems thrown up by IVF and surrogacy practices, intimately linked with our knowledge of reproduction and genetics.

Non-family lawyers see the new knowledge as an aspect of the nature versus nurture debate. To summarise very briefly arguments that have occupied a century of research and debate, in the twentieth century we have accepted wholeheartedly, if intermittently, Durkheim's rule[7] that human behaviour is socially constructed and not the result of underlying inevitable biological tendencies, or in other words, a baby begins life as a *tabula rasa* — a blank slate. But now there is indisputable evidence that behaviour is strongly influenced, at the very least, by genetic inheritance. There are biological explanations not only for diseases — where one can be 100 per cent sure of inheritance — but also for behavioural and personality traits. There may be threats to gender equality arising from this, with an increasing amount of research reporting both human and animal fixed patterns of behaviour differences between males and females in survival and reproduction. The gender equality war is beginning to be fought in IVF treatments: very recently, there has been considerable adverse reaction to the story of a woman aged 60 who gave birth to a baby through artificial reproduction techniques.[8] What was striking was that there would have been no such controversy had a man aged 60 become a father, an everyday occurrence which could lead to an equally adverse outcome for the child in terms of health and upbringing. Or are men just being 'selfish genes', as Dawkins would have us believe?[9] The law has also by and large equated sperm donation, an easy procedure, with egg donation, which involves an operation and drugs.[10]

The interest in this for family lawyers is the new genetic 'determinism'. Is family life pointless? Need it only be a question of rudimentary discipline and protection, if children are wholly genetically pre-determined? If we cannot escape our genetic predisposition, then do parents merely accept the child that they have given birth to

---

4 HFEA 6th Annual Report, 1997.
5 R. Kaufmann et al, 'Preimplantation genetic analysis' (1992) 37(5) *J Reprod Med* 428–436.
6 B. Hoggett et al, *The Family, Law and Society* (London: Butterworths, 4th ed, 1996) 455.
7 *Education and Sociology* (Glencoe: Free Press, 1956); *Moral Education* (Glencoe: Free Press, 1961); S. Lukes, *Durkheim* (London: Allen Lane, 1973).
8 *Daily Telegraph*, 22 January 1998.
9 *The Selfish Gene* (Oxford: Oxford University Press, 1989).
10 Human Fertilisation & Embryology Act 1990, s 12(e).

with some fatalism? Will the 'victim' of an unfortunate genetic mix or his parents be blamed for his genetic make-up? If genetic inheritance is to be used to explain many aspects of behaviour and, to the lay person, *every* aspect of behaviour, will there be a wholesale abandoning of creative responsibility in family life?

Another potential danger of the new knowledge is the struggle to absorb it and use it without prejudice either way. Our current acceptance that nurture and environment are far more important than inheritance has been used to discredit and terminate the eugenic or racist theories prevalent in the late 19th century and in the early part of the 20th century. Once, races were classified and ranked in a hierarchy of desirability. The IQ test ruled and was accepted as inevitable. Hitler's treatment of races was seen as the culmination of the biological view of inheritance and has left today's researchers in a quandary over the handling of their material. One may cite as an example the furore that greeted Herrnstein and Murray's book *The Bell Curve*.[11] It will be difficult, although essential, to acquire and analyse sensitively knowledge about genetics, especially as it affects different peoples and genders. Our earlier rejection of such views could be said to have resulted in today's multiculturalism and tolerance; they are the ultimate rejection of biological determinism and classification of people according to birth. This generation has defined a middle path between, at one extreme, the abuse of genetic knowledge by racists, imperialists and fascists, and at the other extreme total reliance on social engineering and its mass deployment by totalitarianism. We are entering a volatile and powerful new area from which no individual is immune.

So many new issues have been raised with uncertain answers, that in this paper only an overview can be taken on a few topics, and even then questions will be raised without solutions. The conceptual areas of family law that are affected are paternity and maternity, the meaning of parental responsibility, the use of genetic knowledge and adult choice. Some straightforwardly technical laws are affected, but other areas open up deep questions of international law, morality and welfare.

Parenthood

The most direct link between the new genetic knowledge and established family law lies in its effect on the science of parenting.

In the USA, the Minnesota Centre for Twin and Adoption Research has studied 7,000 sets of identical twins raised in different families.[12] The Centre has calculated the 'heritability' of behavioural traits. According to the Centre, heredity is at least as responsible as upbringing for behavioural traits such as alienation, extroversion, traditionalism, leadership, career choice, risk aversion, attention deficit disorder, religious conviction, vulnerability to stress and pessimism.

There are two fundamental caveats about such studies. First, insofar as heritability studies assume that behavioural traits are accounted for by an interaction between a person's genes and their surrounding environment, they simply show the percentage variation in a trait that is accounted for by variation in the genetic make-up of the population being studied. Crucially, such studies do not show that genes alone are responsible for the expression of a particular trait and

---

11 (New York: Free Press, 1994); R. Jacoby and N. Glauberman, *The Bell Curve Debate* (New York: Times Books, 1995).
12 D. Finkel et al, 'Heritability of cognitive abilities in adult twins' (1995) 25(5) *Behav Genet* 421–431; D. Finkel et al, 'Genetic influences on memory performance in adulthood' (1995) 10(3) *Psychol Aging* 437–446.

they do not enable the degree to which genetic (or environmental) factors are responsible for a trait to be quantified. In the case of identical twin studies, we can say that, given a common genome, different traits expressed in the twins must be accounted for by environmental differences rather than by genetic differences. However, we cannot attribute such expressed traits to either environment or genes as such. Secondly, because heritability studies involve some statistical complexity, they can be misapplied in the service of various ideologies (concerning, for example, the superiority or inferiority of persons) and, obviously, this is a cause for concern.

Misapplication of heritability studies might radically alter parental beliefs — for example, the belief that parents have, when they see their new-born, that they can make a better, if not perfect, person of their baby. Why should parents go to the lengths of stimulating, educating and bringing up their children if those children are destined to turn out very much the same regardless of their environment and even had each baby gone home from the hospital cot to the wrong set of parents, little difference would be made? This sort of belief may alter not merely the structure of the family, but the entire role of the family as envisaged in family law. Until recently, the family was assumed to be a nursery in which the new-born person was raised. If it is thought that providing children with an enriched environment makes no difference to their intelligence, then any parenting which is good enough, ie safe from physical hazards and reasonably nourishing, will be acceptable, if we ignore the fact that social and environmental influences may very well tip the balance in cases of heredity.

If it were to be thought that some families were more disposed to violence, or low intelligence and consequent poor upbringing practices, is the law still to strive to better them and encourage them? Is the law to abandon its influence or strive even harder to make a difference? Existing family law is somewhat confused about heredity versus upbringing, about biological responsibility versus social responsibility. For example, the Child Support Act 1991 in general emphasises the financial responsibility of the biological father,[13] but the Children Act 1989 and laws regulating donor insemination protect the social father.[14] The new emphasis on biology or genetics is already manifest in adoption law, where the connection with the birth parents is now more readily valued and discoverable, despite the overwhelming emotional, social and financial contributions of the nurturing parents, that is, the adoptive parents, and possible hurt to them.[15] The outlook for adopters is clouded. Our emphasis on biological origins means that adopters carry out the hard work of raising a child, but the characteristics of the child are nevertheless fixed and the natural parents retain their hold and central place in that child's life.

When the family is at the core of government policy, these are vital questions. It may be thought that the genetic information should be played down, because it is still necessary to educate and form the character of children and not to take away the parents' motives for doing this and doing it well. It is possible that even heavier responsibilities might be placed on parents, whose duty will be seen as the vigorous counteraction of inborn tendencies. On the other hand, governments might rely on the outcome of the human genome project to abandon investment in social policy, blaming all ills and social exclusion on science and inheritance.

13 s 54 includes some other categories.
14 Human Fertilisation & Embryology Act, s 28.
15 Adoption Act 1976, ss 51, 51A.

Why, for example, institute curfews, and laws to regulate alcohol consumption, a ban on unhealthy food, why instigate the work mentality and counteract the 'welfare mentality' of staying at home, when everything could be genetic?

The possibility of scientific confirmation is beginning to play a part in family law, albeit in no uniform way. It has become well and truly accepted in the ascertainment of biological paternity and in permission to trace birth parents of adopted children. In understanding 'responsibility' and financial support, family law answers have been somewhat ambiguous. There is a growing tendency to allocate social and legal responsibility to genetic fathers, witness, for example, the Lord Chancellor's Department's paper on giving automatic parental responsibility to unmarried fathers.[16] This document is marked by the confusion of the benefits of the legal concept of parental responsibility and actual social care and responsibility; in fact, the ascription of one will not necessarily produce the other. At the same time, considerable amounts of social and financial responsibility are allocated to non-biological fathers by divorce law placing duties on the divorcing husband who may or may not be the father of the ex-wife's children,[17] and also by the ascription of legal parenthood in IVF cases by the Human Fertilisation and Embryology Act 1990.[18] In many ways, English family law plays it safe and puts the creation of some responsibility somewhere for the child in the first place, without regard to the logic of whether it should be the social father or the genetic father, thus trying to cover all possibilities without regard to a clear scientific or moral policy in this field.

Paternity law is a good example of the confusion in family law over the ascription of responsibility, as summed up in the word 'father' or 'mother'. DNA testing which can establish with certainty the father of the child was introduced by the Family Law Reform Act 1987,[19] but is confined to blood samples. Its use today is preferable to the old simple 'blood tests', which were able to show by blood groups that a person was definitely eliminated as the father of the child, but did not show that a person was definitely the father. The accuracy of DNA testing is based on the unique genetic identity of each child, composed of the genes of its two parents. It was at first regarded as shocking and almost suspect by judges who, reflecting the mood of the general public, seemed to feel that to *know* who one's father was, was something never intended by nature. It is now regarded as relatively routine and considerable use of such testing is made under the Child Support Act.[20] Knowing who one's father is can therefore — although it has not — put an end to presumptions of legitimacy and paternity arising from marriage. Biological fatherhood certainty has also not ended the practice of ascribing social and financial responsibility to the men who stand in place of the father, that is the stepfather and, after divorce, the mother's ex-husband.[21] The biological father (where not married to the mother) is not given full rights in the Family Reform Act 1987,[22] and in fact this was resisted until recently. In order to acquire his rights, he has to apply to the Court or make an agreement with the mother. This was determined by enactment because it seemed unfair to force the sharing of rights

---

16 *1. Court Procedures for the Determination of Paternity. 2. The Law on Parental Responsibility for Unmarried Fathers, Consultation Paper,* March 1998.
17 'Child of the family', as defined in the Matrimonial Causes Act 1973, s 52(1).
18 ss 28(2), (3), 29(1).
19 s 23 and Family Law Reform Act 1969, s 20.
20 *Re A (a minor)* [1994] 2 FLR 463; *Re H (a minor)* [1996] 4 All ER 28.
21 n 17 above.
22 s 4.

with a man on a woman who at no stage had agreed to marry him or to share rights with him and who, indeed, might have been mistreated by him. Moreover, to give legal rights to an unmarried father is not to ensure that the child enjoys the benefits of the presence of the father and his interest. His rights are abstract entities that may be enjoyed or abused from a distance. This is why it is important not to confuse social responsibility with 'parental responsibility' as granted by enactment.[23] Our belief in the importance of genetics is now growing to the extent that it seems more natural to give the legal concept of 'parental responsibility' to biological fathers, believing that this will be for the welfare of the child and that the legal grant will encourage the father to enjoy the company of his child. Whether this will be the case, remains to be seen.

At the same time English law grants considerable responsibility to the man who takes the role of social father by agreement. For example, section 28 of the Human Fertilisation & Embryology Act 1990 provides that the husband of a married woman who has artificial reproduction treatment is the legal father, unless he did not consent. So the fact that the woman may have been treated with sperm from an anonymous donor is of less importance than the consent of the husband and his legal and social presence in the household. This is reinforced by section 28(3) of the same Act, which provides that an unmarried woman who seeks treatment with a man will in effect be treated legally in the same way, that is, her partner will be deemed the legal father because of his presentation for treatment together with her. This means that sometimes there is no father in any sense at all, as, for example, when a single woman is accepted for treatment by a clinic without the presence of any man at all.[24] The anonymous sperm donor is not the legal father[25] and if a sperm donor is used but the treatment is not under the Act, the sperm donor, if known, will be regarded as the biological father and financially responsible for the child. In all cases the carrying mother or gestational mother is the legal mother, by virtue of section 27 of the 1990 Act. The unmarried partner father, who has received treatment together with the mother, is, as was said, the legal father under the Human Fertilisation & Embryology Act[26] but he appears not to count as the father under the Children Act 1989 for the purposes of parental responsibility,[27] although he does for the purposes of financial responsibility under the Child Support Act 1991.[28] In no case is a deceased father the legal father where artificial reproduction treatment takes place after his death.[29] The surrogate or gestational mother is the mother for the purposes of surrogacy,[30] not the commissioning mother. So if the surrogate mother is married, her husband is the legal father of the child and this will remain the case unless the commissioning couple seek and are granted an order under section 30 of the Human Fertilisation & Embryology Act. There is little consistency here apart from some negation of genetics in the interests of the creation and preservation of an apparently normal nuclear family. The anonymous sperm donor is not treated as the legal father, by section 28(6) of the Human Fertilisation & Embryology Act, presumably in order to encourage sperm donors to assist infertile couples, and also to preserve the image of the normal

---

23   R. Deech, 'The Reform of Illegitimacy Law' (1980) 10 *Fam L* 101.
24   s 28(3), (6).
25   *ibid* s 28(6)(*a*).
26   s 28(3).
27   s 2(2).
28   s 54.
29   Human Fertilisation & Embryology Act 1990, s 28(6)(*b*).
30   *ibid* s 27.

family where treatment has been successful for the couple so treated. There will be an interesting issue one day, perhaps not too far in the future, when children, encouraged by social attitudes, begin to seek out the names or other attributes of the sperm donor.

Sex selection

As explained above, pre-implantation genetic diagnosis may be used to select the sex of an embryo before it is transferred into the womb. Other methods of sex selection have been vaunted or even advertised, but none is known to be as accurate as selection of the embryo, once its sex is known at the eight cell stage. Could this impact on family law?[31] There are a number of areas where the ability to choose the sex of a child might be convenient to parents. Leaving aside mere preference for religious or social reasons, there are legal issues relating to inheritance of property, which may have been entrusted for descendants of one sex or the other, inheritance issues and the descent of titles in the Royal Family and the aristocracy. This issue will become of decreasing importance, at least for the Royal Family, if the Bill introduced by Lord Archer in 1997, which would allow the throne to pass to the oldest child of the monarch, regardless of sex, were to become law.[32] The abolition of voting rights of hereditary peers in the House of Lords might not lessen the love of the title which can only descend to a male heir, even if it will not in the future carry voting rights.

Following a public consultation in 1993, the Human Fertilisation & Embryology Authority banned sex selection in licensed treatment centres if carried out for social reasons.[33] Sex selection is allowed for medical reasons where there is a risk of a child inheriting a serious, life-threatening disorder. The general consensus arising from public consultation was that children should be valued for themselves and not for characteristics such as their sex. There was a general fear that choosing gender could be the beginning of a slippery slope towards selecting the perfect child. 67 per cent of those who responded were opposed to sex selection for social reasons. The HFEA has permitted the use of sex selection for medical reasons, for example in cases where a woman risks having a child with a sex-linked disease, such as haemophilia. The HFEA concluded that sex selection for social reasons was not acceptable because (a) it accepts unequal values placed on the sexes, and would reinforce gender stereotyping to the disadvantage of women; (b) children may be seen as commodities; (c) there may be adverse consequences for a family trying to select the sex of one child whether this is successful or unsuccessful; (d) it is an inappropriate use of medical resources. Nevertheless, there is still strong pressure to select the sex of a child and there are two methods which have been advertised and fall outside the HFEA's remit because they only use the sperm of the husband and the sperm is not stored. The first such method is available in the US and is called flow cytometry procedure.[34] This involves separating sperm cells by applying fluorescent dye to the DNA inside the sperm. The HFEA is concerned

---

31   G. Pennings, 'Ethics of sex selection for family balancing' (1996) 11(11) *Hum Reprod* 2339–2345.
32   Succession to the Crown Bill 1998.
33   *Code of Practice* para 7.20; see also European Convention on Human Rights and Biomedicine (1996), art 14.
34   L. Johnson et al, 'Gender Preselection in Humans? Flow cytometric separation of X and Y spermatozoa for the prevention of X-linked diseases' (1993) 8(10) *Hum Reprod* 1733–1739; B. Reubinoff and J. Schenker, 'New advances in sex preselection' (1996) 66(3) *Fertil-Steril* 343–350.

about this procedure not only for ethical reasons but also because of the risk of inducing harmful mutations into the embryo. There is not sufficient evidence that the technique is safe and people have been urged to be extremely cautious when considering this treatment. The other unsupervised method is centrifugal force to separate X from Y sperm, which has a questionable success rate. The clinics that offer this are often used by couples from ethnic backgrounds where it is important in their culture to have male offspring.

Identity

Growing knowledge of the impact and importance of genetic inheritance is bound to increase the pressure to know one's origins, and this is reinforced by the popularity of concepts such as freedom of information and the search for one's roots. Adoption law has already succumbed in that by section 50 of the Adoption Act 1976, the 18 year old adopted child may, with counselling, seek access to information about his birth parents. There are legal parallels between access to information in adoption and in IVF.

Parents who placed their children for adoption had assumed lifelong confidentiality. This was removed from them by the 1976 Act, the only concession being made was counselling, and that for the adopted child, not the parents. The Human Fertilisation & Embryology Act also protects sperm donors' anonymity. Section 31(5) of the Act states that the HFEA may not be required to give any information as to the identity of a donor if that information was not required to be given when the information was provided. Under section 31(4)(a) the Authority may one day be required by regulations to give information to those who have discovered that they are IVF children. No regulations specifying the detail of information to be collected and given have yet been made, but a consultation exercise is being prepared by the Department of Health on this issue. 'Information' may refer to personality and genetic information, such as the state of health of the donor father, his race and colouring, his interests and profession; or it may even be that the name will be disclosed, although that would require legislation having retrospective effect. There is already considerable material advocating the need of a child to know his or her parents, especially the father, most likely to be the anonymous one in this case.[35] If the arguments bear fruit, boosted as they probably will be by human rights and freedom of information legislation, a new law would bear unduly heavily on the parents and children of artificial reproduction because the duty to disclose information would be a complete breach with the original theory and purpose of IVF and legislation.[36]

Donors are anonymous for the purposes of the parents and their needs, that is, in order to provide a couple where, typically, the husband is infertile, with a child who appears to the outside world to be their own natural child. Such a child may well grow up not knowing that he or she is the product of IVF and not knowing that the mother's husband is not the child's father. It is thought that many donor

---

35   eg A. McWhinnie, *Families Following Assisted Conception* (Dundee: University of Dundee, 1997); V. Adair and A. Purdue, 'DI programmes with personal donors: issues of secrecy' (1996) 11(11) *Hum Reprod* 2558–2563; F. Shenfield and S. Steele, 'What are the effects of anonymity and secrecy on the welfare of the child in gamete donation?' (1997) 12(2) *Hum Reprod* 392–395; M. Freeman, 'The New Birthright?' (1996) 4 *Int Jl of Chn's Rts* 273; and K. O'Donovan, 'A Right to Know One's Parentage?' (1988) 2 *Int Jl of Law Fam* 27.

36   *Committee of Inquiry into Human Fertilisation and Embryology, Report* Cmnd 9314 (1984) para 4.22.

insemination (DI) couples do not tell the children about the history of their conception and a law about disclosure might well encourage continuing ignorance and withholding of this vital information by the social parents. Anecdotally, researchers have found that children in so-called normal families are sometimes not the offspring of the mother's husband. If there is a true 'right to know', we must question whether all children should be allowed to seek DNA orders to establish whether or not the persons whom they believe to be their parents are indeed their biological parents. In other words, if there is a right to know, logically it ought to extend to all parents and all children. Of course, there is no foreseeable way that IVF/DI parents could be forced to tell children of the circumstances of their births.

Under the Human Fertilisation & Embryology Act a register of information is kept and, by section 31(3), a person who is over 18 may enquire whether or not he or she was born by artificial reproduction techniques, and a person over 16 who is to marry may enquire whether or not they are related to their intended spouse.[37] This, of course, will not help those who do not suspect their origins and who may be living together and procreating, as opposed to marrying. The 'right to know' — if pressed too far — may inhibit the use of artificial reproduction, as has proved the case in Sweden, where the names of donors are made available. Initially, the willingness of donors to donate dropped but is now reported to have recovered; on the other hand, would-be parents often go abroad for donor sperm in order to ensure anonymity.[38] The weakening of international barriers increases the likelihood that despite the best intentions of legislators, couples who wish to procreate will seek the forum which suits them best.

There is not yet any clear demand for knowledge in families to reflect total genetic history. No doubt plenty of 'traditional' families tell their children nothing of their perhaps inconvenient origins, or deliberately mislead them. Recent examples of this stem from the need to hide children during the Second World War and for the children not to know that they were Jewish: for example, the current US Secretary of State, Madeleine Albright.[39] Other children may have stemmed from secret liaisons within marriage and recent examples which have received wide publicity involve Paula Yates,[40] Martin Amis[41] and Mazarine Pingeot.[42] Morbidly, the body of the late Yves Montand was recently disinterred in order for DNA samples to be taken for the purpose of proving whether or not an alleged daughter was in fact his.[43] Much as one may support the 'right to know' there are a number of obstacles, not least of which is the difficulty of obtaining evidence after death, and the disruption to an apparently normal family.

The parallel with the right to know in adoption may be taken too far. It is presumed that in disclosure relating to adoption there is a paternal and maternal story worth knowing, because the adoption must have occurred for reasons that are interesting and relevant, and there were mothers and fathers and families who were left behind on adoption. With IVF there is no history that is relevant except the purely genetic one. No story, other than infertility, lies behind the

---

37 s 31(6).
38 D. Morgan and R. Lee, *Human Fertilisation and Embryology Act 1990* (London: Blackstone Press, 1991) 163.
39 *Daily Telegraph* 14 February 1997.
40 *ibid* 12 May 1997.
41 *ibid* 21 June 1996 reported an unknown daughter.
42 *ibid* 12 January 1996.
43 *ibid* 12 March 1998.

non-paternity of the obvious man. There is, presumably, no story to be told to the IVF child save the simple and possibly embarrassing one of the impoverished medical student who became an anonymous sperm donor. There is no earlier family of social relevance in donor insemination. Moreover, as the state moves to impose increased financial responsibility on unmarried fathers, there must be a fear on the part of currently anonymous sperm donors and future ones that disclosure of their names may one day lead to financial responsibility. Are they very different from the young man who becomes a father after a 'one night stand' where the parties barely know each other's names? On the other hand, if genetic inheritance becomes relevant, especially because cures may be available for certain diseases, it may well be seen as totally unfair for a person to have been misled about their paternity.

The European Convention on Human Rights, Article 8, demands respect for the private life of an individual. This might be interpreted to mean that those who have become parents with the assistance of artificial reproduction have the right to keep this a secret; or it may mean that the children ought to be able to establish the details of their identity, as held in *Gaskin* v *UK*.[44] The Data Protection Act 1984 recognises the confidentiality of health records, but the current Freedom of Information proposals[45] will make pressure to disclose as much information as possible even greater.

Surrogacy

Surrogacy throws up some of the most difficult problems concerning truth about genetic origins versus the happiness of infertile couples. It was grudgingly accepted by the Warnock Report.[46] There is a presumption in favour of the surrogate mother as the mother, entitled to security of status, even though she may not be the genetic mother of the child.[47] The surrogate mother cannot be required by the commissioning parents under any contractual arrangement to hand over the child and the woman who is carrying the child is to be treated as the mother of the child under section 27 of the 1990 Act.[48] Welfare of the child is therefore rated more highly than the contractual arrangements, if any, between the commissioning couple and the surrogate mother.[49] The commissioning couple may, however, acquire parental responsibility, almost akin to adoption, under section 30 of the 1990 Act. The HFEA register will not record a surrogate birth where the child was conceived without using a licensed treatment. Surrogacy is perfectly possible on a do-it-yourself basis and the truth about his or her origins can then very easily be kept from the child. A surrogate child may have three mothers, the carrying mother, the commissioning mother and the egg donor mother, and the child may have four 'fathers', the husband in the commissioning couple, the husband of the surrogate, the husband of the egg donor and the sperm donor, if any. There is currently a government review of surrogacy but its remit is largely limited to commercialisation and the use of agencies in this field, rather than the family law

---

44 [1990] 1 FLR 167.
45 *Your Right to Know — the Government's Proposals for a Freedom of Information Act* Cm 3818 (1997).
46 n 36 above, paras 8.10–8.20.
47 Human Fertilisation & Embryology Act, s 27.
48 Surrogacy Arrangements Act 1985, s 1A.
49 *A* v *C* [1985] FLR 445.

problems as such.[50] The attitude of the British public to surrogacy, indeed, the attitude of lawyers to surrogacy is inconsistent. When the surrogacy arrangement appears to work smoothly, no objections are raised, despite the risk of storing up genetic problems in the future. If, on the other hand, the contractual arrangement goes wrong, then surrogacy as such is disapproved by the media, while the attitude to the surrogate mother and the commissioning mother in the case will depend on the facts. It is very difficult for family lawyers to take a straightforward view on this while the practice remains new and controversial.

Consent

Strictly speaking, the practice of storing frozen embryos has no particular genetic impact on family law, save that the gap between fertilisation and birth may be protracted, giving rise in future to questions in the child's mind about his or her origins. Nevertheless, this area has given rise to some of the most interesting cases. Two that are known world-wide are *Davis* v *Davis*[51] in the state of Tennessee and, in Israel, the *Nahmani* case.[52] In both cases, there had been fertility problems during the marriage and treatment for them had resulted in the production of embryos containing the genetic material of husband and wife. The embryos had been frozen pending their use which was not convenient when they were created. In *Davis* v *Davis* a married couple stored embryos with a clinic in preparation for the transfer to the wife's womb. Before this had been accomplished, the marriage ended in divorce. The ex-wife still wanted the embryos implanted in her so that she could have the opportunity of becoming a mother, but the ex-husband, genetically the potential father, no longer wished to become a father. The trial judge held that the embryos were unborn children, that it was in their best interests to be given the chance of life, and that temporary custody should therefore be transferred to the wife in the hope of a successful implantation. On appeal, the Tennessee Court of Appeal vested joint control of the embryos in the former husband and wife. The holding that the wife had the sole right to seek implantation was overturned. The court recognised the right to procreate as a citizen's basic civil right and, conversely, a right to prevent procreation as a constitutionally protected choice. To award the embryos to the wife would violate the husband's right not to beget where no pregnancy had taken place. It would be repugnant to order either parent to bear the consequences of parenthood against his or her wish, according to the court. Finally, the court ordered the parties to agree to donate the embryos to research or to allow them to perish. By that time, the former Mrs Davis had remarried, and wanted only to donate the embryos to another childless couple.

The facts in the *Nahmani* case were identical, save that they had been preceded by Israeli regulations explicitly prohibiting the implantation of a fertilised egg in a woman who was not the prospective mother, that is to say, surrogacy was prohibited.[53] Mr and Mrs Nahmani were married in 1984. Because of a tumour,

50 *Surrogacy: Review for the UK Health Ministers of Current Arrangements for Payments and Regulation, Consultation Document*, Department of Health 1997.
51 *Davis* v *Davis* 842 SW2d 588 (Tenn 1992).
52 *Nahmani* v *Nahmani* (1995) 49(1) PD 485, Israeli Supreme Ct 5587/93. This account relies heavily on an unpublished paper, D. Heyd, 'Whose Pre-embryos are They?', Conference on Medical Ethics, Hull, 2 April 1998.
53 The background is explored in D. Heyd, 'Artificial Reproductive Technologies: the Israeli Scene' (1993) 7 *Bioethics* 263–270; A. Benshushan and J. Schenker, 'Legitimizing surrogacy in Israel' (1997) 12(8) *Hum Reprod* 1832–1834.

Mrs Nahmani was forced to undergo an operation and her uterus, but not her ovaries, was removed. Since she could still produce eggs but could not carry a pregnancy, the couple decided to seek IVF treatment with the intention of implanting the fertilised egg in a surrogate mother. Due to the prohibition on such a procedure in Israel, the doctors refused to provide the couple with the desired treatment. The Supreme Court, as a compromise solution, gave ad hoc permission to the couple to undergo IVF treatment and use a surrogate in another country. The embryos of Mr and Mrs Nahmani were frozen, but before a surrogate mother could be found in the US, the husband left his wife and started living with another woman by whom he had children. The hospital in which the embryos were stored refused to hand them over to Mrs Nahmani without her ex-husband's consent, which he withheld. The first court decided that she could have the embryos, even without her ex-husband's consent. He appealed to the Supreme Court of Israel, which overturned the decision of the lower court. But in a specially summoned second session of the Supreme Court in 1996 in which 11, rather than the usual 5, judges took part, the court reversed its own previous verdict and allowed Mrs Nahmani to take her frozen embryos.[54] The approach of the Israeli court, unlike the approach of the court in Tennessee and the English Court of Appeal, was based on which spouse had the more compelling interests, that of the ex-wife to become a parent or of the ex-husband not to become a parent against his will.

While the Tennessee case played down the rights of the mother, if any, and focused on a person's right not to have his genetic material used without his consent, the majority judgment in the Israeli case ignored the issue of consent, or lack of it, on the part of the father, and ruled on a moral basis. The Israeli decision would mean that if a successful surrogate mother were found a child would be born whose sense of identity and sense of family would be severely undermined by the genetic and social background of the case.

British law has attempted to deal with the fate of stored embryos by covering all possibilities in the Human Fertilisation & Embryology Act 1990. Under schedule 3 of the Act, consent must be given in writing and may be withdrawn at any stage. The consent must specify one or more of the following purposes, namely treatment of certain persons or research. Consent to the storage of any gametes or any embryos must specify the maximum period of storage, if less than the statutory period, which is now up to 10 years in certain circumstances, and state what is to be done with the gametes or embryos if the person who gave the consent dies. So a divorcing husband could promptly withdraw his consent to the storage or use of an embryo that had come into creation by the act of himself and his wife, but of course once the embryo has been used in treatment or for research this is too late. The British attitude is very insistent on consent as the key to dignified and independent use of a person's genetic material. The preservation and protection of the autonomy and dignity of the individual and of the embryo are held thereby to be protected.

The embryo is given special status under the Human Fertilisation & Embryology Act and its disposal must be carried out sensitively. Those who have a conscientious objection need not participate.[55] International conventions would not permit genetic material to be regarded as property.[56] In *Davis* v *Davis*[57] the

---

54 Additional Hearing (1996) 50(4) PD 661. It appeared, however, that the Californian surrogacy agency dealing with them would not allow an arrangement to proceed without the consent of both parties.

55 s 38.

56 European Convention on Human Rights and Biomedicine (1996), art 21, prohibits financial gain from body parts.

57 n 51 above.

American court ultimately held that embryos are not property and a commercial trade in gametes or embryos would widely be perceived as contrary to public policy. In British law individuals have control but not ownership of their genetic material and such material is not property able to be divided on divorce or bequeathed. Sale is prohibited by section 41(8) of the Human Fertilisation & Embryology Act. The preservation of bodily autonomy and control over the destiny of one's own genetic material is paramount. The additional genetic confusion that would be caused if persons were allowed control over and to authorise the removal of another person's genetic material is profound and incalculably damaging.

Cloning

Cloning[58] is the most recent issue to raise questions of genetics and family law in a very dramatic way. A simple definition of a clone is an organism that is genetically identical to another. Mammals reproduce sexually. The reason for the urges that have driven history and fuelled the passions of mankind, are to enable us to combine in the production of a new individual of genetic diversity. Identical twins are, in a way, natural clones, but although they are identical to each other, they are each a combination of their two parents. In 1997 a novel technique of cloning was reported.[59] Cells were taken from the udder of a six year old Finn Dorset ewe. They were fused with 277 unfertilised eggs. The procedure is to remove the nucleus of the cell and fuse it with an egg from which the nucleus has been removed, by a small electric shock, which in this case replaces fertilisation by sex — thus is one of nature's greatest forces dispensed with! Twenty nine 'fertilised' eggs resulted and were implanted in surrogate black-faced ewes. One gave birth to Dolly. Dolly is identical to the sheep from whose udder she was cloned. She is unlike so-called clones where *embryonic* donor cells were used, in whose creation two mammals had already joined together and contributed their genetic material.[60] Now it seems possible that one parent alone, not two, can make a baby, if the Dolly technique were applied to humans. So, too, we could manufacture babies identical to one parent or even contemplate babies with certain 'designer' qualities added to them before implantation.

It is reported that some six per cent of Americans like the idea of cloning themselves. It has been thought that one could replicate a baby in case one was lost by cot death, or recreate an elderly relative. Lesbians could bear children not only without contact with a man, but without even having to resort to the sperm bank. It has even been suggested that cloned embryos from each of two women could be mingled at a very early stage in order to produce a baby that was composed of the genetic make-up of two women, a true union of two females. In fact, men might be quite unnecessary for breeding purposes, as only cells, eggs and surrogate mothers would be needed for reproduction, not sperm. Fear of the elimination of men's role in reproduction and the family may be part of the violent reaction against Dolly.

---

58 See generally *Cloning Issues in Reproduction, Science and Medicine, Consultation Document*, Human Genetics Advisory Commission and Human Fertilisation & Embryology Authority 1998.
59 I. Wilmut et al, 'Viable offspring derived from fetal and adult mammalian cells' (1997) 385(6619) *Nature* 810–813.
60 K. Campbell et al, 'Sheep cloned by nuclear transfer from a cultured cell line' (1996) 380(6569) *Nature* 64–66.

There are several ethical and practical reasons why cloning should not be allowed at the moment. For the purposes of family law, the most relevant arguments relate to the welfare of the child.

Would cloned children be the butt of jibes and be discriminated against? Would they become a sub-caste, who will have to keep to each other? Would they be exploited? Would they become media objects? This is quite possible. Louise Brown, the first IVF baby, born in 1978, is still in the news. Would the life choices of clones be closed off? What would be their place within the family, and what would happen to the family? Would a cloned child be subject to excessive control from its parents or one parent, who already may be too dominating as demonstrated by their choice of a cloning technique? Would cloning mean the desire of one parent to have complete control, blocking out any possibility of a second parent and family, denying the natural independence of the growing child? Would the one parent be severely disappointed in the child if, as so often happens, she does not turn out as expected? Would the mother really be the mother, or are the real parents of the clone the parents of the mother? It would be the grandparents who would have provided the genetic material of the cloned child. What do we mean by mother? Would it be the cell donor or the surrogate or the social mother? Is the mother the mother of the clone or the sister of the clone? What of parental responsibility, in every sense?

Much of our family law and general law is predicated on the basis that adults are creatively responsible for the safety and nature of their growing children. If it were known that a cloned child was genetically identical to one parent, would it mean that adults would wash their hands of responsibility for the growth of this child? If the parent was, for example, musical or a criminal, would it mean that the parent was not responsible for the budding musical talent of the child, and not responsible if it turned out to be a criminal? Or would more responsibility than ever before be ascribed to the one parent, because he or she had chosen to bring into the world a child who was guaranteed to have those talents? The cloned child would have no genetic connection with half of its social family, if it had one, and the effects of the knowledge of its origins on the child might be damaging.

Article 3 of the European Convention on Human Rights guarantees citizens protection against inhuman or degrading treatment. This might be of some assistance to the cloned child, although once it had been born it would be too late and rather meaningless to say that its birth was a matter of inhuman or degrading treatment.

Marriage

The modern law of nullity in the Matrimonial Causes Act 1973 reflects certain elements of genetics, albeit in an early state. A marriage is not valid if the parties are within the prohibited degrees of relationship.[61] This prohibition is universal in some form or other and reflects both a desire to defend the traditional family from jealousy and encroachment and also knowledge of defects that might be inherited by the child born of an incestuous relationship. Grounds (d)(e)(f) of section 12 of the Matrimonial Causes Act 1973 also have a tinge of genetics to them, namely that one of the parties was suffering from a mental disorder or venereal disease or was pregnant by some person other than the spouse. The law about mental disorder is largely grounded on the need for true and informed consent to marriage, but

---

61   Marriage Acts 1949–1986, Sched 1.

might well also have at its root a fear that some mental disease would be passed on to the children; and the nullifying effect of pregnancy *per alium* also preserves the genetic integrity of the marriage undertaken. In sum, English annulment law looks at facts existing before the marriage and at the time of the marriage. In this context, it should be noted that in the USA a blood test is required of intending spouses, to establish freedom from sexual disease.[62] One is therefore not very far removed from a state of the law whereby it is regarded as sensible if not necessary to take precautions before marriage and reproduction to ensure the health of potential children. This attitude has been given a new dimension by the science of PGD, described above.[63] Now that testing for genetic inherited diseases is available before marriage, this may be reflected in the reform of annulment law and in the responsibility of spouses towards each other and their children. To make sense, PGD would be triggered not only by marriage but by any cohabitation that was likely to lead to reproduction.

It is reported that engaged Cypriot couples are encouraged to have genetic testing for carrier status in relation to thalassaemia, a serious blood disease prevalent in the Cypriot and some other populations.[64] Is the eradication of a disease an aim worth achieving when the price is testing, knowledge that one might not wish to have, and the occasional inhibition on reproduction or the end of plans to marry by a couple where one or both is found to be a carrier?[65] Just as it is apparently regarded as irresponsible to neglect one's body because of modern understanding of the effect of smoking, diet and exercise, especially in pregnancy, it may one day come to be regarded as irresponsible to give birth to a baby that was not as perfect as modern science could enable it to be. Will it come to be seen as irresponsible for parents to fail to have testing?

The consciousness of what can be achieved is already quite widespread. For example, the Internet now advertises American cryobanks, (ie banks of sperm for sale) that offer sperm that has been specially screened to suit the requirement of donors of a particular area or group. Fairfax Cryobanks of Virginia advertised in a journal that it had expanded its genetic screening of semen donors to include the breast and ovarian cancer gene in Jewish donors and alpha-one antitrypsin deficiency in all donors. The BRCA-1 is a gene involved in hereditary breast and ovarian cancer. About one per cent of Ashkenazi Jews carry a mutation in the

---

62 H. Krause, *Family Law* (St Paul: West Publishing, 1995) s 3.8.

63 n 3 above.

64 The church in Cyprus became involved with the programme and all couples getting married had to provide a laboratory report indicating their carrier status: ex rel J. Old, National Haemoglobinopathy Reference Laboratory, John Radcliffe Hospital, Oxford; M. Angastiniotis et al, 'Prevention of thalassaemia in Cyprus' (1981) 1(8216) *Lancet* 369–371; B. Modell and A. Kuliev, 'Services for thalassaemia as a model for cost-benefit analysis of genetics services' (1991) 14(4) *J Inherit Metab Dis* 640–651; M. Petrou et al, 'Alpha thalassaemia hydrops fetalis in the UK' (1992) 99(12) *Br J Obstet Gynaecol* 985–989.

65 C. Snowdon and J. Green, 'Preimplantation genetic diagnosis and other reproductive options: attitudes of male and female carriers of recessive disorders' (1997) 12(2) *Hum Reprod* 341–350.

The price of obtaining a healthy family in terms of losses of wanted pregnancies may be too high. The author is indebted to Prof Bernadette Modell, Professor of Community Genetics, UCLMS Dept of Primary Care and Population Sciences, Whittington Hospital, London, for information on Cyprus and the benefits of screening. In Prof Modell's view, it is premature to worry whether at-risk couples will be expected to submit to screening and preimplantation genetic diagnosis in the future, because the service is not generally and equitably available. Limitations in the service are more significant in 'avoidable' births than people not wanting to know or use the information. The main ethical problems seem likely to revolve around unequal access and unequal ability to pay: B. Modell, 'Delivering genetic screening to the community' (1997) 29 *Annals of Medicine* 591–599; Y. Verlinsky and A. Kuliev, 'Progress in preimplantation genetics' (1998) 15(1) *J Assist Reprod Genet* 9–11.

BRCA-1 gene.[66] Women who carry this mutation have an estimated 85 per cent lifetime risk of developing breast cancer and a 50 per cent lifetime risk of ovarian cancer. Men carrying this mutation have an increased risk of prostate and colon cancer. Alpha-1 antitrypsin deficiency is an autosomal recessive disorder affecting about one in 6,700 Caucasians.[67] It is characterised by a greatly increased risk of severe emphysema. Some patients develop hepatitis as new-borns and some develop cirrhosis as adults.[68] Approximately one in fifty Caucasians are carriers. There is a genetic mutation in a high proportion of Jews that doubles the risk of colon cancer and also mutations for Tay Sachs disease. The American Jewish community is already worried about discrimination on the grounds of heavy prevalence of the breast, ovarian and colon cancer gene and is calling for a law against genetic discrimination. A survey of families whose members suffer from hereditary colon cancer has revealed that many were either refused health insurance or had their premiums raised.[69]

Preimplantation genetic diagnosis

The next generation may well resort to PGD for disorders as unspecific as depression, addiction, poor sight or even ugliness. Three-quarters of young American couples in a recent survey[70] said that they would choose abortion if told that the foetus had a 50 per cent chance of obesity. In other words, once couples know that choice is possible, they will avail themselves of it. This takes two forms: pre-marital testing of the couple for genetic disease carrier status with the aim of eradicating those diseases by the avoidance of reproduction, and PGD, opening up the possibility of selection of healthy embryos from amongst unhealthy ones before pregnancy.

An even more remote development is genetic manipulation. This is currently prohibited by law[71] but in the future parents might well wish to ensure that their children had genes installed before birth to ensure that they developed in a particular way and with defences against unwanted diseases and defects.

PGD is used to help people who are at risk of passing on a serious genetic disorder to their children. It already offers couples a chance to begin a pregnancy knowing that their child will be unaffected by the disorder they carry. This procedure is capable of regulation at the moment because it falls under the Human Fertilisation & Embryology Act.[72] The creation of embryos outside the body and the subsequent biopsy, in order to test for a genetic disorder, must take place in a centre licensed by the HFEA. This particular advance in genetics has caused concerns. Will it be possible to pick and choose genetic features and design ideal human beings? Furthermore, genetic tests reveal information not just about the

---

66   E. Schubert et al, 'BRCA2 in American families with 4 or more cases of breast or ovarian cancer' (1997) 60(5) *Am J Hum Genet* 1031–1040; C. Oddoux et al, 'The carrier frequency of the BRCA2 617delT mutation among Ashkenazi Jewish individuals is approximately 1%' (1996) 14(2) *Nat Genet* 188–190.

67   N. Kalsheker, 'Serine proteinase inhibitors on chromosome 14 and the genetics of familial chronic obstructive airways disease' (1990) 31(1) *Med Hypotheses* 67–70.

68   D. Cox. 'Risk for liver disease in adults with alpha-1 antitrypsin deficiency' (1983) 74(2) *Am J Med* 221–227.

69   *GenEthics* News, Feb/Mar 1998. The Human Genetics Advisory Commission is to inquire into discrimination: announcement by the chairman, 7 May 1998.

70   *Life Magazine* April 1998.

71   Human Fertilisation & Embryology Act 1998, Sched 2, para 1(4).

72   *ibid* ss 3, 14.

potential parents but also about their relatives. People who know that they risk passing on a serious genetic disorder to their children face a number of difficult choices. They must consider whether they wish to risk having children who may be affected by the disorder and whether they wish to have pre-natal diagnosis which may bring with it difficult decisions about terminating a pregnancy. They may decide that they will not have children because the risk of having an affected child is too great and they do not want to consider abortion.

The advantage of PGD over pre-natal diagnosis is that the genetic diagnosis will take place at a much earlier stage. As a pregnancy has not been established, couples will not have to consider abortion, which is likely to be a much more difficult and stressful decision than the disposal of affected embryos in their earliest stages of development, before they are transferred. PGD involves creating embryos outside the body by IVF. A biopsy is then carried out to remove a cell or cells from the developing embryo which can then be used to test whether the embryo carries a genetic disease. Embryo biopsy is mainly performed 2–3 days after fertilisation, when there will be 6–10 cells. Removal of two cells at this stage does not appear to be detrimental for subsequent embryo development. Sexing an embryo to avoid sex-linked disorders remains the most common reason for pre-implantation diagnosis worldwide, and testing for cystic fibrosis remains the most common use of PGD for a single gene defect. It is expected that the range of disorders for which PGD is available will increase, as the genes responsible are identified.

There are various problems. Misdiagnosis may occur if the biopsied cell is normal, but the remaining cells in the embryo are affected with the genetic defect. Secondly, the chances of achieving a successful pregnancy are reduced because of failure of fertilisation and possible damage to embryos. The HFEA is concerned to ensure that PGD is practised in a safe and responsible way to the highest standards, while at the same time keeping within accepted ethical boundaries. Because of the legislation in the UK it is possible to draw a line permitting some activities and prohibiting others and it is the role of the HFEA (working with other groups such as the Advisory Committee on Genetic Testing) to devise guidance in this respect. It has, for example, banned sex selection for social reasons.

The wish of a couple for their children to be healthy and free from disability is natural and would not contradict the generally accepted notion that an individual already born with that condition should receive appropriate respect with full civil and human rights. The danger for family law and society in general is that increases in genetic testing and the availability of techniques such as PGD might create a climate where disability becomes avoidable; hence there would be pressure on individuals to have genetic tests and avoid having a disabled child. People may become unwilling to accept children who are physically or mentally disabled.

Some of the conditions for which PGD is available affect the child from birth. Others appear only in later life, so there will be a period when affected individuals enjoy life free from the disorder. An example of such a condition is Huntington's disease which usually has an onset of between 30 and 60 years with a small proportion of cases having an onset at under 15 years. However, can an individual lead a normal life knowing that they will, or are likely to, develop a life-threatening or degenerative disease? Is it ethical to discard an embryo that might develop a disease in 50 years' time?

The technique may spread still further because the ability to test for literally hundreds of genetic disorders may be possible within five years using gene chip technology. Once it becomes possible to detect multiple gene defects quickly and economically, new pressure may emerge to test all embryos to eliminate the risk of implanting one that carries one or more common serious disorders. Is the whole of family life and pregnancy to be thus turned on its head? Or should PGD be limited only to a couple where diseases are clearly indicated in the family medical history?

The Human Fertilisation & Embryology Act 1990 requires that before providing any woman with treatment, clinics must take account of the welfare of any child who may be born or who may be affected as a result of the treatment.[73] The HFEA Code of Practice outlines various factors that should be considered including the medical histories of the couple and their families, their health and consequent future ability to look after or provide for a child's needs.[74] These are particularly relevant in the context of PGD. One can imagine a situation where the clinic learns that the prospective parents have a genetic disease and yet the individual concerned does not know whether they themselves have a defective gene and may not wish to know. Should the knowledge be forced on the parents? Should the clinic refuse to go ahead with treatment?

Supporters of disability rights have objected to the spread of PGD because of the value judgement they believe it makes about people born with a genetic condition. The concern for family law is that there will be pressure on couples to undertake testing but if they refuse to do so the care of a disabled child would fall entirely on those parents, with the view that they brought it on themselves. There must also be concerns about the parent-child relationship if there is choice. Parental disappointment might take on a stronger and more unpleasant meaning.

Hilary Rose in *Love, Power and Knowledge*,[75] questioned parental choice in relation to pre-natal diagnosis. She argued that the choice is manufactured by the technology and that women can find themselves having chosen for example infertility treatments, foetal surgery and embryo and PGD yet feeling that it was not what they wanted. The choice, she argued, is eugenic in that it is premised on the goal of marginalising disabled people, the victims will be devalued and the mothers will be blamed. Principally, there is a fear that modern genetics will create a society in which people are intolerant of anything less than perfection and in which the family becomes the focus of ensuring that that perfection is created in a new generation.[76]

---

73   *ibid* s 13(5).
74   '3.17 Where people seek licensed treatment, centres should bear in mind the following factors: a. their commitment to having and bringing up a child or children; b. their ability to provide a stable and supportive environment for any child produced as a result of treatment; c. their medical histories and the medical histories of their families; d. their ages and likely future ability to look after or provide for a child's needs; e. their ability to meet the needs of any child or children who may be born as a result of treatment, including the implications of any possible multiple births; f. any risk of harm to the child or children who may be born, including the risk of inherited disorders, problems during pregnancy and of neglect or abuse; and g. the effect of a new baby or babies upon any existing child of the family. 3.18. Where people seek treatment using donated gametes, centres should also take the following factors into account: a. a child's potential need to know about their origins and whether or not the prospective parents are prepared for the questions which may arise while the child is growing up; b. the possible attitudes of other members of the family towards the child, and towards their status in the family; c. the implications for the welfare of the child if the donor is personally known within the child's family and social circle; and d. any possibility known to the centre of a dispute about the legal fatherhood of the child.'
75   (Cambridge: Polity Press, 1994), a feminist critique of reproductive science.
76   *Ante-natal and Preimplantation Genetic Diagnosis, Embryo Research and Contemporary Abortion Issues, Briefing Paper*, Genetic Interest Group, 20 December 1996.

Welfare of the child

To a large extent the influence of the HFEA on genetics and family law is circumscribed by the statute,[77] although the statute contains considerable flexibility. One need hardly remind family lawyers that the phrase 'the welfare of the child' is susceptible to many interpretations. Where there is room for disagreement, however, it certainly surfaces. This is clear in the arguments about older mothers and their right to access to fertility treatment. It has recently been reported that techniques have been developed whereby the menopause may be controlled by new drugs designed to extend the age of fertility. Older mothers may become a regular possibility in that embryos could be created while the mother is young and then stored until it was convenient to use them.

Section 13(5) of the HFE Act provides that there shall be no treatment 'unless account has been taken of the welfare of any child who may be born as a result of that treatment (including the need of that child for a father)'. The Act excludes no category of woman from treatment, whether she is married or single, young or old. The Code of Practice specifies the factors relating to the welfare of the child and its need for a father that must be taken account of by the clinics before commencing treatment. Given the variety of meanings that can reasonably be attached to this phrase, it is no wonder that clinics find it a difficult decision even though they have HFEA protocols to follow.

Conclusion

So what can one conclude for the future development of family law? Genetics clearly affects every part of it, and not only those relating to children. The influence of the new genetic knowledge can be seen in questions relating to the formation of marriage, responsibility for and maintenance of children. We see the influence of genetics in adoption law and in our concepts of welfare and raising a child. There are no clear paths forward and no consensus yet, but awareness of the issues must be a good thing.

---

77 Human Fertilisation & Embryology Act 1990.

Insurance and Genetics: The Current State of Play

Onora O'Neill*

Personal insurance: solidarity and mutuality

Seen in the simplest possible terms, insurance is a way of mitigating the effects of harmful events of uncertain incidence by pooling modest premiums which provide the resources to make larger payments selectively to those who suffer such events. Insurance is worthwhile for each person because the incidence of harm is uncertain: each benefits by contributing a premium in return for assurance that if misfortune strikes a claim can be made and met. If the incidence of harm could be fully known in advance there would be no context for insurance: those who knew for sure that they would not experience adverse events of a given type would not insure against them, and insurers would not offer worthwhile terms to those who were certain to experience such events.

These simplicities soon vanish when one considers the variety of possible forms personal insurance can take. The most fundamental division between types of insurance is between those based on *solidarity* and those based on *mutuality*. *Solidarity-based insurance* takes no cognisance of the different levels of risk that different individuals bring to the pool: premiums are set at a uniform level, or based on ability to pay; entitlement to claim if the event insured against occurs is uniform. The NHS and similar health insurance schemes in other countries are examples of solidarity-based insurance provision. Everyone contributes, indeed the better paid may contribute more, but those who are likely to use the health service a lot do not pay more than the robustly healthy. Unsurprisingly, solidarity-based insurance has to be publicly organised: it requires universal or at least very wide participation, hence an element of compulsion (usually via the tax system), since those whose risk is least are required to contribute in solidarity with others. Without an element of compulsion, those with least risk would have reason to leave solidarity-based schemes and seek private insurance which could cover their low risks more cheaply, the average risk (and cost) of those left in the pool would rise, and yet others would then have reason to leave.

By contrast *mutuality-based insurance* differentiates premiums on the basis of the level of risk each person is held to bring to the pool. Typically commercial insurance is based on mutuality. In this case there may be no compulsion (eg home contents insurance), or no more than conditional compulsion to take out insurance if one undertakes some activity (eg motor insurance). In either case there may be no compulsion to join a particular scheme: better risks will purchase their insurance from those who offer them lower premiums; worse risks will purchase despite higher premiums because they can get no better terms. For example, the UK motor insurance industry offers drivers with clean records lower premiums, while those with bad records pay the higher premiums demanded because they can get no lower ones. Of course, the calculation of the risk represented by an individual is unavoidably an approximate matter: some people with adverse risk factors are good drivers. Still, there is little objection to the practice of adjusting

---

* Newnham College, Cambridge.

premiums in proportion to the risk level each driver is held to represent. Driving is optional, and if high premiums keep those whose driving is a menace off the roads, and provides an incentive to safe driving for all, this is a benefit to all.

However, some forms of mutuality-based personal insurance, such as private health, life or travel insurance, raise more difficult ethical and policy questions because they cannot so readily be regarded as optional. If health insurance is organised on a mutuality basis there are likely to be many who can obtain no (or no affordable) private health insurance, who therefore cannot meet the costs of needed health care. It is not surprising that most developed countries have rejected mutuality-based health insurance models, and have established solidarity-based health insurance.

The USA is the obvious exception to this generalisation, and has around 40 million citizens without private health insurance at any one time (about 60 million within any two year period). This exclusion is only partly compensated for by solidarity-based tax-funded health insurance for the poor (Medicaid), since many of those without private insurance are ineligible for Medicaid. This result attests rather than disproves the difficulty of relying on mutuality-based insurance systems to provide cover for basic needs such as health care.[1]

Insurance and genetic information

The revolution in genetics is thought to raise difficult questions for personal insurance, and in particular for mutuality-based insurance, because it may reduce uncertainty about future events of specific sorts, such as suffering from a certain type of cancer, or having a heart attack, or dying within a certain time period. Increasing certainty changes, and at the limit undermines, the context of insurance. If risks can be more accurately known, then mutuality-based insurance systems will be able to apportion premiums to risks more accurately. There need be less pooling of risk and can be greater differentiation of premiums; competitive pressures will encourage both. The upshot could be that those with the highest perceived risk were charged more or unable to obtain insurance.

For example, if insurance companies could use genetic information to predict accurately an individual's age at death, they would know when it was unprofitable to sell an individual life cover extending beyond a given date on normal terms, and would either raise the premiums asked or refuse to provide cover. Or if they could use genetic information to establish that a given individual was likely to suffer an early heart attack or from early cancer they would have reason to raise premiums on health insurance for that individual. It is in the public interest that standard forms of personal insurance be widely available, but the availability of more accurate predictive tests may work against that objective.

Insurance companies have argued that using genetic information to predict risks would be no more than an extension of their current practice: just as they have long required proposers to provide information about medical record and family history (in addition to life-style information about, for example, dangerous sports or smoking), so they should now be allowed to require proposers to provide genetic information, and in particular the results of any genetic tests. Some have even

---

1   See T.R. Marmor, *Understanding Health Care* (New Haven: Yale University Press, 1994) and more recently 'Forecasting American Health Care' (1998) 23 *Journal of Health Politics, Policy and Law* 131.

argued that a 'right to underwrite' entitles insurers to require individuals to take genetic tests and disclose the results.

Such arguments are commonly supported with the observation that insurers already use some sorts of genetic information. When they draw on knowledge of current medical conditions of genetic origin, and when they infer a risk of illness from family history information, they are using genetic information, although of an imprecise sort. The more precise additional information obtained by genetic tests is simply, some argue, an extension of these accepted uses of less precise genetic information.

These very general claims do not hold up under closer scrutiny. The results of genetic tests, by themselves, tell one whether a certain mutation is or is not present, and hence whether or not a certain protein will be expressed. Although it is often said that genetic tests show whether someone has 'the gene for' some disorder, that is not strictly what the test will show. Additional statistical information linking a given test result to the occurrence of some disorder is also needed if a sound prediction of disease or of lowered life expectation is to be made on the basis of a genetic test result. Without information that links genetic test results to incidence of disease or death, they lack actuarial import.

Of course, sometimes robust information linking genetic tests to actuarially significant outcomes is available. The links between the relevant genetic test results and certain *single gene disorders*, such as haemophilia or cystic fibrosis or Tay Sachs disease, are well established. However, this by itself does not show that genetic test results for single gene disorders are of much use to insurers. In all these cases the relevant disorders are of *early onset*, and the genetic test result confirms rather than predicts the presence of the disease. Many of the genetic tests now available whether through clinical genetics centres (or, in a few cases, over-the-counter to the general public[2]) are tests for serious early-onset single gene disorders,[3] so are not very useful for insurers.

To find genetic test results with *predictive* value for insurers one has to look to those that are relevant to *late onset disorders* with high predictive value, and in particular tests for single gene late onset disorders. Two widely discussed instances of late onset single gene disorders are Huntington's chorea and the hereditary forms of breast cancer that can be predicted on the basis of the BRCA1 and BRCA2 tests. (The amount of discussion is quite out of proportion to the rarity of these disorders). In these cases a good deal of actuarial information is already available, which makes it possible to use a genetic test result for predicting later onset of serious, even fatal, disease. However, even in these cases the outcome can vary: the ages for onset of disease and of death of those with genes for Huntington's or with the BRCA1 and BRCA2 genes vary greatly; a few of the former and sizeable fraction of the latter live to old age and die of other causes.

In other cases, the results of genetic tests are not linked to single gene disorders at all. This may be because the gene and its variants code for characteristics which are not disorders. Or it may be because a given gene, or some of its variants, have only a weak statistical link to some *multifactorial disorder*. Where genetic test results are weakly linked to disorders, other genetic, environmental or life-style factors will also be at work. In these cases a given test result may not provide a sound basis for actuarially significant predictions. Some of those with a given gene

---

2 The phrase 'over-the-counter' is a term of art: do-it-yourself genetic test kits are more likely to be sold by mail order, or indeed over the internet, than by chemists.

3 See the *Consultation Report on Genetic Testing of Late Onset Disorders* (November 1997), Advisory Committee on Genetic Testing (ACGT), Department of Health.

that is statistically associated with a disorder may be protected against that disorder by other genes, or by medication, or by lifestyle. For example, clotting factor can protect against haemophilia; a special diet against the retardation associated with PKU.

Although mutuality-based insurance assigns risk levels to different individuals, and sets premiums on this basis, this assignment is often not based on particularly accurate predictive capacities. Just as motor insurers collect information on *current and past* characteristics of drivers and use these as a rough basis for setting premiums, so health insurers use information about *current or past* health or ill health as a rough basis for assigning premiums. Using 'current conditions' or 'pre-existing conditions' to set premiums may seem reasonable because these factors can be quite stable. Where early onset genetic conditions are continuously manifest in medical records, these records can provide better evidence of the likely state of future health than any predictive test could give, and the fact that the illness could have been predicted on the basis of genetic test results is beside the point. If the premiums for health insurance were not to reflect early onset genetic conditions, it would be necessary to set them not merely without reference to genetic test results, but also without reference to current or past health.

Health insurance: the US debate

In the USA debates on genetics and insurance in the last few years have been quite different from those in the UK, and have centred around the supposed need — or lack of need — for legislation that prohibits the use of genetic test results by insurers. This legislative focus largely reflects the fact that health insurance in the USA is commercially organised and mutuality-based. Fears that commercial health insurance may fail for those with adverse risk factors, including adverse genetic risk factors, are not fanciful.

A great deal of recent US legislation, both state and federal, aims to restrict the use by health insurers not only of genetic test results but more broadly of 'genetic information'. Federal legislation enacted in 1996 forbids insurance companies from using genetic information (both test results and family history) to exclude from group health insurance.[4] The state of New Jersey has gone even further and forbids use of any genetic information for any insurance or employment purpose without written consent, and puts an absolute ban on the use of such information to refuse health insurance.[5] Evidently this demand challenges the long standing practice by which insurers have used information derived from medical records and family history, which may include a great deal of *loosely* genetic information. The demand that health insurance not use genetic information, interpreted in this way, is so sweeping that it comes close to a demand that health insurance be based on solidarity rather than on mutuality. In the absence of compulsion, competitive pressures to seek low risk and exclude high risk clients will lead to differentiated premiums. Each insurer will seek to discriminate better from worse risks more accurately, so will seek to insist on the disclosure of pertinent information. Insurers who fail to do so are likely to suffer adverse selection: the poorer risks will accumulate in their portfolios, driving up the premiums they have to charge, driving out the better risks and driving down their sales and profits. Given that so

---

4 US PL 104–191, The Health Coverage Availability and Affordability Act 1996.
5 F. Charatan, 'New Jersey passes genetic privacy bill' (1996) *British Medical Journal* 313.

much is at stake, regulatory bodies aiming to ban the use of all genetic information would have to impose very strong and intrusive regulation on commercial health insurers.

Whether a mutuality-based system of commercial health insurance can in fact be regulated by a ban on so nebulous a category as 'genetic information' remains to be seen. It may be hard enough to ban the use of information resulting from specific genetic tests in commercial health insurance systems. Some would argue that it is arbitrary to exclude use of genetic test results, given that some genetic conditions can be accurately diagnosed by other tests (for example, PKU). Others would point out that even if insurers were forbidden to use genetic test results in setting premiums, provision should be made for individuals who think that it might be to their advantage to disclose such results.

Life insurance: the UK debate

Since the UK enjoys a solidarity-based national health scheme, most of the UK debate about genetics and insurance so far has been about other forms of personal insurance, and overwhelmingly about life cover. Life cover is important not only because it represents a great deal of UK insurance business, but because it is usual to use life policies not only to protect dependents but to back mortgages. There is therefore a strong public interest in the wide availability of life insurance on affordable terms. However, this interest has not so far led to widespread demands for legislation comparable to that against 'genetic discrimination' found in the USA.

Public debate on genetics and life insurance in the UK was initially stimulated by the publication in 1995 of a report of the House of Commons Science and Technology Committee.[6] This was followed in October 1996 by wide press coverage of a meeting at the Royal Society which brought together geneticists, actuaries and others.[7] Since then the debate has been advanced by the publication in December 1997 of two reports. The first was a Draft Code of Practice on genetics and insurance published by the trade association of the UK insurance industry, the Association of British Insurers (ABI), whose members transact about 95 per cent of insurance business in the UK.[8] The second was a report to government by the Human Genetics Advisory Commission (HGAC), a government advisory body reporting to the Office of Science and Technology in the Department of Trade and Industry as well as to the Department of Health.[9]

Both the areas of overlap and the differences between the latter, most recent reports are of interest. One major point of agreement is that nobody should be required to take genetic tests as a condition of obtaining life insurance. Those who prefer not to know aspects of their genetic make-up should not be required to know. This provision is of considerable importance given the strong evidence that persons who fear that they might be at risk of certain, particularly late onset, genetic diseases for which there is no known treatment often prefer not to discover

6   *Human Genetics: The Science and its Consequences*, Third Report, House of Commons Science and Technology Committee, HC 231 (1995).
7   *Human Genetics — uncertainties and the financial implications ahead* (1997) ed R.M. Anderson, *Philosophical Transactions of the Royal Society*, Series B, Vol 352, 1035–1114.
8   *Genetic testing: ABI Code of Practice* (December 1997) Association of British Insurers, London.
9   *The Implications of Genetic Testing for Insurance* (December 1997) Human Genetics Advisory Commission, Office of Science and Technology, Department of Trade and Industry.

conclusively whether they have the relevant gene, and so to leave open the hope that they do not.

The principal area of difference between the two reports is over disclosure of the results of genetic tests taken for other reasons (typically medical or reproductive reasons, sometimes for research purposes). The ABI draft code insists that insurers should be able to require the disclosure of any genetic test result obtained for other reasons. Any other policy would, they claim, open the way for those who have discovered from genetic tests that they are at risk of serious disorders to withhold information, and to take out cover at unfairly advantageous rates. Anything other than a disclosure requirement amounts to permitting adverse selection, and adverse selection harms both insurers and their other clients, who collectively bear the costs of increased payments to those who obtained their cover at unfairly advantageous rates.

The HGAC report argues that too little is yet known about the actuarial implications of specific genetic test results for a uniform policy of permitting insurers to require disclosure to be appropriate. The report points out that adverse selection is not at present an insurmountable problem, as evidenced by the fact that a number of UK companies have indicated that they do not plan to ask for disclosure of genetic test results. Moreover, a blanket requirement of disclosure might inhibit people from taking tests which they might otherwise seek either for medical or for reproductive reasons, and could lead to delay in medical treatment that might ameliorate a disorder, or even prevent its development.

The report recommends that there should be an initial two year moratorium for *all* requirements of disclosure of genetic test results for policies of normal size, after which disclosure could be required only where it could be shown that there was sound evidence that a specific test was actuarially significant for a specific insurance product. Moreover, it insists that sound actuarial evidence that is publicly available should be the precondition of any use of genetic test results, since without this there cannot be a robust appeals procedure that secures normal standards of consumer protection for those who suspect that their premiums may have been excessively loaded, or who have been denied insurance. In effect, the report challenges insurance companies to approach the availability of genetic test results in a way that is consonant with their self-image as parts of a knowledge-based industry.

This demand is not trivial. Linking genetic test results to actuarially significant events may often require new research, in some cases long term research. This research will have to identify the actuarial implications not only of (variations in) certain genes taken one by one, but the actuarial implications of combinations of genes, and of genes in combination with certain environmental conditions or therapeutic interventions. To base actuarial reasoning *solely* on results of tests would be as absurd as basing actuarial assessment of the implications of diabetes solely on knowledge of the outcome of untreated diabetes. For example, it would be absurd to view the outcome of having the PKU gene as invariable retardation, given that a restricted diet blocks this effect, or to overlook the fact that treatment can ameliorate cystic fibrosis and haemophilia, when assessing the actuarial implications of having these genes. There is no automatic way of deriving actuarially useful information from genetic test results.

Delay and caution in using genetic test results in setting life insurance premiums need not, however, prevent insurers from taking account of single gene disorders of early onset, for here they can have access to current medical evidence, as in the past. Other genetic test results (for example those for single gene disorders of late onset and for polygenic conditions) might be important for life insurers, but the HGAC report recommends that they be used only if and as sound actuarial evidence becomes available.

One worry about both of these reports might be that in allowing *any* use of genetic test results for purposes of life insurance they fail to address the predicament of those whose genetic test results have strong and known adverse implications. The point is correct, but not nearly as damaging as it would be in the case of use of genetic test results in health insurance. Life insurance is mainly sold for a limited period of cover to those with dependents and an income that makes buying a flat or house feasible, hence generally to relatively healthy people. Those with serious early onset disorders are less likely to aim to buy life insurance.

Debate about the use of genetic test results in setting premiums for life insurance is far from over in the UK. The ABI plan to review their own code in the light of the HGAC report. Both the HGAC and groups such as the Genetic Interest Group (GIG) will no doubt pay close attention to any attempts by insurers to use genetic test results whose actuarial significance has not been clearly established. There will probably be calls to ban all use of genetic test results in insurance, whether or not they are of actuarial importance, possibly by legislation similar to that enacted in the US. There will also be public interest in the success, or otherwise, of the ABI in ensuring that its members live up to the standards of their own code of practice, in the robustness and transparency of whatever appeals procedure is established, and in the policies of those insurance companies which are not members of the ABI.

Other personal insurance: the coming debate

The wider UK debate on other forms of insurance and genetics has hardly begun: what remains to be done is far more than a matter of choosing among, refining and following through recommendations already on the table. There are some personal insurance products which raise harder questions about the use of genetic test results than life insurance does. As the US debate shows, health insurance raises more difficult issues. While the UK can avoid parts of this debate so long as it sustains a solidarity-based health insurance system, it may be hard to avoid the whole of it.

It has, for example, been suggested that individuals should be required to take out long-term care insurance to cover the costs of residential or nursing care in their old age. However, should genetic test results make it possible to predict with some degree of confidence who was likely to need such care for longest, insurance to cover its costs might not be affordable by the very people most likely to need it. For example, if genetic test results made it possible to determine each person's likelihood of developing Alzheimer's, or Parkinson's, or other conditions needing long-term care, with some degree of confidence, then those whose risk was judged highest might find that they could not afford to purchase long-term care policies (particularly if those thought to have least risk concluded that they had no reason to purchase any long-term care cover). The recently established Royal Commission on Long Term Care will no doubt have to consider this issue, which may be a good deal more difficult than the issues of life insurance which have been the main topic of debate in the UK to date.

Less grave, but nevertheless considerable, difficulties may arise if companies selling other forms of personal insurance, such as travel insurance or critical illness cover, were to try to use genetic test results to avoid insuring, or to load, bad risks. There is already evidence that people with chronic genetic conditions, such as sickle cell disease and inherited forms of diabetes, can have trouble in obtaining elementary travel insurance.

The initial concentration of the UK debate on genetics and life insurance, which was no doubt entirely appropriate given the existence of the NHS and the importance of life cover, has in fact focused on the easy case. Life insurance is unlike other forms of personal insurance in that it is mainly bought in the prime of life by healthy people; other sorts of personal insurance are most needed by the less healthy. The most difficult debates may lie ahead.

'I Blame the Parents': Fitting New Genes in Old Criminal Laws

Celia Wells*

Inborn defects — genetic errors — can dispose certain people to act in a way unacceptable to society. How the law should deal with that remains as uncertain as in Lombroso's
day.[1]

This essay seeks to contribute to our understanding of how the 'genetic revolution'
might affect our thinking about criminal law. Would a developing belief that there
is a genetic basis to behaviour lead to a different basis for the way we think about
criminal law, and in particular about criminal responsibility? Although that is a
very large question, not least because there are many, contradictory ways of
approaching crime, criminal law and criminal justice, it is not an especially novel
one. The nature-nurture debate has appeared in many forms in the development of
criminological theories, and theories of criminal law and punishment have long
been locked in a struggle between individual responsibility or free will versus
social or biological determinism. To this debate we can then add the (belated)
contributions of feminist theorists on the gendered nature of crime and criminal
law and the important insights of social and cultural theorists in relation to the
meaning of blame and responsibility.

Drawing on debates about the relationship between law and science, the paper
distinguishes between theories which explain abnormality and those which tell us
something of 'normality', and concludes that notions of criminal responsibility are
generally resistant to explanations (whether from internal or external
circumstances) which seek to excuse behaviour. The thesis developed is an
essentially negative one, both in its rejection of the idea that the genetic revolution
poses particular questions for criminal law and in its reminder that criminal law
itself reflects generally the worst things about a society. Like any other available
'knowledge',[2] genetics will be a resource to be exploited as the handmaiden of the
coercive and controlling tendencies of the criminal justice system. Insofar as the
genetic revolution tells us something about ourselves, it will be reflected in
criminal law.

What kinds of questions might genetic 'knowledge' raise for criminal law? A
non-inclusive definition is that criminal law is a system of censure and sanction for
some types of antisocial behaviour.[3] Taking the term 'criminal law' here to include
the procedural as well as the substantive aspects of the system, we can begin to

---

* Cardiff Law School, Cardiff University.
I am grateful to the Law School for funding, and to Oliver Quick for his assistance with, research, and to
Matilde Betti, Bill Felstiner, Nicola Lacey, Bob Lee and Derek Morgan for listening to my thoughts out
loud on this paper. I bear responsibility for all of its shortcomings.

1 Steve Jones, *In the Blood* (London: HarperCollins, 1996) 218.
2 E. Doyle McCarthy, *Knowledge as Culture* (London: Routledge, 1996) 4.
3 A. Ashworth, *Principles of Criminal Law* (Oxford: Clarendon Press, 1995) 1. It is debatable whether
   it is right to qualify 'behaviour' with 'antisocial'.

assess the impact that genetic information might bring to bear by taking an example: X has caused Y harm (as defined by criminal law) to Z. One set of questions is concerned with issues of detection and proof, 'who is X?' A second type of question centres on the explanatory and attributional, 'why did X cause Y?' This might also take us to a third question, do we have the information which might prevent X from doing Y in the future or, could it have been anticipated, can we predict that X or people like X will do Y? This question of prediction might have two sorts of implication: in relation to X, would it justify some preventive measure? And in relation to Z, what obligations or responsibilities are owed to Z or other potential victims? These are all questions with which criminal law or the criminal justice system are already engaged, and they broadly break down into three sets: genetics and criminal process, genetics and responsibility, and genetics and punishment or disposal. While old-fashioned fingerprinting itself depends on genetic differences, the introduction of DNA profiling does raise important different questions.[4] However, I propose here to leave aside matters related to detection and proof and to concentrate on perhaps less obvious questions about the broader role of crime in society, about the construction of responsibility in criminal law and related issues. The 'genetic revolution' prompts an exploration of the assumptions underlying some of the core aspects of criminal law. The central question is one of attribution — who or what should be held responsible, what weight should be given to genetic abnormalities, or for situational misfortune such as poverty or emotional deprivation, and how should such factors be reflected in punishment or disposal? To approach this question we need first to think about the role of criminal law in society, about science, and about what we know of biological causes of behaviour.

To say that criminal behaviour is behaviour prohibited by criminal law only takes us so far,[5] and to make sense of a debate about genetics and criminal law we have to reframe the question. It is about genetics and some types of behaviour *which happen to be criminal* (for example, intentional violence or sexual abuse), rather than about a category called *criminal offences*.[6] To look for a genetic predisposition or explanation for bigamy or for parking on double yellow lines, or owning a dangerous dog, would make little sense — although to look for a predisposition to lying or for risk-taking might be different.[7] Even if we were to take intentional violence as our starting point, there is still a social constructional element in determining the acceptability and tolerability of different types of violence. This is not fixed, violence to wives and partners is less tolerated than previously, bullying at school is less tolerated. Even taking an apparently clear category — such as homicide — we will find variations in its perception depending on who does it, where it is done, and who the victim is.

When we talk about criminal behaviour, criminal responsibility and criminal punishment, what model of criminality and criminal law does the debate assume?

---

4   N. Lavranos, 'DNA Profiling and Information Technology: A New Weapon for Crime Detection and Prevention?' (1994) *European Jnl of Criminal Law* 595; M Redmayne, 'Science, Evidence and Logic' (1996) 59 MLR 747.

5   Ashworth, n 3 above, Introduction.

6   Those who argue the biological cause often limit their inquiries to violent and/or sexual offenders. For an example see A. Moir and D. Jessel, *A Mind to Crime: The Controversial Link between the Mind and Criminal Behaviour* (London: Michael Joseph, 1995).

7   Farrington found that the factors associated with criminal careers also correlated with behavioural traits such as daring, sexual intercourse and drinking at a young age. D. Farrington, 'Human Development and Criminal Careers' in M. Maguire, R. Morgan and R. Reiner, *The Oxford Handbook of Criminology* (Oxford: OUP, 1997) 361.

Traditionally conceived as a system of state-imposed punishment, criminal law is chameleon-like, adopting or mimicking the compensatory, reparatory and mediatory roles of civil law.[8] It is impossible, and undesirable, to hold constant one model of criminal law — it shifts as we speak, it means different things depending on our subjective position — as victim, as tax evader, as child abuser, as school teacher, as debater, whether we are thinking about types of punishment, whether — take the Louise Woodward case as an example — we have very small children or are the parents of a 19 year old au pair. The layers of meaning within the institution of criminal law and justice are not mutually exclusive and are often contradictory, allowing it to be conceived as 'a system of imposed social control; a system based on reciprocity of obligations and the recognition of certain universally held rights and interests; a system which reproduces and reinforces certain shared meanings; a system which manages or suppresses certain kinds of social conflict; and many other things besides.'[9]

The remainder of the essay is divided (somewhat fluidly) into four sections: genes and 'knowledge'; criminal behaviour; criminal law and risk society; and thinking about criminal responsibility.

Genes and 'knowledge'

The 'genetic revolution' includes, among other things, knowledge about and potential uses of that knowledge, genetic factors which help to explain, predict and alter human behaviour. Without meaning to underplay all the nuances and assumptions about concepts of knowledge, a simple distinction can be made between the types of knowledge to which we might have access. On the one hand there is the explanatory sense of knowledge or understanding. We now 'know' more about our genetic make-up including an increasingly detailed account of the different genetic sites for various disorders, physical or mental, or personality traits. This knowledge is similar to other 'discoveries' about the state of the world, such as the explanation of the planetary system advanced by Copernicus or of gravity by Newton, in the sense that it explains an existing phenomenon. New knowledge of this kind affects our understanding of the world and ourselves but can be distinguished from a second sense of knowledge, one which is taken much more for granted in modern societies than it would have been earlier, which introduces the notion and therefore the possibility of manipulating the knowledge to change that which otherwise would occur. The potential to alter — to use the knowledge to make a different knowledge — brings in its wake shifting boundaries between natural and 'man-made' events, a distinction which permeates discussions of miracles, disasters and many areas of life. This in turn affects our thinking about blame and responsibility. In spelling out the significance of this last observation, it may be helpful first to make some comments about the social construction of scientific knowledge and the interaction between 'expert' and 'lay' knowledge.

The socially constructed nature of scientific knowledge,[10] means that it reflects dominant ideas, for example that human equals man. Human psychology is often ignored as well; scientific accounts of risk may fail to take account of the equally important human perception of risk. The 'technical/engineering world-view of risk, hazard and safety differs markedly from that of the social science/management

---

8   L. Zedner, 'Reparation and Retribution: Are They Reconcileable?' (1994) 57 MLR 228.
9   N. Lacey, 'A Clear Concept of Intention: Elusive or Illusory?' (1993) 56 MLR 621.
10   R. Dreyfuss and D. Nelkin, 'The Jurisprudence of Genetics' (1992) 45 Vand LR 313, 321.

school.'[11] There is great potential for a diffusion of understandings and meanings.[12] And, however great the differences between them, 'feminist critics are similar in their insistence that science be understood and examined as a thoroughly social and cultural activity'.[13] The 'flakiness' of knowledge goes beyond the argument that science is bounded. Scientific or expert knowledge interacts with our own understanding of the world. 'Tacit' knowledge derived from ordinary life plays a significant role and is often in fundamental tension with the 'basic culture of science.'[14] This makes the enterprise of thinking about 'genetics and criminal law' both fascinating and challenging. For tacit knowledge about the causes of crime, about the biological and social influences on behaviour or about the deterrent effect of punishment, is often in fundamental and inevitable conflict with the operating principles of criminal law. This underlines the dangers in assuming that 'new' information will affect existing social institutions in a predictable or 'rational' way. The puzzle is in working out how genetic information, knowledge, and behavioural explanations will affect a further social and cultural process — the practice of criminal law and punishment.

The interaction between our own knowledge and 'scientific' explanation, is part therefore of the process by which notions of cause and blame develop and change. Knowledge affects the way we think about all sorts of things, including blame and responsibility. Blame is more likely when we believe an outcome has a human cause. Yet the dualisms of nature versus nurture, and natural versus 'man-made' phenomena, are built on shaky foundations, the categorisations are shifting as we develop different understandings of the world around us. We will begin to think differently about river flooding once we come to believe that its causes are not simply derived from physical geography or climate, but include the impact of land use practices, and as we begin to appreciate that even climatic factors are (or may be) affected by human activities. Increasing knowledge about the effects of genes on human behaviour, and the possibilities of altering them, and parallel advances in understanding of many areas of life, render inherently unstable our concepts of blame and responsibility, which are after all the broad underpinnings of any system of criminal law. The processes are uncertain, since as McCarthy comments: 'If the sociology of knowledge achieves anything at all, it makes the matter of our connection with reality a rather complex issue.'[15] We are in a process of constant re-negotiation of the boundaries of understanding, and of our reactions to events within our constructed fields of competence. The integrity of the criminal law 'system' would be severely challenged by any wholesale recognition of determinism.

Knowledge is equated with progress, but often brings unwanted secondary effects, which may threaten the trust we have placed in others. It may be that the Human Genome Project turns out to be one of the 'ironies' of progress,[16] alongside technological 'improvements' which threaten local environments, and the use of growth drugs for cattle which feed people but also expose them to the risk of cancer, or of animal feed which transmits diseases such as BSE and CJD. And, as

---

11   D. Blockley, 'Hazard Engineering' in C. Hood and D. Jones, eds, *Accident and Design* (London: UCL Press, 1996) 31.

12   The current ESRC programme 'Public Understanding of Science' would be much more appropriately named 'Scientific understanding of the public.'

13   McCarthy, n 2 above.

14   J. Ravetz, *Scientific Knowledge and Its Social Problems* (Oxford: Oxford University Press, 1971) and B. Wynne, 'Knowledges in Context' (1991) 16 *Science, Technology and Human Values* 111.

15   McCarthy, n 2 above, 6.

16   D. Nelkin (ed), *Controversy: Politics of Technical Decisions* (London: Sage, 1992).

more of those ironies are revealed, our relationship with scientific knowledge will itself alter, such that debate about scientific issues with implications for public policy may correspond 'with a perceived erosion of trust in some domains of scientific expertise.'[17] Thus a dual process takes place: our thinking about science, or expert knowledge, is subject to change, and at the same time, our ideas of responsibility, of whether or whom or what to blame for some untoward occurrence will change also. The lay (non-scientific) community perceives only confusion when the 'miracles' of science fail to deliver. As Giddens argues, trust in expertise plays a fundamental role in psychological survival, yet the processes of modernity constantly throw any such trust into question.[18] The construction of expertise itself is also affected since it is built on certainty and trust: 'the reflexive processes of modernity undermine the certainty of Knowledge'.[19] I shall return to this particular argument in the third section.

How does law relate to science or expert knowledge? David Nelken describes three dominant positions in the debate on the relationship between law and science.[20] The 'trial pathology' approach, perhaps the most familiar to criminal lawyers, is concerned with accommodating expert evidence and often takes much of that expertise for granted. A second level of analysis conceives law and science as competing institutions, competing for space and bearing many similarities in the approaches each takes to their determinations.[21] Thirdly, some theorists conceptualise law and science as incompatible discourses, an approach which Nelken describes in this way:

> On the one hand, [law's] concepts and practices need the stamp of scientific credibility in a world where science has the legitimated monopoly of truth claims; on the other hand, its efforts to align its ideas with those of science are destined to fail as it reproduces itself according to its own code so that it only succeeds in generating 'hybrid artefacts'.[22]

The reception of expert evidence in cases of insanity and diminished responsibility provides a vivid example. Law tries to define mental disorder in pseudo-psychiatric terms forcing an Alice-in-Wonderland exchange, each compromising their field of expertise to accommodate the other.

The purpose of this section has been to remind ourselves that there is something highly problematic in the underlying premises of any of the 'genetics and...' debates. Science and knowledge do not come handed to us in packages hermetically sealed from social and cultural influences, and the representation of scientific 'discoveries' in media accounts feeds into preoccupations with 'dangerous' individuals and the seemingly inevitable assumption that we live in more violent times than ever. An explosion of attention on genetics, on the Human Genome Project, and on the implications for understanding human behaviour, brings into sharper focus the contradictions and complexities of criminal law as a social institution. Popular accounts of genetic discoveries often overplay the capacity for prediction and genetic modification,[23] yet new challenges, such as cloning, appear to take us by surprise. There is a tendency for the imagination to

17 T. Horlick-Jones and B. de Marchi, 'The Crisis of Scientific Expertise in fin de siecle Europe' (1995) 22 *Science and Public Policy*, 139, 141.
18 A. Giddens, *The Consequences of Modernity* (Cambridge: Polity Press, 1990).
19 U. Beck, *Risk Society: Towards a New Modernity* (London: Sage 1992); Horlick-Jones and De Marchi, n 17 above, 140.
20 D. Nelken, 'A Just Measure of Science' in M. Freeman and H. Reece (eds), *Science at Court* (Aldershot: Dartmouth Press, forthcoming) (manuscript).
21 *ibid.*
22 See n 20 above, 6.
23 S. Jones, *The Language of Genes* (London: Flamingo, 1994); Dreyfuss and Nelkin, n 10 above.

run away with the possible implications of the 'genetic revolution'.[24] This is not an excuse for complacency, however, for the social processes of criminal law, blame and punishment continually confront our sense of rationality and fairness. Knowledge, blame and trust interlock and interweave in unpredictable and often unmanageable ways.

'Criminal behaviour'

A conventional account of the relationship between genes and criminal behaviour would be along the following lines. First, there would be a reminder that theories suggesting that particular human features may be hereditary have a very long history. What distinguishes this century's contribution to theories that 'like begets like' is, first, proof that many diseases are hereditary and, secondly, the ability to read the DNA code and as a result to begin to treat some of them.[25] Lombroso of course took heredity in a different direction, and argued that observable physical features disclosed a propensity to criminal behaviour.[26] Influenced by Darwinian theories of inheritance, Lombroso nonetheless accepted that society played a role, and merely asserted that it was possible physically to identify those who were more susceptible to its stresses. Today the argument has moved from physically observable characteristics to suggestions that heredity influences behaviour, but it is not clear that either explanations of criminality or the implications for criminal law and punishment are much further advanced than in Lombroso's day.[27]

What contemporary evidence is there about inheritance and crime? The *Oxford Handbook of Criminology*, now in its second edition, is a rich 1,200 page collection of 32 high-quality essays, a 'state-of-the-art map' covering 'all the principal topics ordinarily included in criminology and criminology-related courses'.[28] There is no index entry for DNA, or heredity and only one for genetics. This surely tells us something about the contemporary lack of concern with, perhaps even avoidance of, determinist theories of crime.[29] David Garland distinguishes two distinct concerns from which modern criminology has grown: the Lombrosian or aetiological project of differentiating the criminal and the governmental or managerial project of governing crime and criminals.[30] He confirms that most aetiological studies this century have de-emphasized the biological determinants which Lombroso took to be fundamental. If genetic explanations gain a foothold, they will travel into the managerial project, a concern explored further in the third section.

A mix of genetically based and social background factors are identified with criminal behaviour: poverty, alcoholism or drug abuse, low socio-economic status, low IQ, poor discipline and psychiatric disorder are all implicated as risk indicators

---

24   *ibid.*
25   R. Porter, *The Greatest Benefit to Mankind* (London: HarperCollins, 1997) 586.
26   In itself an ancient idea, Jones, n 23 above, 218.
27   *ibid* 218.
28   Maguire *et al, Oxford Handbook of Criminology*, n 7 above, Preface.
29   A recent newspaper article on behavioural genes reported a criminologist who said 'I'd rather they didn't even study genetics and violence. The very act of spending money on it...validates it as being important whereas it has no practical consequence except for a very important ideological one.' Decca Aikenhead 'Your behaviour is not all in your genes' *The Guardian* 3 April 1998.
30   D. Garland, 'Of Crimes and Criminals: The Development of Criminology in Britain' in Maguire *et al, Oxford Handbook of Criminology*, n 7 above, 11.

in criminality.[31] There are studies which purportedly show a link between biology and criminality. A Danish research project, comparing the criminal behaviour of 14,427 adoptees with those of their natural and adoptive parents, showed an increased rate of criminal activity amongst those whose natural parents had criminal convictions.[32] 13.5 per cent of adopted sons were convicted of at least one criminal offence where neither natural or adoptive parents had a criminal record. The rate increased to 20 per cent for those whose natural parents had criminal convictions, and to 24.5 per cent where both natural and adoptive parents had convictions. The disparity could be explained by non-hereditary theories such as adoption selection policies tending to match similar socio-economic family backgrounds. And whatever we make of these findings, they still leave a large proportion of the group who did not follow their parents' example.

Does the gender imbalance in crime give any more credence to genetic theories? The fact that crime is largely committed by men went unremarked, and probably unnoticed, until the later part of this century, as Heidensohn points out, a paradox for a discipline· concerned to observe the characteristics of those engaged in particular types of behaviours.[33] If crime is mainly committed by men, it can be tracked down to the single short sequence on the Y chromosome that causes a foetus to develop into a male. To that extent, the trend towards biologising behaviour, for assuming a genetic base to male criminality and to female lack of it, may be justified.[34] But how strong is the link is another question; it is probably too distant to have meaning and it is difficult to imagine what we might do about it. Men are more likely than women to commit offences, but that does not mean that most men are persistent criminals.[35]

While noting that for many people the role of inheritance compared with that of experience is an obsession which goes back long before genetics, Jones reports that

> Most modern geneticists find queries about the relative importance of nature and nurture in controlling the normal range of human behaviour dull, for two reasons. First, they scarcely understand the inheritance of complex characters (... like height, weight or behaviour...) in simple creatures like flies and mice...Second, they know that the perpetual interrogation — nature *or* nurture? — is largely meaningless.[36]

Turning more specifically to violence, there are suggestions that some individuals (men and women) are more vulnerable to psychopathology as a result of either an inherited or acquired tendency or a combination of conditions.[37] More testosterone tends to more violence, while less oestrogen tends to less violence. Fishbein reports that although the relationship between PMS and violence is still controversial, recent research on violent behaviour implicates certain neurotransmitter systems in the development of hyperaggression.[38] But here, the problem of the phenomenon

---

31   R.G. Steen, *DNA and Destiny* (New York: Plenum Publishing Corp, 1986) 217–238; Farrington, n7 above, 361.
32   S. Mednick, W. Gabrielli and B. Hutchings, 'Genetic Influences in Criminal Convictions: Evidence from an Adopted Cohort' (1984) 224 *Science* 891–893.
33   F. Heidensohn, 'Gender and Crime' in Maguire *et al*, *Oxford Handbook of Criminology*, n 7 above, 761.
34   S. Jones, n 23 above, 238.
35   *ibid.*
36   *ibid* 226 (emphasis in the original).
37   D. Fishbein, 'The Psychobiology of Female Aggression' (1992) 19 *Crim Justice and Behaviour* 99. See generally M. Levi, 'Violent Crime' in Maguire *et al*, *Oxford Handbook of Criminology*, n 7 above, 841.
38   n 37 above, 116.

we are seeking to capture invades our efforts. Taking rape as an example, the social, cultural and political climate profoundly affects our accounts of behaviour. The meaning of rape was in earlier times regarded as a form of property theft against men and neither the product of a sex-starved maniac nor as an expression of political domination. It could not have had the same meaning, for men let alone women, Shorter argues, at a time when

> Early modern women were already so completely under male domination that it is hard to imagine what further inroads into their autonomy or independence might have been sliced. Short of falling into slavery, these women could scarcely have been more victimized by the male-controlled social, economic and political systems in which they found themselves.[39]

Violence is historically contingent, and the compression of time through modern communication and transport networks changes its conceptual 'field'.[40] New forms of violence are identified — the silent telephone call of the stalker is one example.[41] There is a shiftingness, a contingency, of the very terms we seek to employ. Now, I think, we need to take a step back and take a somewhat more critical stance to the whole project.

Criminal law and risk society

Is criminality an expression of deviance and therefore inherently abnormal, or indeed is it so normal that it is an essential element in the functioning of societies?[42] Of the five million or so recorded offences in England and Wales each year, only about 300,000 result in convictions and 200,000 in cautions, and many offences are never recorded. Therefore what we read into statistics on those few offenders who do end up being formally processed through conviction or caution we must treat with care. The ratio of convictions to recorded offences is so low that it makes all the more surprising the fact that one in three men in the UK will have a conviction for a serious offence by the age of 31 (for women it is one in 13).[43] Of those who are convicted or cautioned, 82 per cent are male and 45 per cent are under 21.[44] Disproportionate numbers of those sentenced to imprisonment come from ethnic minorities, and have experienced some time in local authority care. Self-report studies suggest that the 97 per cent of known offences which do not result in a conviction are committed by a wider range of the population. Elmhorn found 92 per cent of teenage boys in Stockholm admitted to at least one offence and a recent international self-report study suggested over half of young people have committed at least one criminal offence.[45] If criminal behaviour is almost

---

39 E. Shorter, 'On writing the history of rape' *Signs* 3, 1977, 471, 475.

40 S. Cotta, *Why Violence?* (Gainesville: University of Florida Press 1985) 9–11.

41 *R v Ireland, R v Burstow* [1997] 4 All ER 225.

42 E. Durkheim, *The Rules of Sociological Method* (Glencoe, Ill: The Free Press, 1958).

43 Home Office, *Digest 3 Information on the Criminal Justice System* (London: HMSO, 1995). This includes all indictable offences and certain summary offences such as assault on a constable and criminal damage.

44 Maguire, 'Crime Statistics, Patterns and Trends' in Maguire *et al*, *Oxford Handbook of Criminology*, n 7 above, 135, 173.

45 *ibid* 175. He adds, at 177, that 'The most recent British contribution to the debate is the Home Office survey . . . which confirmed the common finding — at least among surveys based on self- completion questionnaires — of no significant association between social class and admissions to offending *as a whole*, but of a strong association, for both males and females, between social class and admissions of *more serious* offending.' Graham and Bowling, *Young People and Crime*, Home Office Res Study No 145 (London: HMSO, 1995).

normal for males under the age of 25, that makes it normal for all men since they were all young once. So there is, depending on one's perspective, a troubling or reassuring normalcy about criminal behaviour by young men.[46] The same cannot be said for women; the male-female ratio of convictions has remained static over the last 100 years.[47] As Kai Erikson wrote in *Wayward Puritans*, the interesting question is less about who commits crime and more about the reasons that some deviancy leads to a person acquiring the identity and label of deviant and not others.[48] Few respondents to crime surveys report persistent offending. The development of a 'criminal' or deviant career is not a matter of individual determination, it reflects a range of broader cultural and historical factors.

Durkheim argued that crime is functional, that societies make criminals rather than criminals unmaking society. 'Social rules and the violation of them are an intrinsic aspect of social organization, a part of the human condition'.[49] Others have taken up the argument arguing that deviance offers social systems 'a dialectical tool for the clarification of threats, ambiguities, and anomalies in classification systems'.[50] A powerful theme in recent theorising about criminal law draws on Ulrich Beck's 'risk society' thesis which provides insights into the role and focus of blame in contemporary society.[51]

Risk itself is about external danger: disaster, technological breakdown, and human misbehaviour are all examples. Knowledge about risk has been assisted by the twin developments of statistical analysis and the technology to communicate the results of that analysis. Concern with risk is not merely to do with knowledge of probability, it is to do with cultural attitudes to the acceptability of different hazards. For Douglas, risk perceptions affect the ways in which societies respond to different threats, how they distribute institutional authority, and also provide the focus for debates about morality and identity.[52] What is regarded as risky by social groups is selected not given. The BSE crisis as it has developed in the UK over the last five years provides an example of preoccupations with risk and its deployment as a cultural resource, including its potential to provide a vocabulary with which to make sense of seemingly uncontrollable hazards. On the one hand, technological innovation has transformed the agrarian base of the food economy into a major international business reliant on mass-production methods and transportation — hence the emergence of the risk of widespread (invisible) contamination. On the other, our familiarity with and reliance on risk analysis leads to the belief that danger is quantifiable and predictable. BSE has shaken those beliefs and confirmed that bringing hazard under control is both individualized and reliant on expert knowledge. Much of the risk society literature is couched in complex and sophisticated terms but at bottom there is a simple argument about our transition from localised self-sufficiency through industrial paternalistic societies to the emergence of societies where risk is privatised and a matter for individual judgment. However, individual situations are also institutional, Beck argues,

---

46   See T. Newburn and E. Stanko, *Just Boys Doing Business: Men, Masculinities and Crime* (London: Routledge, 1994).

47   *ibid* 177.

48   K. Erikson, *Wayward Puritans* (New York: John Wiley, 1966) ch 1.

49   D. Garland, 'Of Crimes and Criminals: The Development of Criminology in Britain' in Maguire *et al, Oxford Handbook of Criminology* n 7 above, 21.

50   P. Rock, 'Sociological Theories of Crime' in Maguire *et al, ibid* 254 — referring here particularly to the work of Mary Douglas, *Risk and Blame: Essays in Cultural Theory* (London: Routledge, 1992) and Erikson, n 48 above.

51   U. Beck, n 19 above.

52   M. Douglas, n 50 above.

because 'the liberated individual is dependent on a series of secondary agencies and institutions.'[53] Risk society thus raises issues of trust, accountability and personal responsibility. The social institutions associated with law — of which the criminal justice system is emblematic — themselves play a significant role in risk management and the production of risk knowledge.[54] How then do these arguments apply specifically to the risks, dangers or hazards of 'crime'?

I have used these arguments to provide a framework for understanding the rise of corporate criminal liability, and corporate manslaughter.[55] This seems as powerful an instrument for disowning the link between genetics and criminal behaviour as we are likely to find. A corporation is a non-human, yet juridical, person. Corporate manslaughter has been the vehicle on which cultural attitudes towards large-scale disasters have been riding over the last decade. However, the argument cannot be evaded quite so easily for two reasons. First, an emerging theme in recent writings on corporate liability emphasises the importance of tracing responsibility back to human actors, and secondly, risk society analysis, with its dependence on the production of knowledge about risk, alerts us to the real dangers inherent in linking genetics and crime.

In their study of the police as knowledge workers, Ericson and Haggerty describe how the police supply risk information to a web of institutions — insurance companies, regulatory agencies, financial institutions, amongst others. Criminologists 'know' that the popular image of policing as portrayed in TV and film, and even as reflected in news reporting, is wildly biased in favour of action, detection and contact with 'criminals'. Arresting suspects is a relatively rare event for most police officers, even detectives spend almost half their time in the office recording investigative work rather than engaging in it. Much of this recording, this production of knowledge, is for internal purposes. If you haven't arrested someone you can at least produce a paper trail explaining what you have been doing. If you have arrested someone, then preparation of papers in relation to custody decisions, in relation to interrogation, or in preparation for prosecution, is necessary. The provision of information to a complex web of other institutions is a major function of police work. Other social institutions, such as education and health, are similarly engaged in the production and communication of risk knowledge. 'Institutionalized communications systems form the foundation of contemporary society and provide the governing basis of social life'.[56] The information is used to establish and monitor, amongst other things, identities: achieved identities such as careers are monitored through record-keeping (in relation to offenders and victims) and through licensing (gun ownership for example), while ascribed identities (age, race, gender etc) are maintained and constructed through the use of categories into which people are fitted. Often these categories of identity are determined externally and the police mould the individual to fit the pre-determined boxes. Youth is one obvious identity here. Police interaction with agencies such as schools takes a number of forms but is characterised by systems of risk selection (which areas, which schools, which pupils). Here the interplay between institutions is apparent with knowledge exchanged between schools, social services, individual parents and the police.[57]

---

53 Beck, n 19 above, 130–132.
54 R. Ericson and K. Haggerty, *Policing the Risk Society* (Oxford: Oxford University Press, 1997).
55 C. Wells, 'Corporate Manslaughter: A Cultural and Legal Form' (1995) 6 *Criminal Law Forum* 45–72.
56 n 54 above, 426.
57 The Police Act 1997 when implemented will establish a Criminal Records Agency. For a useful summary, including an account of the current system of criminal record collection, see S. Uglow, 'Criminal Records under the Police Act 1997' [1998] Crim LR 235, 236–237.

Arguing that 'Communication formats are the focal points for an institution's selection and definition of risks',[58] Ericson and Haggerty suggest that things only become mobilised as police work if they fit the risk knowledge requirements of external institutions. In place of deviance, control and order are risk, surveillance and security. The role of criminal justice systems in controlling problem populations has been well documented.[59] This is the context into which the genetics argument slides. As Cohen argues, a number of institutional frameworks, legal and quasi-legal, diversionary and alternative, administrative and professional, mark out their own territories of jurisdiction, competence and referral. Each produces a set of expert knowledge from which derive new categories and typifications which, for all their differences, are bound by the principle of binary opposition, 'how to sort out the good from the bad, the elect from the damned, the sheep from the goats, the amenable from the non-amenable, the good risks from the bad risks, the high prediction scorers from the low prediction scorers'.[60] Genetic theories may prove a powerful ally in this process: 'Individualization delivers people over to an *external control and standardization* that was unknown in the enclaves of familial and feudal subcultures.'[61]

This section on criminal law and risk society has sought to demonstrate the contingency of the boundaries of deviance. 'Deviance is not a propensity inherent in any particular form of behaviour; it is a propensity conferred upon that behaviour by the people who come into direct or indirect contact with it.'[62] First, behaviour has to be interpreted as 'criminal' — witness the way that health and safety deaths or some types of fraud or drink driving have come to be perceived as 'really' criminal only over the last decade. What has changed is not 'law in the books' but the type of events to which it is applied. Secondly, law in the books does change as well, of course. Witness most obviously examples such as insider trading, money laundering and, over a slightly longer time span, the misuse of drugs.

Thinking about responsibility

Finally, I turn to a consideration of the internal criminal law questions about responsibility and the external criminal law debate about what should be done with (or should it be to?) a person who is held to be responsible.

Possibly one of the most remarkable features of modern criminal law has been its resistance to notions of excuse based on individual characteristics or circumstances, in other words a resistance to precisely the kind of claim which genetic knowledge might found. A number of reasons can be advanced for this, some of which relate to the particular characteristics of legal decisions themselves. As David Nelken points out, legal decisions have many intended audiences.[63] Unlike scientific disciplines which are typically addressed mainly to academic peers, legal decisions are directed at other judges, lawyers, the jury, and, at least indirectly, the general public.

---

58   n 54 above, 430.
59   M. Foucault, *Discipline and Punish: The Birth of the Prison* (London: Allen Lane, 1977); D. Melossi, *The State of Social Control* (Cambridge: Polity Press, 1990); S. Cohen, *Visions of Social Control* (Cambridge: Polity Press, 1985) ch 2.
60   Cohen, *ibid.*
61   Beck, n 19 above, 132 (emphasis in original).
62   Erikson, n 48 above, 6.
63   D. Nelken, n 20 above.

Law refuses to deal with hypotheticals, rarely spells out defeasible empirical propositions, has different ways of arguing from authority and precedent, and special techniques of analysis such as reasoning from analogy. Lawyers and judges are involved in processing already categorised data, events which have been generated by non-academic actors, judges, litigants etc. Legal practice cannot therefore aspire to develop the sort of cumulative knowledge characteristic of certain scientific disciplines.[64]

This has profound implications for any descriptive analysis of principles of responsibility.

The mixed audience to which they are addressed and the mixed aetiology of the sorts of cases which enshrine principles of criminal law ensure that they refract rather than reflect cultural ideas of responsibility. It is important for criminal doctrine to limit the role of excuse. Children are excused, some categories of mental disorder lead to excuse, some powerful external pressures such as threats of violence may excuse. As soon as the phenomenon which is sought to excuse moves away from the exceptional, the harder it is for criminal law to see it. Intoxication is one example here. The severe limits placed on duress or provocation as potential excusing factors bear witness to the overwhelming need to keep the lid on Pandora's box. Factors such as family background, social and economic circumstance, all of which may have both an explanatory and an excusing force, are nonetheless out of bounds. Excuses create problems of line-drawing and threaten the social control or managerial functions of the system.

Criminal law proclaims individual responsibility for actions, with the requirement of voluntariness functioning as the foundation for this notion of responsibility.[65] I use two examples here which show how limited criminal law's commitment to this foundational principle turns out to be when it is challenged by individualised excuses. Barry Kingston, a man with paedophiliac tendencies, sought to have his conviction for indecent assault overturned on the ground that his co-defendant had administered sedative drugs to him which meant that he did not realise what he was doing.[66] The terms in which the House of Lords rejected this claim, one that the Court of Appeal had incidentally found attractive, gives some indications as to the reception a genetics based defence might receive. 'To recognise a new defence of this type would be a bold step,' Lord Mustill said. 'The common law defences of duress and necessity (if it exists) and the limited common law defence of provocation are all very old...I suspect that the recognition of a new general defence at common law has not happened in modern times.'[67] Although he went on to say that the criminal law could not stand still and that novelty itself is not an objection, the signs of resistance were plain.

The unhappy relationship between insanity and automatism is a further example of the ringfence criminal law places round the 'fundamental' notion of voluntariness, one which may be thought more compelling since Kingston's claim might be thought to be one of non-voluntariness rather than in-voluntariness.[68] Here, however, the foundational doctrine of the voluntary act finds itself in competition with the social protection goals of criminal law. When the cause of the involuntariness is inherent as in mental disorder, then insanity steps in: 'Even if D's bodily movements were uncontrollable or proceeded from unconsciousness, the doctrine of automatism will not normally be available if the cause of D's

---

64 *ibid* 15 (manuscript).
65 A. Ashworth, n 3 above, 240.
66 *R v Kingston* [1995] 2 AC 355.
67 At 372.
68 Ashworth, n 3 above, 215.

condition was a mental disorder classified as insanity.'[69] The 'external factor' principle has resulted in an absurd line being drawn between diabetics who, taking too little insulin, come within the insanity bracket and those who, taking too much (and therefore externally causing their episode of unconscious action) come in the protection of automatism. Not all external factors will help the defendant — an unconscious state caused by alcohol and drugs will fall to be caught by the voluntary intoxication rules.

Is it likely therefore, that a genetic basis to alcoholism would be admitted as an excusing factor except in the most limited of circumstances? In fact quite the opposite conclusion should be drawn, underlining the dangers of arguing for a genetic 'excuse.' The role of the insanity defence has been to tighten the circle of control of mentally disordered offenders directly by subjecting them to detention or indirectly by that prospect deterring them from raising the defence. Similar lessons can be observed with provocation, the partial defence to murder. The idea behind an excuse based on loss of self-control is itself interesting, implying as it does that there is an underlying aggression in all of us which is capable of release under certain circumstances. (Of course, speaking of 'all of us' is inappropriate given the gendered history and present of law generally, and of criminal law and provocation especially.)[70] This seems to buy into (at least impliedly) notions of determinism. The other fascinating feature of provocation is the tension between the essentially individualised notion of loss of self-control and its mediation through the standard of the reasonable man.[71] This tension has become particularly acute since the courts abandoned the completely 'objective' abstract reasonable man. Once the reasonable man could be younger, or gendered, or imbued with other personal characteristics, it was hard to know where to stop. Courts have struggled in the last few years to contain the 'reasonable man', veering between a version which all but emasculates him as (s)he merges into the defendant, and rebuilding him into the 'straight citizen'.[72] Meanwhile, the admission of evidence of Battered Wife Syndrome in aid of women who have killed their abusive partners, has been shown to be fraught with dangers. Not only does such evidence seek to argue that the reasonable or normal is abnormal (women who comply with expectations of fidelity and responsiblity for maintaining a home for their children are the victims of a syndrome), it also seeks to make the abnormal, normal by implying that women who use violence in response to violence are living out an inevitable response to persistent abuse.[73]

Provocation acts as a useful exemplar for criminal law as a whole. Alan Norrie argues that crime has been depersonified, that the conception of criminal law as a systematic attempt to govern conduct by rules — a conception that is central to the legitimacy of the modern state — is flawed because the model of the abstract juridical individual at its heart constantly comes into conflict with the socio-political realities of the individual crime.[74] The legitimacy of criminal law is

---

69   *ibid* 98.
70   N. Lacey. *Unspeakable Subjects* (Oxford: Hart Publishing, 1998) ch 7.
71   s3, Homicide Act 1957 '...the question whether the provocation was enough to make a reasonable man do as he did shall be left to be determined by the jury; and in determining that question the jury shall take into account everything both done and said according to the effect which, in their opinion, it would have on a reasonable man.'
72   N. Lacey and C. Wells. *Reconstructing Criminal Law*, 2nd ed (London: Butterworths, 1998) 591.
73   D. Nicolson. 'Telling Tales: Gender Discrimination, Gender Construction and Battered Women Who Kill' (1995) Fem Leg Stud 185–196.
74   A. Norrie. *Crime, Reason and History* (London:Butterworths, 1993) 196.

maintained by this process of decontextualisation with its emphasis on fairness. As Nicola Lacey aptly summarises the argument:

> This decontextualised and formalised mode of attribution serves to keep out of the courtroom the muddying social and political issues which are in fact deeply implicated in a broader understanding of how behaviour comes to be defined as criminal: it keeps out of sight those facts which produce the embarrassing truth that criminalising power in fact disciplines a sector of the population vividly marked by socio-economic status, by race, or ethnicity, and by sex.[75]

The argument is reminiscent of Hay's analysis of 18th century criminal justice policies — the threat of capital punishment tempered by the exercise of mercy at the point of execution — as a successful strategy for maintaining order.[76] Departures from the strict doctrine of individual responsibility temper any suggestion that criminal law is blind to individual circumstance.[77] Ashworth notes that the courts appear to be concerned to keep the ambit of defences as narrow as possible, 'so as to capture only the full or extreme cases of excuse,'[78] deliberately handing over to be reflected at the sentencing stage lesser degrees of exculpation. Nonetheless, it might be interesting to speculate on the reasons for the broadening of the excuse-base over the last 150 years or so.

For most contemporary criminal law scholars, individual responsibility rests on the principle of capacity and a fair opportunity to act otherwise developed by Hart.[79] Any argument that the fair opportunity was compromised by social deprivation or from genetic predisposition runs up against the difficulty that not everyone succumbs to criminal behaviour. Defences of duress and provocation are easier to accommodate for two reasons. First, they are particularised events rather than general conditions, such that the empirical question of whether others would succumb is irrelevant and indeed can be converted into the defence itself — into a prescriptive inquiry as to whether a person of reasonable firmness would have acted similarly. Secondly, the moral equation that the circumstances arose from another's wrongdoing (the duressor or the source of the provocation), is attractive at an intuitive level.[80]

If justice is blind to individual circumstance at the liability stage, when it comes to sentencing all sorts of factors are considered. It is worth reminding ourselves again that only about two per cent of crimes eventually leads to a sentencing decision.[81] Although there has been a move towards a more principled base for sentencing over the last five years, there still remains an inevitable confusion of aims and purposes. Norrie suggests that the tensions at the heart of criminal law are also found in the theory of deterrence, which assumes a free willed actor. On the one hand, the theory of the rational, calculating individual stands in opposition to the contextualised nature of social action, and the tendency of prison to attract the poorest, and most marginalised, the very group least deterrable by general deterrence. On the other, the logic of punishment according to the dictates of individual action comes up against the logic of the broader political end of general deterrence.[82] The gap between practice and theory is not much clearer under a

---

75 N. Lacey, n 70 above, 198.
76 A. Norrie, n 74 above, 18; D. Hay, 'Property, Authority and the Criminal Law' in D. Hay *et al*, *Albion's Fatal Tree* (Harmondsworth: Penguin, 1977).
77 N. Lacey, n 70 above, 199.
78 n 3 above, 241.
79 H.L.A. Hart, *Punishment and Responsibility* (Oxford: Clarendon Press, 1968).
80 Ashworth suggests this is a coherent justification, n 3 above, 245.
81 A. Ashworth, *Sentencing and Criminal Justice* (London: Butterworths, 1995) 57.
82 A. Norrie, n 74 above, 204.

retributive scheme. The ideal rational person would agree to punishment as a moral necessity but would never need to be punished because they would not be so irrational as to commit crime; while the irrational person would not grasp the necessity of the punishment. 'Punishment is justified to *nomenal* beings who do not commit crimes, but unjustified to *phaenomenal* beings who do commit them.'[83]

Stirred into the melting pot of sentencing rationales are rehabilitation and incapacitation, and it is the latter which is the most likely beneficiary of any genetically based theory of behaviour. Here be dragons. The more that individual predisposition becomes accepted, as we have seen with the treatment of those with mental disorder, the greater the likelihood of compulsory measures of social protection. Concerns about paedophilia are the current manifestation of these ideas. Picking up the arguments made in section three about controlling suspect populations, or perhaps closing the loop, we can see that the production of knowledge about past offenders is increasingly used to justify control. The Sex Offenders Act 1997 requires anyone convicted, cautioned, or found not guilty by reason of insanity in respect of a sexual offence[84] to notify the police of their current address. The obligation lasts for between five and 10 years in the case of those sentenced to less than 30 months imprisonment, and indefinitely where the sentence was longer, or the person was made subject to a restriction order.[85] Although the circumstances under which the public have access to such information are limited, it is naive to believe that the existence of registers of this kind do not increase dramatically the opportunities for agencies to write a person's biography and thus determine their access to legitimate employment, educational or other institutional benefits. Recently the Court of Appeal upheld the decision of North Wales police to reveal the identity of two former sex offenders to the owner of a caravan site on which they were living.[86]

Notes of conclusion

When I began this paper, I expected to learn a lot about genetics and behaviour. Instead, I have developed a different understanding of criminal responsibility. Genetic theories have the potential to cast a long, though essentially familiar, shadow over criminal law and justice. Predisposition yields only 'probabilistic information and the relationship between predisposition and actual expression generally remains unknown.'[87] Genetic essentialism acts as a counterweight to assumptions about free will,[88] but that does not necessarily mean that it puts into question much of the law concerning responsibility, intent, condemnation, and punishment. 'Free will' is itself an ideological expression understood to be a metaphor for the need for society to set boundaries. While genetic ideas are unlikely to affect the exculpatory pillars of criminal responsibility, they may well

---

83   *ibid* 208.
84   Ranging from rape to indecent assault, indecency with children and possession of indecent photographs, *inter alia*, Schedule 1.
85   See F. Russell, 'Getting the Balance Right' (1998) 148 *New Law Journal* 84; K. Soothill, B. Francis and B. Sanderson, 'A Cautionary Tale: The Sex Offenders Act 1997, the Police and Cautions' [1997] Crim LR 482.
86   *R v CC of the North Wales Police, The Independent* 26 March 1998. In *R v Norfolk CC, ex parte M* [1989] 2 All ER 359 it was held unlawful to inform an employer that a person was listed on the child abuse register when they had not had an opportunity to refute the basis of the complaint.
87   Dreyfuss and Nelkin, n 10 above, 318.
88   *ibid* 321.

reinforce the tendency of criminal justice systems to control, categorise and label people.

As Jones suggests, the acceptance that genes influence so many human attributes brings for law the question not whether to accept the idea of an inborn propensity to such crimes, but how far it will go. 'For the first time, science is entering a province which the law sees as its own; the relationship between individuals and society.'[89] Law, because we ask it to mediate between society and individuals, cannot afford to admit defences of poverty or inherited disposition but, conversely, because it mediates between individuals and society we expect it to intervene to control those who represent the outsiders. Because this is a cultural process, the identification of those groups will be achieved through the use of the resources available, and genetic information may prove alarmingly useful.

---

89   n 1 above, 220.

The Inscription of Life in Law: Genes, Patents, and Bio-politics

Alain Pottage*

'Bio-colonialism' in New Guinea

In 1989, Carol Jenkins, an American medical anthropologist attached to the Institute of Medical Research in Papua New Guinea, extracted a set of blood samples from some members of the Hagahai, a small group of hunter-gatherers living in an inaccessible mountain range: 'I told them we wanted to see a 'binitang' — an insect — in their blood'.[1] The suspicion that this peculiar 'insect' existed had arisen from research carried out by scientists from the US National Institutes of Health (NIH), who were conducting a survey of the distribution of variants of the HTLV-I virus in Melanesia.[2] In her own (retrospective) accounts of the transaction that was taking shape, Jenkins identified herself as a disinterested intermediary, whose primary concern was to ensure that the Hagahai received the proper commercial or therapeutic return for their participation. Her original research interests had little to do with the genetic properties of their blood. In a paper describing the methods and objectives of her medical-anthropological survey, written before these particular blood samples had been extracted, Jenkins heralded 'a rare opportunity to document the effects of contact on a previously isolated population in Papua New Guinea'.[3] Apparently, the Hagahai had avoided direct contact with 'globalised' society until 1983, when the effects of various illnesses became so severe that they came to a missionary outpost in search of assistance. The missionaries had their own ambitions for the Hagahai, which were not necessarily in the best interests of the health of the group,[4] and the first effective measures of medical assistance arrived only when Jenkins and her colleagues began their study. Indeed, Jenkins' published account states that 'the ethical obligation to intervene with medical aid was immediately obvious to the researchers'.[5] However, although the protocols of research and publication did not exclude an active concern for the health of the Hagahai,[6] it remains the case that the governing objective of Jenkins' programme was 'to investigate the causes

---

* Law Department, London School of Economics.

I am grateful to the participants in a research seminar at Griffith University for their comments on a version of this article.

1 Carol Jenkins, quoted in *The Detroit News* 20 April 1996.
2 Jenkins and two other members of the Papua New Guinea Institute of Medical Research were co-signatories, together with researchers from the National Institute of Neurological Disorders and Stroke (a branch of the US National Institutes of Health) of a letter to a medical journal describing the isolation of the strain of the virus (Richard Yanagihara *et al*, 'Isolation of HTLV-I from Members of a Remote Tribe in New Guinea' (1990) 323 *New England Journal of Medicine* 993).
3 Carol L. Jenkins, 'Health in the Early Contact Period: A Contemporary Example from Papua New Guinea' (1988) 26:10 *Social Science and Medicine* 997, 997.
4 The missionaries' first response was to send a helicopter bearing sweets and toys. More important, in attempting to convert the Hagahai to a more settled, sedentary, life style, the missionaries rendered them more vulnerable to infection by unfamiliar viruses and bacteria.
5 Jenkins, n 3 above, 1004.
6 In fact, through her publications Jenkins actively raised some of the funds needed to buy essential vaccines and medical supplies for the Hagahai.

of their decline and to monitor the consequences of increased contact to their biological and cultural survival'.[7] The extensive array of tests carried out on the members of the group facilitated various therapeutic objectives, but they also provided a criterion against which the course of their decline could be plotted. The prognosis was far from encouraging. Jenkins' research paper states, somewhat tersely, that 'the net population increase is negative and the Hagahai are dying out'.[8]

Jenkins' medical-anthropological publications are written in the language of traditional ethnography; they betray none of modern anthropology's ethical or epistemological anxieties about the status of its objects. Medical anthropology deals with subject profiles fashioned from parasitological surveys, mortality rates, comparative assessments of growth rates, cranial measurements, and so on. These techniques were entirely appropriate to the research programme, which identified the Hagahai population as a site of epidemiological negotiation, where culture-borne viruses and antibodies were exchanged or cancelled. The question of how culture was reproduced, or of how 'biology' was bound to 'culture' in that process of reproduction, was no part of this programme, whether one takes the 'culture' in question to be that of the Hagahai or that of the researchers. Similarly, for the NIH scientists the Hagahai were interesting only as the human carriers of a rare viral strain and its correlative antigens. Both perspectives condensed the social or cultural agency of the group into a set of biological ciphers. Given that these reductive accounts supply the basic fabric of even the most 'critical' interventions, it is not surprising that most versions of the story adopt the notion of genes as 'patrimony', a notion that obscures the most vital issue in the patenting of 'life', namely, the question of how societies (re-)invent the distinction between the social and the biological. In this context, it is particularly important that these processes of (re-)invention should be made explicit, rather than being allowed to condense into inarticulate ciphers, because the most vital aspect of biotechnology patents is their role in forcing the re-negotiation of traditional elaborations of the distinction between nature and culture.

The precise nature of the extracted 'insect' was identified in the laboratories of the NIH, where analysis of one particular culture, taken from a young man, revealed the existence of antibodies to a variant of the HTLV-I leukaemia virus.[9] This culture was used to develop an immortal T-cell line, 'persistently infected' with the HTLV-I strain, which was the basis for a patent application relating to the cell line, the infecting virus, and a set of ancillary diagnostic test kits.[10] Carol Jenkins was identified as one of the five inventors of the PNG-1 cell line, a status which seems to have been attributed almost entirely in recognition of her role as the agent of 'her' population. According to Jenkins' account, the terms of the

---

7   Carol L. Jenkins, 'Medical Anthropology in the Western Schrader Range, Papua New Guinea' (1987) 3:4 *National Geographic Research* 412, 413.

8   *ibid* 412.

9   Yanagihara *et al*, n 2 above.

10 'The present invention relates to a human T-cell line (PNG-1) persistently infected with a Papua New Guinea (PNG) HTLV-I variant and to the infecting virus (PNG-1 variant). Cells of the present invention express viral antigens, type C particles and have a low level of reverse transcriptase activity. The establishment of this cell line, the first of its kind from an individual in Papua New Guinea, makes possible the screening of Melanesian populations using a local virus strain. The present invention also relates to vaccines for use in humans against infection with and diseases caused by HTLV-I and related viruses. The invention further relates to a variety of bioassays and kits for the detection and diagnosis of infection with and diseases caused by HLTV-I and related viruses' (Abstract, US Patent Application No 05397696, assigned to the National Institutes of Health, granted 14 March 1995. The full text is available at <http://www.rafi.ca/pp/patent.txt>).

agreement which she made with the Hagahai were considerably more sophisticated than the euphemistic reference to 'insects' might suggest. Not only did the Hagahai 'leaders' have 'a clear understanding of the concept of ownership',[11] but they were sophisticated enough to appreciate the advantages of patenting the cell line.[12] The patent was supposed to secure an appropriate return for their participation: as Jenkins put it, 'despite what exploitation may take place around the world, in this case the rights of the Hagahai people have been specifically safeguarded'.[13] Apparently, the terms of the 'agreement' were that the Hagahai should receive some (unspecified) share of the commercial profits of the invention. However, in late 1996, the patent was officially disclaimed by the NIH, after a heated international controversy during which Jenkins was apparently threatened with deportation from Papua New Guinea.[14] The NIH Office of Technology Transfer explained its abandonment of the patent in general terms; the Institutes would retain patents only in relation to those inventions with significant commercial potential, and they would no longer file patent applications on 'primary research tools'.[15] Although Jenkins and her advisors had considered assigning the unwanted patent to the Hagahai themselves, the administrative costs would have been entirely disproportionate, given that the invention had almost no prospects of commercial exploitation.

In these 'public' accounts of the PNG-1 patent, the Hagahai themselves are absent other than as the passive objects or mute clients of their observers and advocates. Of the latter, the most significant was a Canadian organisation called the Rural Advancement Foundation International (RAFI), which dramatised their 'exploitation' as a story of 'bio-colonialism':[16]

> Pieces of indigenous and remote rural peoples' very bodies are now, without any doubt, the 'intellectual property' of the corporations and governments researching them in the North. The Papua New Guinea patent dramatically underscores why groups like the Human Genome Diversity Project can no longer hide behind claims to be collecting only for historical, cultural, or medical research. It is now clear that they are also potentially shuttling the cells, DNA, and other biological materials of people into the intellectual property portfolios and cashboxes of the life industries.[17]

Coloured with this polemical theme, the story of the PNG-1 patent becomes an exemplary account of the methods which globalised industry has used to appropriate the genetic wealth of indigenous peoples. In some cases their bodily tissues are themselves the raw materials for some commercial process, but in other cases the exploitative relation is more oblique. For instance, traditional endogamous family structures make it considerably easier to identify and isolate the genetic polymorphisms which are thought to be active in producing certain

---

11 'Scientists Attacked for "Patenting" Pacific Tribe' (1995) 270 *Science* 1112.

12 'Anthropologist Cleared in Patent Dispute' (1996) 380 *Nature* 374.

13 Carol Jenkins, quoted in 'Bio-pirates Face Challenge in Pacific Blood Feud' Gemini News Service Report, <http://www.oneworld.org/gemini/wk42-gemini-bio.html>.

14 *The Independent* 29 March 1996; 'Anthropologist Cleared in Patent Dispute' (1996) 380 *Nature* 374.

15 'US Drops Patent Claim to Hagahai Cell Line' (1996) 384 *Nature* 500.

16 '[A]ccusations came from a small Canadian-based group known as the Rural Advancement Foundation International, which says it is dedicated to the socially-responsible development of "technologies useful to rural societies". By distributing the release via the Internet — a medium prized by scientists for its ability to disseminate information, but one proving equally adept at spreading misinformation — RAFI ensured a wide and rapid airing' ('Scientists Attacked for "Patenting" Pacific Tribe' (1995) 270 *Science* 1112).

17 RAFI Communique, Mar/Apr 1996, 'New Questions About Management and Exchange of Human Tissues at NIH' (text available at <http://www.cptech.org/ip/rafi.html>). See also Aroha Te Pareake Mead, 'Resisting the Gene Raiders' (1997) 293 *New Internationalist* 26.

illnesses.[18] 'Bio-colonialism' encompasses processes of commodification which appropriate not only the 'bodily' genetic resources of indigenous peoples, but also their traditional cultural artefacts. Multinational pharmaceuticals companies have identified the 'biotechnological' bases of those therapeutic or agricultural benefits which indigenous traditions have attributed to plants such as the turmeric root, the neem tree, or basmati rice.[19] The basic mode is to (re-)attach traditional applications to an 'invented' molecular structure; or, in other words, to stretch 'the veneer of [technological] modernism over traditional prior art'.[20]

'Bio-colonialism' discloses an asymmetrical process of exchange in which the wealthy but genetically impoverished nations of the North exploit the genetic patrimony of the vulnerable South. One might ask whether this version of events is as 'true' to the agency and identity of indigenous peoples as it claims to be. For example, it is sometimes argued that (even where they are 'successful') claims to cultural property reconstruct traditional cultures in the 'inauthentic' language of property and patrimony.[21] However, given that traditional cultures are always already included or implicated in globalised society, it is not clear who would be placed to adjudicate on authenticity.[22] For that reason, it may be more productive to ask how accounts are settled within globalised society; either quite literally, by considering how the commercial profits of bio-colonialism should be (re-) distributed, or, more abstractly, by considering the ways in which these stories of exploitation express global society's own anxieties about the 'commodification of life'. This article begins with the second, more abstract, question. Therefore it has little to say about the dynamics of particular local disputes, or about the broader, technical, question of how international regulatory frameworks structure economic asymmetries. Rather, it explores the ways in which themes such as 'biocolonialism' articulate a set of productive misunderstandings about the workings of the patents process and of property processes in general. The element of misunderstanding arises because arguments about the 'commodification of life' reckon with concepts that afford only a limited understanding of how property norms bind events, but these conceptualisations are nevertheless productive because they facilitate the very processes that they misrecognise. It is instructive to consider how critical themes such as 'biocolonialism' are metabolised by the very technological and economic processes which they claim to hold at some sort of critical distance.

Patents and bio-politics

Despite its unpromisingly technical and bureaucratic tone, patent law is politically and socially significant because it constitutes a nexus in which some deep-running anxieties about the relation between 'nature' and 'culture' are negotiated. To the extent that one might treat generalised ideas about life, body, or even property, as

---

18 'Tribal Groups Attack Ethics of Genome Diversity Project' (1996) 383 *Nature* 208; 'Gene Hunters Home in on India' (1996) 381 *Nature* 13.
19 'GATT adds Fuel to Patents Controversy' (1993) 366 *Nature* 625; 'US Patent Office Withdraws Patent on Indian Herb' (1997) 389 *Nature* 6; 'India to Challenge Basmati Rice Invention' (1998) 391 *Nature* 728. Of these, the last example is by far the least plausible.
20 Correspondence, (1995) 378 *Nature* 532.
21 Rosemary Coombe, 'The Properties of Culture and the Politics of Possessing Identity: Native Claims in the Cultural Appropriation Controversy, (1993) 6(2) *Canadian Journal of Law and Jurisprudence* 249.
22 On these issues, see Lisa Wilder, 'Local Futures. From Denunciation to Re-valorisation of the Native Other' in Gunther Teubner (ed), *Global Law Without a State* (Aldershot: Dartmouth, 1997).

the components of an 'indigenous (Euro-American) social theory', which facilitates social transactions by articulating a traditional, local, version of the distinction between nature and culture,[23] the dramatisation of bio-technologies as a peculiarly novel and transgressive form of science poses the sharpest and most persistent challenge to this 'indigenous' theory. And, because biotechnology patents are so often understood as proprietary claims to 'life itself' — claims that breach the boundaries set by 'indigenous' social-theoretical distinctions between nature and culture — the legal and bureaucratic administration of biotechnology patents has become the most intensive site of this confrontation. The threat to generalised conceptions of 'life' is that they might be forced into a mode of reflexivity to which they are quite unaccustomed; that is, they are increasingly being forced to address the question of how or why they draw the distinction between nature and culture in this way rather than another. Moreover, these generalised, indigenous, interpretations of the distinction between nature and culture are complicit with legal doctrine, in the sense that while indigenous simplifications are readily absorbed into legal doctrine as resources for thematising the attribution of disparate rights and duties, legal doctrine repays the favour by lending its institutional and ideological *imprimatur* to some of these cultural simplifications. So although many social anxieties about biotechnology are cast as complaints against law, the complicity between doctrine and indigenous theory is such that these complaints betray a confusion within law itself. Legal doctrine is faced with the problem of how to re-invent the motifs that have traditionally explained or justified the attribution of rights. The ethical or ecological arguments which give voice to social anxieties are apt to seem extravagant. For example, an application to patent the expressed nucleotide sequence for the protein relaxin, which is produced during pregnancy, was opposed by the Green Party on the grounds that it enslaved the women from whom the original samples had been extracted; it involved 'the dismembering of women and their piecemeal sale to commercial enterprises throughout the world'. More abstractly, the application was 'immoral' within the terms of the European Patent Convention because 'the patenting of human genes means that human life is being patented'.[24] Yet, despite their eccentricity,[25] and although they have made no obvious or immediate impression on legal doctrine, these objections have identified a structural failing in patents doctrine. The familiar conception of property, whether it is reconstructed in formal legal doctrine or elaborated in the looser languages of 'indigenous' theory, is unable to account for biotechnological manipulations of 'life'.

The 'bio-colonial' dimensions of patents such as the PNG-1 cell line offer the most immediate and compelling dramatisation of the problems that biotechnology poses for doctrinal and indigenous understandings of property. The ownership of 'genes' is represented as a form of appropriation that is even more threatening than other contemporary forms of bodily 'enslavement'. Whereas slavery perverts property by treating a person as a thing, biotechnology undoes the very distinction that makes property, and hence slavery, possible. The basis of most critiques of

---

23   See Marilyn Strathern, 'New Knowledge for Old? Reflections following Fox's Reproduction and Succession' (1994) 2:3 *Social Anthropology* 263, esp at 270–276.

24   See the decision of the EPO Opposition Division in *HOWARD FLOREY/Relaxin* [1995] EPOR 541, point 6.1. of the reasons.

25   As in, for example, the curious proposition that to permit the patenting of gene sequences would be to 'privatise humanity in the European Union' (representative of the German Green Party of the European Parliament, comments reported in (1994) 372 *Nature*, at 310). It may be that this sort of argument will not survive the 'modernisation' of the Green Party's perspective on biotechnology (see for example (1998) 392 *Nature*, at 213).

'bio-colonial' commodification is the familiar distinction between those entities which lose nothing essential in the process of legal and economic exchange, and those which are somehow 'degraded' by the medium of money. This distinction may yield little more than the familiar idea of gene ownership as a form of slavery. However, even this banal interpretation is significant because it shows how both legal doctrine and its critics have responded to the challenges of biotechnology by attempting to re-institute the old idea of property. The proprietary distinction between persons and things serves as a basic criterion for the interpretation and evaluation of biotechnological manipulations. And, precisely because they begin with this criterion, ostensibly critical themes such as 'bio-colonialism' or 'commodification' bind patent law and its opponents to the very distinctions between nature and culture, or discovery and invention, that biotechnology has rendered transparent or implausible.

Most critiques of biotechnology patents seek to restore the proper bounds of property; the common basic practical response consists in the 'juridification' of human life, granting it a form of legal immunity from commodification. In political argument, this juridical model surfaces only in metaphorical form. For example, the quite common notion of genetic or ecological 'patrimony' implicitly draws on the technical connotations of the concept of patrimony in civilian jurisdictions, where it is conceived as an abstract, indivisible, and inalienable fund, possessed of a juridical personality that secures it against appropriation by any particular individual. Hence the objections made by Greenpeace to genetically-modified plants on the ground that 'plant genetic resources are the heritage of mankind, and should remain available to all without restriction and be preserved intact for future generations'.[26] When the concept of patrimony is re-appropriated within legal theory, these political metaphors do seem rather simplistic. Instead, the virtues of 'patrimony' are attributed to its status as a 'hybridised' legal form,[27] that allows for a 'dialectical' oscillation between local and global, present and future expectations, or property and personality, and which therefore allows nature to be treated as a commodity for some purposes, a non-commodifiable fund for other purposes, and the substance of human personality for yet others. This is a more complicated adaptation of the juridical relation between persons and things, but the distinction is nevertheless preserved. For some tastes, patrimony is too feeble and equivocal a barrier to the commodification of life; in effect, it makes nature a potential commodity which economic forces would soon colonise. 'Dignity' may seem to be a less fallible criterion. So, for example, Bernard Edelman defends French legal principle against the 'cynical pragmatism' of Anglo-American law[28] by arguing that French legal tradition, which instituted the body as the inalienable foundation of 'legal individualism', offered a surer protection for personal dignity than a regulatory framework premised on the 'liberal' principles of informed consent:

> The body is the means of existence of the human person, and as such it cannot be sold, leased, or given away without immediately reviving slavery. In other words, a contract relating to the human body would be inconceivable in law, because it would offend against human dignity: in that respect, the inalienability of the body is of the same order as the inalienability of freedom [or] citizenship... In short, we can enjoy our freedom, but we cannot dispose of it.[29]

---

26 *PLANT GENETIC SYSTEMS/Glutamine synthetase inhibitors* [1995] EPOR 357, 363.
27 Francois Ost, 'Le patrimoine, un concept dialectique adapté à la complexité du milieu' (forthcoming).
28 Bernard Edelman, 'Génétique et liberté' (1991) 13 *Droits* 31; *idem*, 'Expérimentation sur l'homme: une loi sacrificielle' (1991) 235 *La Recherche* 1056.
29 Edelman, 'Expérimentation sur l'homme: une loi sacrificielle' *ibid* 1061.

This is the most uncompromising argument for 'juridified' life. The body as the substrate of individuality is a legal artefact; or, more precisely, the dimension occupied by or incarnated in the 'body' is a medium of subjective existence that is instituted and normalised by law, even before the law begins to attribute rights and liabilities.

These conceptions of juridified life reinstate the boundaries of property, the better to preserve human life from commercialised science. They do so by re-affirming the distinction between persons and things (even if that distinction is complicated by the quasi-Hegelian notion of a domain of things that is so thoroughly infused with 'personality' as to be unavailable to economic transactions). This is a somewhat conservative manoeuvre. Doubly so, since the objective is not only to re-institute property, but also to re-institute law itself. The dimension of 'life' or 'nature' that critiques of commodification seek to protect is bound to a particular definition of legal power, so that the project of rescuing nature is implicitly associated with the project of (re-)instituting a form of legal 'sovereignty'. If, in terms of the familiar theoretical distinction between 'sovereignty' and 'bio-power', the patents process is almost the paradigmatic example of a bio-political programme, the model of 'juridified' life is obviously on the side of sovereignty. Although 'sovereignty' so readily connotes repression, nevertheless it implicitly guarantees the imperilled distinction between persons and things, life and law, nature and society, or invention and discovery.[30] Only within the theme of sovereignty is it possible to sustain the idea of a pre-given natural substrate from which society or personality can be distinguished.

Sovereign power, as the precursor of bio-power, based itself upon a fundamental difference between law and nature, or between norms and the 'life' to which they refer. The association between sovereignty and repression arises from sovereignty's representation of itself as a normative power ranged against 'life', but this very asymmetry also secures the status of life or nature as a domain that is radically distinct from law or society. Sovereignty was not what it took itself to be. Although it wholeheartedly identified itself with one term of the distinction between 'law' and 'life', this distinction was sovereignty's own creation. 'Normalisation' — interpreted both etymologically and conceptually — consists less in a process of intervention in nature, than in the process of establishing the very perspectival horizon within which such interventions are conceived.[31] In effect, there was no such thing as nature until it was instituted as such by the exercise of sovereign power. For that reason, each exercise of sovereign power effectively intervened in its own representations. This form of self-referentiality was plausible and sustainable only for so long as forms of institutional aesthetics allowed it to be reconstructed as a brazen tautology, dignifying the simple say-so of the sovereign as an unquestionable source or cause of order. However, this tautological mode of self-reference unravelled as the institutions of power began to address their own conditions of existence, prompting a transformation in the way in which power was rationalised; more specifically, a shift from the blind investment

---

30   Appropriately, the common form of these distinctions is most convincingly demonstrated by Hegel, for whom the acquisition of property and accession to language are quintessentially juridical processes.

31   'Law is normative in character; it functions as a norm (in the etymological sense of a set square) not because it commands or prescribes but because in the first instance it establishes the framework of its own reference to real life — it normalises life' (Giorgio Agamben, *Homo Sacer. I: Le pouvoir souverain et la vie nue* [French translation of *Homo Sacer. I: Il potere sovrano e la nuda vita*] (Paris: Seuil, 1997) 34).

in excess to a bio-political economics of income and expenditure.[32] 'Sovereignty', and the distinction between life and law that it sustained, was therefore dissolved by a set of bio-political or governmental techniques which undramatically addressed the problem of operational self-reference. As suggested further on, bio-political programmes do not identify themselves with one side of the distinction between norm and nature; rather, they treat the distinction itself as a provisional programme which serves to govern their own operations. In these terms, the anxieties surrounding biotechnology patents stem from the fact that implosion of sovereignty — and its correlative distinction betweeen law and nature — has only belatedly become transparent. The insistence on a proprietary distinction between persons and things as a defence against commodification might be seen as an attempt to re-institute law as sovereignty, and, by definition, nature as the correlate of sovereign legal power.

Critiques of commodification assume that the language of property norms is descriptive of its own actualisation. In other words, the old legal-philosophical account of how 'things' are subjected to legal norms is mistaken for a quasi-sociological account of the performativity of norms. Of course, themes such as 'sanctity' or 'dignity' are routinely deployed in legal argument, but their functional value consists in processes of expression or actualisation that escape juridical thematisations of power. The ontological assumptions of traditional property semantics, assumptions about scarcity, exclusivity, or distinctions between form and matter, have been overtaken by social evolution.[33] The language of property norms does not command or describe the processes by which those norms are actualised in the world. So, whereas critiques of commodification represent biotechnological sciences as a threat to the integrity of property, or as a peculiarly delicate problem of proprietary regulation, property has already lost the integrity which it is supposed to have. In fact, biotechnological models of gene expression offer an instructive analogy for the processes or strategies through which property norms are socially (or sociologically) actualised in modern society.

Biotechnological practices resemble proprietary practices in that they slice across the distinctions between form and matter, or difference and identity, that are essential to the lawyer's conception of property. It is true that molecular biology has reliably identified the molecular structure of many expressible DNA sequences; precisely those structural sequences that are the basis of many biotechnology patents. For that reason one might be tempted to identify 'genes' with these determinate molecular structures, in which case the basic operations discovered or invented by biotechnology would be referable to precisely the sorts of things — or 'thing-analogues' — that are presupposed by traditional theories of property. However, the identity or quiddity of 'genes' becomes increasingly elusive as the specification of molecular structures improves. The difficulty is that a gene, however it is defined, consists not in a structure but in the process that 'expresses' or actualises a given molecular strand. The specification of a particular gene's molecular composition, or the question of what counts as an integral part of that composition, can be addressed only by referring to the process of gene expression. If attention is shifted from structures to the processes that animate them, the question 'what is a gene?' becomes somewhat more problematic. For example, because the function of a particular transcription unit is determined by

---

32   This transformation is especially well described by Alain Guery in 'Le roi dépensier. Le don, la contrainte, et l'origine du système financier de la monarchie française d'Ancien Régime' (1984) 39 *Annales ESC* 1241.

33   See my (somewhat compressed) account of this shift in 'Instituting Property' (1998) 18 OJLS 331.

regulatory sequences that may be quite remote from the transcription unit itself, it is inadequate simply to identify the molecular structure of genes with transcription sequences. More interestingly, the same DNA sequence can be cut and spliced in different ways to produce functional RNA. For example, the structural composition of an expressible nucleotide sequence may be the result of a selection made by the process of protein expression, so that the same element of a 'raw' DNA sequence can function either as an intron or as an exon depending on the way the sequence is spliced in the process of gene expression. Similarly, the process of protein manufacture itself is often regulated by a cybernetic feedback loop, which retroactively adjusts the 'input' codes of gene expression to their actual 'output'.[34] The molecular structures that are commonly identified as 'genes' are a highly selective interruption of these processes. And, although lawyers or scientists might for that reason prefer to deal with an expressed sequence — that is to say a functional nucleotide sequence that reliably yields a given protein — rather than a 'gene', it is not possible entirely to sever these smaller and more determinate mechanisms from the broader set of environmental or ecological conditions in which they are embedded.

For an enterprise such as population genetics, the tension between local structures or mechanisms and their general conditions of existence surfaces as the problem of how to bind genetic types or variations to their human carriers (see below). The conditions of existence of genetic traits are understood as natural-historical processes, and the work of binding genes to carriers is pursued through techniques such as the statistical sampling of selected populations. For commercial biotechnology, the question of how to bind molecular structures to social actors presents itself in a different form. The conditions of existence of biotechnological artefacts are not 'natural-historical'; rather, they consist in those economic, legal and political processes that shape the environment of biotechnological inventions. And, although molecular biology can specify structures or determinate mechanisms of expression, these elements are charged with the value or 'potential' that they are attributed by the reproduction of these processes. The story of the application made by the NIH for a patent relating to a number of cDNA sequences nicely illustrates, from the perspective of the patents process, this continuous re-invention or re-valuation of molecular structures. The NIH application was rejected on the basis that it failed to satisfy the utility requirements of US patent law. And although the NIH in America and the Medical Research Council in Britain decided not to pursue their applications, the decision by the US Patents and Trademarks Office generated some uncertainty as to the patentability of gene sequences.[35] Many of these uncertainties had to do with the identification of 'artefactual' gene sequences. Did a patent relate to the molecular structure of the gene sequence or to some functional characterisation of that structure? Or rather, given that structure is never sufficient 'in itself' to warrant a patent, how was one to distinguish structure and function, or how was one to decide what sort of functional supplement would make a gene sequence patentable?[36] These questions suggest how the quiddity of a gene — or even a particular nucleotide sequence — is not reducible to a determinate mechanism or structure, but that these structures

---

34 See François Jacob, *La logique du vivant. Une histoire de l'hérédité* (Paris: Gallimard, 1970) esp at 299–306.

35 'US and British Researchers Agree not to Seek Gene Fragment Patents' (1994) 367 *Nature* 583.

36 If anything, these uncertainties were only amplified by the US Patent Office's subsequent determination that expressed sequence tags (short nucleotide sequences which are used to identify transcription units that have been expressed as functional RNA) were patentable.

are variables that acquire different values according to the expectations that are invested in them. The role of the patents process is to bind these expectations in such a way as to facilitate the reproduction of the 'patents vector'.[37]

There are two ways of relating property to biotechnology. First, there is the sense in which biotechnology serve as an analogy for property practices. 'Hybridity' as the *modus operandi* and *opus operatum* of recombinant DNA technologies — which splice 'homologous' DNA sequences into 'heterologous' expression vectors — is a sort of working model for sociological concepts of 'hybridity', which describe how social artefacts are characterised by the processes which machine them rather than by any prior 'essence'. Or, in simpler and more abstract terms, biotechnological artefacts are 'hybrid' objects; 'objects whose essence is not prior to their existence'.[38] From that perspective one might say that the semantic elements of property norms are articulated by operations that are just as liquid and productive as the practices of biotechnology. Secondly, however, there is a different sort of relation, in which property practices are not merely analogical to biotechnological processes, but are operationally bound to biotechnology. If one provisionally takes the side of property, this relation might be described as a parasitic or symbiotic bond through which proprietary strategies exploit the indeterminacy of biotechnological practices. For example, the most basic manoeuvre of litigation strategies is to dissolve scientific artefacts (back) into their constituting processes, which are in turn filtered through doctrinal themes such as novelty, obviousness, or utility. In this way, legal concepts are strung together by a process of argumentation which 'parasitically' abstracts the energy or complexity of biotechnological operations by using the latter as a dynamic, re-vivifying, expression vector for legal language. In semantic terms, these proprietary strategies may not be especially 'novel', given that they deploy the familiar legal conception of ownership as priority or exclusivity. The novelty or complexity lies in the process by which lawyers adapt legal semantics to the dynamic relationships between political, scientific, and economic expectations. These semantic elements make up the basic repertoire of patent law but, again, their functional value is given only by the processes which adapt them to economic and legal expectations. Although the particular example of DNA sequences may no longer be commercially significant, given that gene sequences with no assigned function are now rarely seen as economic commodities, it does suggest how the indeterminacy of 'genes' — here expressed as a tension between structure and function — allows patent law to fold itself into the complexity of biotechnological programmes. Indeed, it is also the way in which the semantic energy of biotechnological models is abstracted by political debates. The ethical or ecological debate surrounding the European Union's 'Biotech Directives' exploited the indeterminacy of genes in a similar manner, emphasising either structure or function depending on the objectives of the argument.

An invented virus?

Patent law is bound to its own version of the traditional, 'proprietary' distinction between law and nature. Indeed, the distinction itself is considered sufficient to disqualify any ethical or ecological objection to the 'commodification of life'. According to Henry Greely, a member of the Ethics Committee of the Human Genome Project, and legal advisor to Carol Jenkins in the latter phase of the

---

37 See below for an extended discussion of this latter concept.
38 Bruno Latour, *Nous n'avons jamais été modernes* (Paris: La Decouverte, 1996) 118.

controversy over the PNG-1 patent, ecological activists had failed to grasp the simple distinction between a cell line and the materials from which it was derived:

> [T]he patent doesn't patent a person. It doesn't even patent human genetic material. It's the cell line, a viral preparation derived from the cell line, and three different bioassays to see whether people are infected by this virus. And the idea that the US government owns this person or his genetic material is absolute rubbish. [T]he donors involved can continue, obviously, to use their own DNA to run their bodies. They could also, if they chose, patent anything they wanted to patent that was an 'invention' from their DNA.[39]

The legal claims of the Hagahai were on no different or better footing than those of John Moore, who unsuccessfully claimed a share of the profits of a cell line abstracted from his diseased spleen. Moore failed because the medical and commercial value of the Mo-1 cell line was entirely attributed to the inventive art of the scientists who had identified and isolated his 'golden cells'.[40] This use of a banal doctrinal distinction to disqualify political or ethical objections is quite routine in patent law. Perhaps because the constitution of the European Patent Office has exposed it to politically-motivated interventions, the decisions of the EPO frequently resort to this manoeuvre. For example, faced with the Green Party's claim that the Relaxin application did violence to 'life' in general, and more specifically to the donors from whom the source tissues had been taken, the Opposition Division of the EPO responded in terms that amounted to little more than the proposition that an invented artefact is not the same thing as a natural substance.[41] The same strategy informed the Commission of the European Union's attempts to resolve the uncertainties created by the initial rejection of its long-contested Biotech Directive.[42] A personal, and somewhat more polemical, account of this bureaucratic strategy suggests that many objections to biotechnology patents are the result of 'technical misunderstandings which arise from a wilful refusal to understand the difference between discovery and invention'.[43] The first chapter of the Commission's revised,

---

39   'Scientists Attacked for "Patenting" Pacific Tribe' (1995) 270 *Science* 1112.
40   *Moore* v *Regents of University of California* 111 S Ct 1383 (1991); Bernard Edelman, 'L'homme aux cellules d'or' (1989) 34 *Receuil Dalloz Sirey* 225. A simpler example of the distinction between invention and discovery is found in *Diamond* v *Chakrabarty*, where it was held that an engineered bacterium 'plainly qualified as patentable subject matter' because the patentee's claim was 'not to a hitherto unknown natural phenomenon, but to a non-naturally occurring manufacture or composition of matter — a product of human ingenuity' (*US Supreme Court Reports* 65 L Ed 2d (1980) 144, 150). In *Chakrabarty* the distinction between nature and artifice is unhelpfully stark, not least because the majority in the Supreme Court chose to reduce the case to a formalistic exercise in textual interpretation.
41   First, the application related to a DNA sequence which was structurally different from the sequence as it was found 'in nature', because a 'natural' sequence will express a given protein only if functionally redundant introns have been spliced out. Secondly, even if the application had claimed a molecular structure that was identical to the nucleotide structure in its 'natural' form, the technological interventions which allowed the sequence to be identified and isolated were sufficient to turn a discovery into an invention. More fundamentally, having already characterised the nucleotide sequence in question as a 'DNA fragment' rather than a 'gene', the Opposition Division asserted that '...DNA is not "life", but a chemical substance which carries genetic information and can be used as an intermediate in the production of proteins which may be medically useful' (*HOWARD FLOREY/ Relaxin* [1995] EPOR 541, point 6.3.4 of the reasons).
42   'Proposal for a Council Directive on the Legal Protection of Biotechnological Inventions', COM (88) 496 final, OJ 1989 C 10/3. Another, less explicit strategic reason is the desire to maintain the fiction that the implementation of the directive would not alter established patent laws or practices, but that it would merely harmonise existing practices.
43   Dominique Vandergheynst (Commission of the European Union, DG XV), with reference to the argument that gene sequences or derivatives should be patentable only if they were essentially different from sequences or elements as they were naturally found in the body ('Brevet sur le vivant: une nouvelle invention juridique?' in Libois and Strowel (eds), *Profil de la création* (Brussels: FUSL, 1997) 65, 88).

and successful, proposal for a Biotech Directive corrected these misunderstandings.[44] Taking the view that political oppositions had arisen only because the original formula — according to which 'the human body as such or parts of the human body as such' was not to be patentable — was ambiguous, the revised formula specifies that 'the human body and its elements in their natural state shall not be considered patentable inventions'.[45] Supposedly, this formulation improved on the first because it clarified the point that, as knowledge of the human body in its natural state could only qualify as 'discovery' rather than 'invention', natural processes are automatically secured against commodification.[46]

The story of the PNG-1 cell line makes these doctrinal 'clarifications' seem quite implausible. The text of the PNG-1 patent application implicitly concedes the point that, despite their technical sophistication, recombinant DNA and hybridoma technologies remain dependent on the extraction and exchange of 'raw' human materials.[47] A good part of the application is dedicated to the task of differentiating the PNG-1 virus from neighbouring or potentially antecedent strains of HTLV-I. The object is to establish the exclusivity of the PNG-1 viral strain and the peculiarity of the population(s) which might benefit from the various bio-assays in which the invention was embodied:

> Unlike strains of HTLV-I from Japan, the West Indies, the Americas, and Africa, which share a 97% sequence homology, the PNG-1 variant is only about 92% identical to a Japanese prototype HTLV-I. [The] PNG-1 variant, in turn, differs by approximately 4% from that of the variants from Melanesian Solomon Islanders, indicating the existence of a new HTLV-I quasispecies.[48]
>
> Due to the genetic variability between HTLV-I isolates from Melanesia and other geographical locales, the widespread screening for infection in human populations in Melanesia can be best served by using a virus strain which is indigenous to that area.[49]

---

44 '[I]n particular, to determine the difference between inventions and discoveries with regard to the patentability of certain elements of human origin' ('Proposal for a European Parliament and Council Directive on the Legal Protection of Biotechnological Inventions' COM (95) 661 final, OJ 1996 C 296/4, 5). At the time of going to press, the text of the Directive as approved by the European Parliament had not appeared in the *Official Journal*. However, this formula reappears in recital 14 of the approved text.

45 ibid, article 3(1). The text of the Directive makes a sharper distinction between 'discovery' and 'invention'. See article 5:

> 1. The human body, at the various stages of its formation and development, and the simple discovery of one of its elements, including the sequence or partial sequence of a gene, cannot constitute patentable inventions.
> 2. An element isolated from the human body or otherwise produced by means of a technical process, including the squence or partial sequence of a gene, may constitute a patentable invention, even if the structure of that element is identical to that of a natural element.
> 3. The industrial application of a sequenced or a partial sequence of a gene must be disclosed in the patent application.

See also Alain Gallochat, 'Directive on Legal Protection of Biotechnological Inventions: Another (or Last) Chance for Europe?' (1996) 82 *Patent World* 13, esp at 15: 'This improvement should be wholeheartedly approved. It relates back to a fundamental principle in the patents field, a principle that has been somewhat forgotten, namely, that a discovery cannot be patented while an invention can...' (The author is counsel for the Pasteur Institute, one of the more aggressive European public sector holders of biotechnology patents).

46 See the account of the directive's ambitions in Vandergheynst, n 43 above, 80–82.

47 See generally RAFI Communique, Jan/Feb 1997, 'The Human Tissue Trade' <http://www.rafi.ca/communique/fltxt/19971.html>.

48 Abstract, PNG–1 Patent Application, n 10 above.

49 *ibid.* Some sense of the significance of these figures can be gathered by referring to the contest between Luc Montagnier of the Institut Pasteur and Robert Gallo of the National Cancer Institute as to who enjoyed priority — both 'intellectual' and 'proprietary' — in the discovery of the AIDS virus. One of the evidential facts in this contest was the small degree of sequence variation between the two

First, the designation of Carol Jenkins as one of the five 'inventors' of the cell line indicates that the cell line was not conceived as an entirely 'scientific' artefact; it could hardly have been argued that Jenkins had made a direct contribution to the formulation of a conception of the molecular structure.[50] Her formal status highlights the function of the PNG-1 patent — and perhaps patents in general — in concretising a fluid and open-ended process of co-operation between various social actors into a singular scientific 'fact'.[51] Secondly, given that the innovative content of this 'invention' seemed to owe more to the natural components of the extracted materials than to any technological process of extraction and purification,[52] the idea that the production of the cell line involved a radically inventive process seems especially implausible.[53] Unlike the more complex and precarious achievements of recombinant DNA technology, the production of an immortal cell line demands little more of the 'inventor' than the mastery of a routine scientific technique.[54] The 'inventive' process seems merely to transcribe a natural code into a new medium. In these cases, the dogmatic distinction between discovery and invention gives way to a more flexible and more plausible distinction between form and substance, which characterises biotechnological programmes as either novel or natural by referring to the use which they make of

discovered viruses. The nucleotide sequences of LAV (the Pasteur isolate, which had been forwarded to the NCI) and HTLV–III (the strain isolated by Gallo) varied by only 1.5 per cent, a factor of difference which was so minimal as to suggest that the NCI strain was identical to the Pasteur strain, any divergence being attributable to spontaneous mutations in culture (see Rebecca S. Eisenberg, 'Proprietary Rights and the Norms of Science in Biotechnology Research' (1987) 97:2 *Yale Law Journal* 177, 226–229, and esp n 260).

50   In US law, an 'invention' is predicated upon the conception of a molecular structure: 'conception of a DNA sequence, like conception of any chemical substance, requires definition of that substance other than by its functional utility' (*Fiers* v *Sugamo* (Fed Cir) (1993) 25 USPQ 2d 1601). For an illustration of how this notion of invention can become an issue where the commercial stakes are significant, see the dispute over the BRCA1 patent and specifically the question whether NIH scientists who had participated in the inventive programme should be recognised as inventors (reported in (1995) 373 *Nature* 649).

51   The nature and the limits of Jenkins' role are implicitly disclosed in the assertion made by NIH scientists, that 'at no time did NIH investigators have direct interactions with the Hagahai' (response to a Freedom of Information Act request, made by RAFI, cited in RAFI Communique Mar/Apr 1996, n 17 above).

52   In some cases there may be a technical or doctrinal answer, which is that the process itself is the invention. One example is the story of the 'polypeptide expression' application. One of the reasons given by the EPO's Examining Division for rejecting the patent was that this particular recombinant DNA process 'could not be identically repeated since the source of DNA in humans varied with the individual'. In response, the Technical Board of Appeal emphasised that the patent was a process, which could be used to transform various materials — a 'general methodology which is fully applicable with any starting material' — and that this process was sufficiently described, and repeatable, so long as the methodology itself functioned reliably: 'generally applicable biological processes are not insufficiently described for the sole reason that some starting materials or genetic precursors therefor, eg. a particular DNA or plasmid, are not readily available to obtain each and every variant of the expected result of the invention provided the process as such is reproducible' (*GENENTECH I/Polypeptide expression* [1989] EPOR 1, point 3.3.3 of the reasons).

53   '[T]he element isolated is the result of the technical processes used to identify, purify and classify it and to reproduce it outside the human body, techniques which human beings alone are capable of putting into practice and which Nature is incapable of accomplishing by itself' (COM (95) 661 final, n 44 above, 5).

54   Of course, some elements of the 'routine' might consist in a form of 'tacit' knowledge, which is tied to the circulation of laboratory technicians and post-doctoral researchers. For example, an intuitive 'feel' for the development of a cell culture, or a sense of just when and how to shake a flask or test tube, often plays an important part in even the most sophisticated procedures (see, for example, A. Cambrosio and P. Keating, 'Going Monoclonal: Art, Science, and Magic in the Day-to-Day Use of Hybridoma Technology' (1988) 35 *Social Problems* 244, and also the role of laboratory procedures in the 'discovery' of PCR (Paul Rabinow, *Making PCR. A Story of Biotechnology* (Chicago: University of Chicago Press, 1996).

the body. Hence the argument that biotechnological inventions should not be patentable if they treat the human body 'as a structured entirety of cells, tissue and organs', and, more specifically, that cell lines and hybridomas should be patentable only if 'both the individual and the point in time of the extraction of the cells were selected by chance, ie not for the mere or predominant purpose of obtaining valuable substances'.[55]

There is something quite unsatisfactory about these endless permutations of 'nature' and 'artefact'. Each perspective exposes its opponent's particular 'fetish'[56] by trading on a distinction between two types of causal genealogy — natural mechanism and human intervention. This same distinction allows political arguments to undo patent law's fetishistic attachment to scientific idols, while legal doctrine repays the compliment by disclosing the artefactual sinews of ecological 'nature'. This process of mutual misunderstanding is interesting and instructive only because the exchange exposes a common 'blind spot'. On the one hand, in attempting to press a political or ethical distinction between 'commodifiable things' and 'non-commodifiable things' into a narrow doctrinal distinction between discoveries and inventions, the strategy behind the second European 'Biotech Directive' misrepresented the nature of the problem. Political oppositions are not a function of doctrinal confusion. Rather, although their force is blunted by legal proceduralisation, political arguments show how legal doctrine mistakes its own interested definition of 'nature' for nature 'as such'. From this perspective the doctrinal distinction between inventions and discoveries is itself a form of violence against nature.[57] On the other hand, the technical definitions of patent law reveal the unacknowledged complexity of ecological 'nature'. The technology involved in the production of cell lines seems unremarkable only because science is all too successful in reproducing itself as 'nature'. The apprehension of 'natural facts' is now mediated by multiple layers of social representation, and the more deeply embedded these layers, the more readily they congeal into a substance that is misrepresented as 'nature'. The common failing of both perspectives is their addictive attachment to the idea of nature 'as such', a pre-given substrate that guarantees the existence of artefacts, and which, depending on one's point of view, defines the proper sphere of human invention. This attachment obscures the fact that there are no such things as inherently 'natural' things, no more than there are entirely 'invented' things. Interestingly, that lesson might have been learned from the Hagahai themselves, whose hybridised social relations disclose the contingency of any distinction between nature and culture.[58]

---

55 Observations reported in Rainer Moufang, 'Patenting of Human Genes, Cells and Parts of the Body? — The Ethical Dimensions of Patent Law' (1994) 25:4 *IIC* 487, 510–511. The more precise formulation consists in a distinction between 'inventions' relating to lymphocytes extracted from 'sensitised test persons', which would not be patentable, and those which arise from a 'one-time and incidental extraction' of myeloma cells, which would be patentable.

56 See generally Bruno Latour, *Petite réflexion sur le culte moderne des dieux faitiches* (Paris: Les empêcheurs de penser en rond, 1996).

57 See, for example, the argument of a 'bioethicist' quoted in a RAFI text: 'The product of nature doctrine has been rendered vacuous by allowing that the isolation, purification, or alteration of an entity or substance from its natural state turns it into something "not found in nature"' (see RAFI Communique, Jan/Feb 1994, 'The Patenting of Human Genetic Material' (text available at<http://www.rafi.ca.communique/fltxt/19941.html>).

58 Jenkins' account of the Hagahai contains the observation that the women of the group would breast feed both their children and their piglets, the piglets being the more privileged of the two classes of dependant. For an account of how these 'transgenic' social practices 'hybridise' the distinction between nature and culture, see generally Marilyn Strathern, *The Gender of the Gift* (Berkeley: University of California Press, 1988).

The distinction between the 'natural' and the 'social' is itself a social artefact, continuously re-invented by discursive programmes that emerge from a point 'between' the terms that they distinguish. Recombinant DNA technologies are 'transgressive' not because they intervene in natural processes more violently or more effectively than other forms of technology, but because they begin 'before' any distinction between nature and technology. In that respect biotechnologies are again representative of discursive processes generally. The incorporation of the 'natural' into the 'social' is not the result of a process of normative authorship, in which 'social' forces are imprinted upon a 'natural' substance. Bio-political rationalities employ the distinction between the natural and social to regulate themselves, but they cannot be identified with either term. Bio-political programmes are sustained by a reflexive process of intervention in their own distinctions, which serve as criteria by which to steer operations and by which to observe the effects of those operations. They are neither norm nor nature, occupying instead the indeterminate point 'between' those terms, and consisting in nothing more than this process of recursive self-observation.[59] This proposition does not depend on the claim that there is no such thing as material reality.[60] Rather, it confines itself to a description of how events are thematised within discursive programmes. 'Natural' events, just like their 'social' counterparts, are ascriptions which these programmes use as prompts or occasions for their reproduction.[61] Nor does the proposition imply that the distinction betwen nature and artefact, or the social and the biological, is entirely illusory. Scientists, lawyers, sociologists, and politicians routinely assign events to one or the other of its terms. The world is semantically 'materialised' by the reproduction of social programmes which may deploy some version of the distinction between nature and artefact, or things and persons, in their interpretation of observed events. The more interesting question concerns the way in which these distinctions work within the reproduction of bio-political norms.

The theme(s) of authorship or invention might be seen as the components of a legal technique of 'purification'.[62] In this sense, 'purification' describes the way in which discursive processes manage social contingency. It is, so to speak, a way of 'interrupting' or 'patterning' the flow of events. Themes such as 'discovery and invention' turn processual events into localisable facts by fastening them to a conceptual structure which grants them a determinate identity and a stable pattern of causal co-ordinates. The purification of events therefore transcribes contingency into a stable, manageable, topography. However, because there is a radical distinction between these 'purifying' themes and the operations in which they are expressed, so that a theme cannot account for its own expression, 'purification' merely reproduces the processes which it seeks to interrupt. It is therefore a particular technique of hybridisation.[63] For example, the patents process purifies scientific and economic events by characterising them in terms of concepts such as

---

59   For this shift from tautology to recursivity, see my argument in 'Power as an Art of Contingency: Luhmann, Deleuze, Foucault' (1998) 27:1 *Economy and Society* 1.

60   '[M]eaning could not outlast the destruction of life or of its chemical and physical basis [but] this dependency is not an operative premise of meaning events themselves' (Niklas Luhmann, *Social Systems* (Stanford: Stanford University Press, 1995) 66).

61   See 'Power as an Art of Contingency', n 59 above.

62   This concept is borrowed from Bruno Latour, but it should be noted that my appropriation diverges significantly from Latour's use, in that the model of differentiation presupposed by my argument does not allow the various 'purifications' to be referred to a single, common, hybrid object (cf Latour, n 38 above, 197).

63   *ibid*, 107.

obviousness, sufficiency of disclosure, or industrial application, which are in turn re-characterised by economic and scientific strategies. This version of 'purification' emphasises the thoroughly productive capacity of proprietary themes. It also suggests why biotechnological artefacts are so troubling from the perspective of traditional property law. The problem is not that property is losing its mastery of things, quite simply because it has never enjoyed the mastery imagined by legal philosophy. Rather, it is becoming more and more obvious that the old purifying themes have outlived their usefulness, so that the relationship between themes and operations has to be re-negotiated. For example, there is a basic incompatibility between ethical and political arguments and the scientific-rational character of the patents system, which can accommodate 'ethical' themes only if they are translated, or betrayed, by some form of risk calculus.[64] The questions asked of property law increasingly require it to adjudicate on this sort of incompatibility. That may be why both law and science have converged on themes such as informed consent which seem to have the ability to bind scientific or economic characterisations of persons and events to the legal conception of the autonomous individual. For example, returning to the tension between ethical themes and impersonal calculations of risk, questions of risk can be treated as criteria by which to assess the adequacy of disclosure (or the extent to which a particular act of consent is properly 'informed'), thereby preserving the legal fiction of the consenting subject from the more complex representations of agency that are implicit in scientific or economic assessments of risk.

Commodification as co-variation

If one focuses on processes rather than their purification, what kind of objects or artefacts do biotechnological inventions become? If appropriation is seen as a form of discursive inscription rather than a mastery of 'things themselves', how does the patents process function in the reproduction of these artefacts? One answer is suggested by the concept of patents as 'vectors':

> [A]s patent law functions to draw boundaries around information, it allows research to be treated as a form of property or as an asset. In so doing, it enables research to become part of the commercial currency; for it to be mortgaged, insured, included on the balance sheet, and used as a basis upon which decisions about investment can be made. In this sense patents act as vectors which enable operational links to be forged between higher education institutes and industry, and between public and private spheres of research.[65]

There are several versions of the argument that patents regulate the flow of scientific information. One might, for example, ask to what extent the norms of

---

64   The question of risk is excluded just as readily as it is included, by the argument that 'potential risks in relation to the exploitation of a given invention for which a patent has been granted cannot be anticipated merely on the basis of the disclosure of the invention in the patent specification' (decision of the EPO Technical Board of Appeal in *PLANT GENETIC SYSTEMS/Glutamine synthetase inhibitors* [1995] EPOR 357, point 18.4 of the reasons). In other words, the risk is accepted as a legitimate criterion in principle, but one which is inapplicable in practice because the risk falls to be assessed during the lifetime of the patent rather than at the point at which the application is made. Consequently, any form of risk assessment would be the proper concern of regulatory bodies other than the EPO. See also *HARVARD/Onco-mouse* [1991] EPOR 525, point 4 of the decision, and the Commission's new Biotech Directive, n 44 above, para 23, at 6. Certainly, the proposition that 'ethical considerations permeate the entire normative structure of the patent system' seems somewhat naive (Moufang, n 55 above, 514).

65   Brad Sherman, 'Governing Science: Patents and Public Sector Research' (1994) 7(3) *Science in Context* 515, 525.

patent law work as the functional equivalents of Merton's norms of scientific culture.[66] However, this question still represents the agency of property norms in conventional legal or regulatory terms; the relation between patent laws and scientific processes is understood as a relation between a normative template and the world to which it is applied. And, although scientific practices might be allowed a capacity to resist, or to evolve forms of 'creative compliance', these processes of negotiation are understood in terms of the prescriptive content of norms rather than the discursive operations that articulate prescriptive themes. In other words, the process of regulatory negotiation is deciphered by measuring evasive activity against the propositional content of regulatory norms. From the start, the field of regulatory events or activities is 'framed' or delimited by these propositional contents rather than the more complex and heterogeneous tissue of discursive operations. The model of intellectual property rights as 'vectors' is distinctive because it represents the nexus between law, economy, and science as an emergent bond, in which no participant enjoys a privileged perspective from which to observe and intervene in the others. Hierarchical distinctions such as the distinction between norms and facts are embedded in the discursive programme which employs them. In other words, the social plane is folded into a set of local hierarchies, none of which, not least that of the sociologist or social theorist, can claim any sort of epistemological or practical priority. So, although science has always been dependent upon particular institutional or economic configurations, and upon the ability of scientists to develop and exploit these networks,[67] the idea that patent law has been reduced to an 'expression vector' for commodified science is entirely misplaced. The nexus between law, economy and science is emergent in the sense that each of these practices exists only in and through its relation to its partners, so that money, norms, and scientific facts are already bound into relations of mutual representation and mutual convertibility. This more fluid theoretical model is not too far removed from the perspective of the participants in the patents process. For example, the research director of SmithKline Beecham, defending the company's use of patents to structure access to its projected map of the human genome, observed that: 'there's absolutely no reason why our genes can't be used as "currency" in negotiating creative alliance frameworks with various partners'.[68]

The concept of an emergent process implies that (patented) artefacts are produced by the ongoing articulation of discursive processes. Some sense of how this might work is suggested by Marie-Angèle Hermitte's interpretation of the requirement that a plant variety right — a *droit d'obtention végétal* — should be granted only in relation to those plant varieties that are distinguishable from all previously known varieties by at least one significant characteristic.[69] There is no closed categorisation of distinguishing characteristics, which allows the process of identification to be responsive to economic and scientific imperatives:

> If varieties are classified according to a limited range of characteristics it is relatively difficult to create a new variety but each existing variety enjoys a broad and stable market position. To extend the list of classificatory characteristics, something which the examiners consider they are entitled to do even in the course of an examination, makes it much easier

---

66 Rebecca S. Eisenberg, n 49 above.
67 Or, borrowing again from Bruno Latour, one might say that a scientific concept is 'a strategic entity' that allows one to 'interest' and hold on to one's allies (*Le métier de chercheur — regard d'un anthropologue* (Paris: INRA, 1994) 28).
68 Quoted in (1994) 371 *Nature* 365.
69 For example, the length of the stem, the number of seeds, the time of fruiting, and so on.

to create new varieties, even if these enjoy a less stable and much narrower market position.[70]

Hermitte's argument is that economic interests infiltrate the taxonomic categories of intellectual property, causing them to become more or less rigid in response to market strategies. If that were so, the role of patent law and the law relating to plant variety rights would indeed be to serve as nothing more than a receptive medium for the active conversation between economic and scientific criteria. The role of law would simply be to facilitate this exchange rather than to impose its own definition of what should qualify as a sufficient distinguishing characteristic. According to Hermitte, intellectual property laws therefore become a form of 'soft' law, which retains the external institutional attributes of a system of legal norms, but whose internal mechanisms have been thoroughly colonised by an economic rationality. There are various problems with this analysis, which have to do with the priority accorded to economic programmes,[71] but the basic formulation points beyond itself, towards a model of how patentable inventions are constructed by the 'co-variation' of legal, scientific, and economic programmes. A patent is a legal artefact, referable in the first instance to law's particular perspective on this process of co-variation. However, even if one privileges law to this limited extent, the essential point is that a patented invention is produced by the legal characterisation of a fluid process, in which law is itself implicated, rather than the legal description of an identifiable fact or mechanism. The general category of the invention, which emerges from the articulation of various criteria of inventive priority, is a sort of virtual entity, sculpted by the legal characterisation of economic and scientific expectations. As this representation of the nexus of expectations is progressively woven into the language of inventive step, obviousness, industrial application, and so on, it gradually comes to be expressed as an intangible 'thing'. However, the materiality of this intangible artefact consists in nothing more substantial than the legal apprehension of a fluid nexus of expectations. More precisely, the intangible *res* is the referent of propositions or prescriptions that consist in the co-variation of legal discourse and its companion discourses. In that sense, the patents process 'commodifies' not by binding pre-constituted things or mechanisms, but by representing its discursive binding of expectations as an intangible 'thing'. In these terms, a model that Hermitte uses to argue for the concept of intellectual property law as a form of 'soft law' instead becomes the model of a relation in which each participant patterns the nexus of expectations in accordance with its own purifying themes; a proprietary 'vector' is reproduced as a dynamic process in which scientific programmes accommodate themselves to an economic accommodation of legal criteria, and so on, in a circular movement of overlapping observation.

The general category of a patentable invention — or the notion of 'the addition of a new idea to the existing stock of knowledge'[72] — therefore precipitates from the various themes which the law uses to decipher scientific processes, and more especially to observe the complex relations between scientific and economic processes. This process of legal invention involves a relentlessly corrosive mode of purification, in which scientific commodities are decomposed into competing

---

70 Hermitte, 'Le rôle des concepts mous dans les techniques de déjuridicisation. L'exemple des droits intellectuels' (1985) *Archives de Philosophie du Droit* 334, 344.
71 cf Alain Pottage and Brad Sherman, 'Création et appropriation' in Libois and Strowel (eds) *Profils de la création* (Brussels: FUSL, 1997).
72 *Biogen Inc v Medeva* [1997] RPC 1.

accounts of their emergence.[73] If science turns artefacts into facts, patent law turns scientific facts back into artefacts. Litigation strategies deploy the familiar proprietary themes of identity and continuity[74] — which are here diffracted into various sub-themes such as (non-)obviousness, (in)sufficiency of disclosure, or, in the context of biotechnological inventions, the distinction between biological and micro-biological processes[75] — so as to unravel the patents vector, reconstructing between scientific and economic parts of the bundle in legal terms. So, for example, the distinction between 'obvious' and 'obvious to try' allows litigators to shift between a genealogy based on a 'purely' scientific representation of the process and a representation of the scientific process as it is mediated by economic or corporate expectations. More important, these legal themes have to take account of law's immediate implication in the patents 'vector'. For instance, concepts such as 'sufficiency of disclosure' allow lawyers and judges to advertise or accommodate economic concerns about the 'breadth' of a proposed patent, and thereby to bind scientific and economic expectations in a way that anticipates the longer-term effects of patent law upon the systems that it binds. 'Commodification' consists in this process of unravelling and recomposing the fabric of expectations.

The uses of 'bio-colonialism'

In functional terms, the patents 'vector' is a technique that binds events through processes of bio-political normativity rather than 'juridical' power. This theoretical distinction is hardly novel, but the example of biotechnology patents offers a clearer specification of the concepts of 'bio-power' and 'governmentality'. The concept of 'purification' is an essential part of this specification. For example, an important implication of the preceding arguments is that concepts of 'bio-colonialism' or 'commodification' constitute a form of political or legal purification; they press complex processes of co-variation into simplifying templates fashioned from traditional conceptions of property and political power. The interesting observation about these templates is not that they are selective or out-dated, but rather that they serve to reproduce the very processes that they criticise. Thus, critical representations of bio-colonialism have been incorporated into the commercial strategies of multinational pharmaceuticals corporations, not just because they facilitate the process of exploitation, but more importantly because they ease the articulation of commercial vectors.

Complaints about commodification are often met by the argument that biotechnology patents do not place human individuality at stake: 'the effect of a patent on human genes is restricted to the exclusion of others from using the genes in an industrial process and, thus, does not affect at all the personality of human

---

73   '[I]t is less the facts of science that are at issue in a patent trial [sic] than the scientific process itself' (Alberto Cambrosio *et al*, 'Scientific Practice in The Courtroom: The Construction of Sociotechnical Identities in a Biotechnological Patent Dispute' (1990) 37:3 *Social Problems* 275, 275).

74   For an excellent analysis, see Cambrosio *et al, ibid.*

75   This distinction was essential to the HARVARD/Onco-mouse claim; the engineered mouse was not the product of a biological process because the decisive interventions or manipulations happened at a 'micro' level: 'the oncogene is inserted by technical means into a vector (eg a plasmid), which is then micro-injected at an early embryo stage' ([1990] EPOR 510, point 4.9 of the reasons). Of course, this simpler distinction became more complicated when these micro-biological interventions were supplemented by biological processes of reproduction (see *PLANT GENETIC SYSTEMS* [1995] EPOR 357).

beings'.[76] Superficially, this is quite correct. However, examples such as that of the PNG-1 cell line patent reveal the sort of difficult questions that biotechnology patents ask of modern conceptions of human individuality. Even if the basic notion of embodied individuality remains unquestionable,[77] the reproduction of this conception of individuality has been complicated by the manner in which biotechnology undoes the distinction between nature and culture, (re-)opening the 'socio-biological' question of how to attach human individuals to their genetic components.

Scientific studies of genes are not directly interested in individual human beings; instead they deal with a very different kind of individual. Genetic types or traits have biographies that unfold through particular human lives, and those biographies are shaped by processes of fertility and mortality which exceed the temporal or geographical limits of embodied human existence. 'Genes' exist primarily as laboratory artefacts or statistical figures, and as such they occupy a dimension that has only an oblique and problematic relation to the dimension of social individuality. Indeed, recombinant DNA technologies have so thoroughly appropriated the molecular matter of genes that the notion of an 'original' human source is of little or no relevance. DNA fragments have acquired a malleable individuality of their own, and one might well ask whether, for example, it is appropriate to 'identify a gene which expresses in the human liver with the label human'.[78] In this respect genetic technologies have amplified a problem that had already become apparent in relation to the simpler question of the legal status of human tissues. As medical-technological resources, human tissues such as blood, gametes, organs, or hospital waste have been assigned to different medical sectors and accorded different regulatory statuses.[79] Each of these statuses implies a particular representation of the body, and a particular technique for (re-)attaching tissues to bodies. The bond between each kind of tissue and its body of origin is reconstructed as a specific compound of social or technological expectations, which determine who is authorised to give consent, what makes consent actual or effective, whether or not some form of payment is appropriate, what is in the best interests of research, and so on. The difficulty then is to find some way of stitching these different regulatory statuses (back) together, as a coherent representation of individuality. 'Informed consent' is a particularly successful answer to this difficulty because it works with a model of individuality that is so vacuous and pliable as to be almost infinitely adaptable. In themselves, the questions of what counts as consent, whether 'actual' or 'counterfactual', or of what counts as adequate disclosure, allow for the construction of quite different categories of consenting subject.

---

76 Joseph Straus, 'Patenting Human Genes in Europe — Past Developments and Prospects for the Future' (1995) 26:6 IIC 920, 927.

77 'It goes without saying that one must assume that individuality in the sense of a self-propelling, psycho-physical unity, and above all in terms of each person's individual death, is something accepted by all societies' (Niklas Luhmann, *Love as Passion. The Codification of Intimacy* (Cambridge: Polity Press, 1986) 14).

78 See for example the observations of one German scientist, quoted in Straus, n 76 above, 927: 'the human genome has a label which I think is appropriate because man is defined in a certain way, at least with respect to its macroscopic structure, by the total structure of a genome. But we are talking here and in all other cases about little bits of DNA and if the source comes from plants, or does it come from bacteria or from humans, then we give an etiquette which is not appropriate.... I think when we talk in terms of biology, then, of course, its only the genome which defines a certain species'.

79 See Marie-Angèle Hermitte, 'Le corps hors du commerce, hors du marché' (1988) *Archives de Philosophie du Droit* 323, esp at 329–341.

In one sense, the tension between social individuality and genetic materiality is simply the modern form of a very old question: how does one reconcile physical materiality, bodily integrity and social individuality?; or, more abstractly, how can embodied individuality be defended against 'process'?[80] However, the difficulty of the question is acutely accentuated by the fact that life and death have become bio-political concepts, so that the issue is no longer that of how to attach 'social' individuality to 'biological' processes, but rather how to construct a model of individuality that takes account of the radical contingency of the bond between the social and the biological.

Legal themes, and specifically the notion of informed consent, are quite successful in addressing these difficulties. In fact, they intervene even before one reaches formal legal procedures such as patent applications, in such a way as to reproduce the basic scientific material of 'genetic patrimony', not least viruses such as the PNG-1 strain. These more discreet functions are evident in the way that population genetics — exemplified in the work of the Human Genome Diversity Project — has come to style itself as a form of 'sincere' science, conscious of the broader ethical implications of its activities. The sincerity of population genetics is advertised by its basic normative programme, which is to establish a historical geography of the human family that begins with the egalitarian and apolitical substance of genes rather than a divisive and asymmetrical category such as 'race'. In practical terms, this involves the construction of a genetic 'family tree' that shows how humanity became differentiated into its existing (genetic) populations, or of how 'genes, peoples and languages have diverged ... through a series of migrations that apparently began in Africa and spread through Asia to Europe, the New World and the Pacific'.[81] In order to retrace the evolution of genetic types, population geneticists begin with existing populations, and calculate their proximity to one another — or the 'genetic distance' between them[82] — by calibrating the variations in the molecular sequences of certain genes. In other words, affinities inferred from variations in genetic sequences are traced to a point of division or divergence: '[w]hen other matters are equal, genetic distance increases simply and regularly over time. The longer two populations are separated, the greater their genetic distance should be'. It should therefore be possible to identify the temporal and geographical point at which two existing populations diverged, and thence to reconstruct the entire genealogy of the human family. However, these affinities are difficult to infer where one is dealing with heterogeneous populations in which the pure lines of evolutionary drift have been complicated or contaminated by intensive cultural exchange.[83] For that reason,

---

80   See Caroline Walker Bynum, *The Resurrection of the Body in Western Christianity, 200–1336* (New York: Columbia University Press, 1995).

81   Luigi Luca Cavalli-Sforza, 'Genes, Peoples and Languages' (1991) 265 *Scientific American* 72, 72.

82   'If we know that there exist different genetic types of a specific protein or other strictly inherited character, we can count individuals carrying one type or the other and establish the proportions of that type in the population being examined. These proportions vary from one population to another because they change over time in each population in a relatively unpredictable manner. The change in proportions of these types over time is the *evolutionary process* itself' (L.L.Cavalli-Sforza *et al*, *The History and Geography of Human Genes* (Princeton: Princeton University Press, 1994) 4).

83   Therefore, the larger part of the theoretical resources of population genetics is devoted to the work of isolating the pure diachronic line of 'evolution itself' from a skein of social relationships in which the diachronic is enmeshed in the synchronic. The great advantage of genes is that they promise a pure measure of human history: 'Genes, always transmitted from parents to children, describe a vertical path through the generations. Culture can also pass vertically from generation to generation, but unlike genes, it can also be transmitted horizontally, between unrelated individuals' (Cavalli-Sforza, 'Genes, Peoples and Languages' n 81 above, 78). The trouble with this approach is that it overlooks the fact that any diachronic purification is the result of understandings and selections that are embedded in society as it is constituted here and now.

population geneticists prefer to begin with populations that have retained a 'pristine genetic constitution'.[84] If the great virtue of 'pristine' populations is that they constitute the only reliable co-ordinates for the evolution of genetic types Papua New Guinea, for the population geneticist as much as the doctoral student in anthropology, is the very ideal of purity and complexity.[85] Indeed, the investigative programme which resulted in the 'invention' of the PNG-1 virus and its correlative antibodies implemented the basic schema of population genetics; so much so that the virus itself was identified by its own genealogical 'dendrogram', which discreetly constituted the 'genes' that formed the 'genetic patrimony' of the Hagahai, and an essential part of their identity.[86]

The Human Genome Diversity Project is faced with the problem of how to (re-) incorporate the molecular substance of genetic types into human society. There are two aspects to this problem. First, how does one persuade the members of pristine populations that their participation in the project would be of benefit to themselves and to the 'human family' in general? Secondly, how can the abstract elements of genetic evolution — statistical populations and molecular sequences — be bound to social personality in such a way as to produce a plausible story of 'human' evolution? In other words, if there is indeed some 'evolutionary' correlation between genes and languages as the representatives of, respectively, biology and society, how are people to recognise and orient themselves by reference to this abstract distinction? These difficulties are resolved by the Human Genome Diversity Project's ethical protocols, which also take full advantage of the indeterminacy of the concept of informed consent:

> It is important to identify the most appropriate persons with whom to communicate, the persons from whom clearance should be obtained, and the appropriate content and media of communication. Research will need to take account of the group's social organisation, goals and aspirations, cultural values and mores, and laws (both statutory and customary).[87]

These protocols allow indigenous peoples to be represented 'as partners in the work rather than merely subjects of it'.[88] This is, of course, a particularly

---

84   Luigi Luca Cavalli-Sforza, *ibid*, 76.
85   'In no other place can one find almost intact ways of life that disappeared from Europe and most of Asia thousands of years ago, and from Africa centuries ago … From the point of view of population structure, information on tribal customs, demographic properties, and especially migratory changes can therefore be extremely interesting. The basic problem, what fraction of genetic variation is due to differential selection or random genetic drift, requires knowledge of these factors' (Cavalli-Sforza *et al*, n 82 above, 351–352). See also the Report of the Sub-committee on Bioethics and Population Genetics, UNESCO International Bioethics Committee, section 1.2.3: 'Samples could be, and frequently are, analysed from all over the world. However, for genetic studies the more isolated homogeneous human groups are thought to be the most informative'.
86   The uniqueness of the PNG-1 cell line was established by recourse to many of the techniques used in population genetics. For example, the claim that 'alignment and comparison of the nucleotide sequence of each provirus with the published sequence of a prototype [HTLV-I virus] revealed the existence not only of highly divergent variants of HTLV-I in Melanesia but of new quasi-species within this HTLV-I variant' (see the text of the patent application, n 10 above) was supported by a viral genealogy, a sort of family tree; or, in the more specialised language of the patent application, a 'dendrogram' allowing one 'to deduce the evolutionary relationships among members of the HTLV-I family'. For an explanation of 'phylogenetic tree analysis' see Cavalli-Sforza *et al*, n 82 above, 30–39).
87   Report of the UNESCO Sub-committee on Bioethics and Population Genetics, n 85 above, section 2.2.1. (See also the comment of one of the members of the UNESCO Sub-committee: 'The latest measures produced by the HGDP planners contain some of the most ethically sophisticated and detailed procedures for obtaining informed consent from individuals and groups in population genetics research' (1996) 379 *Nature* 11).
88   Cavalli-Sforza, cited in *ibid* section 3.1.4.

inequitable kind of 'partnership',[89] which has evolved more as a way of ensuring the survival of the project than as a way of recognising indigenous peoples.[90] Moreover, in representing the participation of individuals in these terms, ethical protocols yield an unexpected scientific or cognitive benefit; the contractual bond of informed consent is essential to construction of a 'scientific' relation between evolutionary genetics and individuals.

In the population geneticist's story of genes, peoples, and languages, the reference to 'peoples' is somewhat opportunistic. It represents 'people' as the vital medium of a relation between genes and languages. First, the hypothesis of a causal connection between the transmission of genes and the transmission of languages supposes that people are the common 'carriers' of both codes. Secondly, 'people' themselves are supposed to derive their cultural identity from this compound of genes and languages; indeed, in one sense they simply are this compound of genes and languages (which is why the story of how genes are reproduced can be represented as a story of how humanity itself is reproduced and differentiated). The trouble is that because population genetics reckons only with molecular structures, linguistic classifications, and statistical populations, each of which is a theoretical abstraction with no self-evident relation to 'real' people, it is unable to explain just how genes characterise 'people'. Population genetics takes on the difficult task of determining how genes and culture are bound together by some process of co-evolution or co-variation; how, that is, genes affect social individuality, or of how personality serves as a medium through which 'culture' is re-absorbed into 'genes', particularly in a culture that has come to thematise itself in terms of its genetic components. Yet it does no more than retrace two similarly-shaped developmental 'curves', without explaining the mechanisms by which each affects or responds to the other. Obviously, 'people' are supposed to constitute the medium or mechanism of this exchange, but the nature of this role is inferred rather than explained. And, although this inference gains explanatory consistency by being fashioned into a scientifically-constructed genealogy of human populations — and, by implication, people — one immediately encounters the problem that, like all family trees, the population geneticist's 'dendrogram' is a highly selective model. For example, the populations from which the genetic history of humanity is inferred are highly selective groupings, referable not only to the geneticist's preference for 'pristine' populations, but also to the statistical sampling techniques which allow these populations to serve as co-ordinates for the evolution of humanity as a whole. In other words, the genetic past which is supposed to characterise modern humanity as a whole is just the retrospective elaboration of an arbitrary representation of contemporary humanity.

Population genetics creates a role for 'people' that it cannot explain within its own frame of reference, and then compounds the problem by turning a weak hypothesis into a grand genealogy. The ethical practice of requiring informed consent functions in such a way as to reinforce this fragile genealogical

---

89   The violence of this is plainly expressed in a photograph of Professor Cavalli-Sforza, which, according to the caption, shows the author taking 'a genetic sample' from 'a member of the Aka tribe of African pygmies' ('Genes, Peoples and Languages', n 81 above, 78). The population geneticist occupies the focal spot of the photograph; he smiles directly at the camera, while the woman subject from whom he is about to take a sample sits with her arm limply extended over a table, bound by tourniquet, her facial expression signalling only utter, abject, resignation.

90   See Donna J. Haraway, *Modest_Witness @ Second_Millenium. FemaleMan©_Meets_Oncomouse*[TM] (New York: Routledge, 1997) 249: 'the people to be sampled might give or withhold permission, to be more or less carefully sought and thoroughly explained, but they were not regarded as partners in knowledge production who might have ends and means of their own in such an undertaking'.

characterisation of human beings. Because consenting participants are already identified in terms of the genetic population to which they belong or which they represent (simply by virtue of the fact they they are recognised as the appropriate individuals or representatives to give consent to a particular project) their subscription to the project already makes of them what the project would like them to become, namely, the 'people' who ensure the articulation of genes and languages, or the 'social and the biological'. Thus, a legal, contractual, relation binds participants into a vital scientific or theoretical role that is presupposed by scientific explanations but which cannot be accounted for by the science of population genetics itself. This is only one of the ways in which 'ethical', legal, protocols are constructively re-appropriated by the processes they are supposed to regulate, thereby reconstructing the individuals or populations who are ostensibly accorded recognition or protection. The theme of 'bio-colonialism' has also suffered this fate, and informed consent is again the principal vehicle of re-appropriation.

There is of course a somewhat crude sense in which ethical or ecological objections to biotechnology patents are appropriated within the patents process itself. The existence of ethical opposition to a patent is a factor that can be mobilised in legal argument. Plainly, the options are somewhat less interesting for the patentee, who can only attempt to minimise the long-term damage caused by adverse publicity,[91] than they are for the infringer, who can turn publicity to strategic advantage.[92] However, informed consent facilitates a rather more subtle and interesting technique for the incorporation of ethical themes in the patents process. For example, the case of the PNG-1 patent has been superseded by commercial practices such as those adopted by Merck or Hoffmann LaRoche, in which industrial corporations have negotiated the assignment of some of the anticipated profits of pharmaceutical inventions to indigenous groups in return for their approval or endorsement.[93] Even from the perspective of those organisations who have done most to expose 'bio-colonialism', informed consent is considered to be an effective remedy to the violence of bio-colonial commodification. For instance, the Rural Advancement Foundation International readily accepts informed consent as an approved procedure for commercial science; researchers should disclose 'any intention to seek patents and the prospects of commercial gain', and 'prior informed consent is required from both the subjects of medical research and their communities or governments before materials or information arising from the research can be commercialised in any form'.[94]

Informed consent, and the contractual procedures that it has inspired, constitute a particularly effective way of integrating the theme of 'bio-colonialism' within bio-colonial transactions. And again, as with the Human Genome Diversity Project's ethical protocols, this process of integration involves more than the simple

---

91 'Opposing the involvement of a visible and respected public interest group can frequently generate adverse reactions in the market' (William S. Feiler, 'Devising and Implementing an Effective Biotechnology Litigation Strategy' (1995) 72 *Patent World* 34, 35).

92 'When the client is a defendant in a biotech suit, enlisting the participation of high profile public interest groups can be a potent stratagem' (*ibid*).

93 See generally (1998) 392 *Nature*, at 525 and 535–540. Although it concerns a group or nation that is less obviously 'indigenous', the partnership between Hoffmann LaRoche and the Icelandic genomics company deCode Genetics, under the terms of which 'the Icelandic nation' is to receive free of charge any pharmaceutical products of this corporate collaboration, offers a practical example of how 'pristine populations' might be compensated or enriched by these new forms of 'bio-colonial' transaction. See the account given by deCode at its website (http://www.decode.is/news.html).

94 RAFI Communique Mar/Apr 1996, n 17 above.

conscription of indigenous participants. As the extended debate over the European Biotech Directive suggests, commercial enterprises cannot entirely insulate themselves from political opposition; this has less to do with the force of political arguments than with the fact that biotechnologies have corroded the different purifiying themes which facilitate the reproduction of proprietary 'vectors'. Ethical or ecological arguments against 'bio-colonialism' betray tensions or incompatibilities existing within the compound structure of 'bio-colonial' transactions. Here again, the virtue of 'informed consent' is that it is a highly 'deformable' theme, which readily negotiates the complexity produced by the increasingly transparent differentiation of concepts of individuality and body. Because it consists in an open-ended relation between 'subjects' and 'information', each of which is already a complex, indeterminate, category, the procedure of informed consent is sufficiently malleable to reconcile the quite different conceptions of agency that are found in law, science, politics, and economics. And, because the category of 'information' is based upon the translation of complex economic or scientific assessments of 'cost' and 'benefit' into a set of criteria that would make sense from the perspective of the fictitious consenting subject, it performs a dual mediating function. First, it makes abstract conceptions of agency or individuality commensurable with the familiar juridical notion of subjectivity; secondly, and perhaps more importantly, it makes these abstractions commensurable with each other, relegating the juridical notion of subjectivity to the role of a simple common denominator. And, as with the role played by informed consent in constituting an ostensibly scientific account of the relation between genes, peoples, and languages, the act of consenting characterises the subscriber in terms of a prefabricated role. If one asks who, for example, is qualified to give consent to a 'bio-colonial' transaction, the protocols adopted by the HGDP and advocated by RAFI suggest that consent should be given by the population as a whole, or the government, or the relevant individuals, or by all of these 'actors'. The indeterminacy of these specifications means that from the start they are apt to incorporate and reproduce precisely those scientific and economic processes which informed consent is supposed to regulate. Indeed, definitions of populations and individuals are so thoroughly infused with economic and scientific expectations that the options available to the consenting actor have already, even before consent is given or withheld, been configured by commercialised science.

Again, the act of consent yields some unexpected benefits. For example, the judicial arguments in the case of *Moore* v *Regents of UCLA* reveal how procedures of informed consent (which were ostensibly developed to secure the interests of patients) ensure the reconciliation of economic, scientific, and therapeutic rationalisations of medical practice. The rise of commercialised biotechnologies has accentuated the differentiation of medicine, producing some sharp divisions between 'Hippocratic' therapy, laboratory research, and commercial profit. Increasingly, the function of legal regulation and adjudication is to mediate between these overlapping representations of the patient. By drawing on the almost inexhaustibly adaptable resource of legal subjectivity, the procedure of informed consent manages to bind these representations to a common denominator. The patient's consent is the common term of each separate transaction; the fiction of the informed patient translates competing representations into a basic calculus of costs and benefits, thereby unifying or absorbing the tensions between rationalities. Of course, informed consent is not a property law concept, and these observations might be taken as evidence for the proposition that human dignity and autonomy should be granted a more fundamental form of protection. Whereas informed consent does no more than impose conditions on the commercialisation of human beings, the more radical argument for dignity would quite simply prohibit commercialisation. The most obvious practical means of granting protection would be to create an exceptional category akin to the Roman law concept of a *res extra commercium*. However, to create or defend an exception is to concede the claims of the rule. In other words, the technique of exemption is plausible only if one accepts the traditional account of how property norms bind things. As soon as concepts such as dignity or autonomy are treated as purifying themes rather than effective descriptions, the question is not whether dignity should be enforced, but how the theme of 'dignity' would be absorbed into commercial vectors. Here, somewhat crudely, it might be observed that the claims of 'dignity' are somewhat less plausible than those of 'informed consent'. The 'cynical pragmatism' of Anglo-American law is especially troubling to Bernard Edelman because French law has come to adopt informed consent as the means of proceduralising its conceptions of dignity. However, the undoing of dignity is not entirely the fault of informed consent. Conceptions of dignity presuppose some mode of proceduralisation, if only to determine what counts as 'pure' research, how conflicts between research and therapy should be addressed, under what conditions it would be appropriate for patients to take part in randomised drugs trials, how the donation of tissues should be regulated, and so on. These unavoidable practical questions require a mode of proceduralisation which shares the flexible mediating skills of the concept of informed consent. Again, the simple point is that legalistic representations of genetic technologies have to take account of law's immediate implication in biotechnological processes.

Index